Power, persistence and change

International Library of Sociology

Founded by Karl Mannheim

Editor: John Rex, University of Warwick

Arbor Scientiae
Arbor Vitae

A catalogue of the books available in the **International Library of Sociology** and other series of Social Science books published by Routledge & Kegan Paul will be found at the end of this volume.

Power, persistence and change

A second study of Banbury

Margaret Stacey,
Eric Batstone,
Colin Bell and
Anne Murcott

Routledge & Kegan Paul
London and Boston

First published in 1975
by Routledge & Kegan Paul Ltd
Broadway House, 68–74 Carter Lane,
London EC4V 5EL and
9 Park Street,
Boston, Mass. 02108, USA
Set in Times Roman
and printed in Great Britain by
Unwin Brothers Limited
The Gresham Press,
Old Woking, Surrey

ISBN 0 7100 7995 8 (c)
ISBN 0 7100 8018 2 (p)

Contents

Figures

Tables

Appendix tables

Acknowledgments

We wish first to acknowledge our debt to the people of Banbury, their voluntary leaders, their elected representatives and all who work in and for the town. We are aware that, partly because of Banbury's accessibility to the Midlands and the South-East of England, but also because of the attention attracted by *Tradition and Change* since its publication in 1960, the town has experienced more than its fair share of investigation. Market researchers, planners, students, as well as sociologists, have found Banbury a suitable place to survey. We wish to express our gratitude to all the townspeople who offered hospitality to the field-workers and who so willingly co-operated in the second study. For the most part the townspeople must remain anonymous, but we would like to acknowledge our debt to two local historians, Ted Brinkworth and Barrie Trinder. *Tradition and Change* is widely read and studied by sociologists, political scientists and planners in many parts of the world. We hope that this, the report of our second study, will prove as useful to scholars and may in that way repay part of our debt to the people of Banbury.

Our debt to our academic colleagues, past and present, is obvious. The debt to those whose writings we acknowledge is recorded in the text. We are particularly grateful to colleagues in the Department of Sociology and Anthropology at the University College of Swansea for their encouragement and criticism over the years. We would like particularly to mention Professor W. M. Williams, Dr J. B. Loudon, Mr C. C. Harris, Dr M. Kenna, Mr J. Hutson and Mr Richard Startup. We are also specially grateful to Dr C. S. Smith, of the Civil Service College, who was one of the field-workers in the first study, for his insights into certain changes over time, his help in the development of concepts, and for his support and encouragement. Colleagues in seminars in various universities and academic societies have also been most helpful.

ACKNOWLEDGMENTS

There are many people who have worked for and with us over the past seven years without whom this book would never have been compiled: the interviewers and coders in Banbury and district who collected and coded the sample survey data; Elizabeth Chambers who was researcher as well as secretary; Mrs Betty Evans of the Swansea Sociology Department who punched the cards and helped with some of the sorting; the many secretaries, clerks and typists who for shorter or longer periods in Banbury, Swansea and elsewhere have typed and retyped manuscripts and tables, filed and refiled data; Mrs Camille McCulloch who painstakingly checked all quotations and references and prepared the bibliography. To these and all other helpers we would say: thank you.

We gratefully acknowledge our debt to the Nuffield Foundation, whose grant of £20,000 made the research possible. We would also like to thank the Foundation and its officers for their understanding of the vicissitudes of the academic enterprise and for their courtesy and patience.

Note on the text

The names used throughout the text are fictitious. Except in the case of public figures, descriptions of social circumstances have been modified where individuals might otherwise have been identifiable. We hope that these changes, essential to maintain confidentiality, have not distorted the sociological implications of the data. In the case of public figures, who inevitably may be identified, no data has been included which is not already public knowledge.

Introduction

The first study of Banbury was undertaken between 1948 and 1951.[1] It aimed to see how the interrelationships between major social institutions, economic, religious, familial, worked out in local social relations. At the time of that study, social and sociological theory was on the grand scale, dominated in Britain by Ginsberg's interpretation of Hobhouse and influenced principally by the European thinkers, Comte, Durkheim, Spencer, Marx and, to a lesser extent, Weber. Perhaps Ginsberg was unusual in Britain at that time in stressing the importance of the individual in sociological understanding and explanation.

On the empirical side the scene was dominated by the reform school, whose research had origins in work such as that of Booth and Rowntree. The reform school stressed notions of abnormality, suffering, and inequality, and was mostly about the working class. The empirical work bore little relation to the contemporary sociological theory.

In social anthropology, on the other hand, there were interesting developments where social processes were examined by the 'case method'[2] established by Malinowski and where theories of the structure and process of societies were closely related to the field data. The studies of, for example, Evans-Pritchard, Meyer Fortes and Max Gluckman provided interesting examples of the way in which such work could be undertaken.

In more complex societies a tradition of 'community studies' was also developing.[3] Many of these, like that of Arensberg and Kimball in Ireland, related to rural areas.[4] The work of the Lynds in Middletown was, however, an outstanding example of the detailed study of social structure and social process in an American town.[5] The studies inspired by Lloyd Warner had been continuing from the early thirties and were an attempt to apply the techniques and approach of

1

social anthropology to American urban society. The Yankee City series was in process[6] and Davis and Gardner's study of the deep south already published.[7]

The difficulties of unfocused holistic study of western urban areas were already becoming plain. So that while a focus of the first Banbury study was to test some of the holistic ideas of the grander theorists on a smaller canvas and the model used was found in the Middletown studies, the Banbury study focused on a particular aspect of change in the town. 'The purpose of the research was to study the social structure and culture of Banbury with special reference to the introduction of large-scale industry.'[8]

In the report of the research, after giving an impressionistic sketch of the town and the surrounding countryside as it was around 1950 and of the history of the town, certain social institutions were examined in some detail. Thus there were chapters on earning a living, politics, religion, voluntary associations, houses and neighbours, the family, social status and social class.

Although attention was focused from the beginning on the possibility of tension between Banburians and immigrants, and indeed some such tension was found, this turned out not to be the most important aspect of the social and cultural analysis. What emerged was an important division between 'an established group, a group bound together by common history and tradition, with a recognized social structure and having certain common values',[9] and a number of other groups which were outside this established group. This last was referred to as the traditional Banbury society, the remainder as non-traditional. The traditional society included some immigrants and not all the natives, although Banburians were in a majority. This society was based on a long-standing network of relationships between families and friends, for whom conformity, stability, conservation of established institutions were keynotes.

As this society was based on a series of face-to-face relationships it could only accept a limited number of newcomers at a time. The arrival of the aluminium factory and the associated influx of immigrants therefore represented an abrupt change. 'Non-traditionalism, which had begun to emerge before the days of the aluminium factory, was reinforced and extended.'[10] The opposition between traditional and non-traditional, which contained within it some of the problems of immigrant assimilation, was seen as an important key to understanding the social structure and culture of the town. But the division was not a dichotomy, as some have supposed. Non-traditionalists were not one group and there was no consensus among them: 'they do not share any common social system or system of values and customs for they are composed of many different, and sometimes opposed, groups; they include those who have come in [to Banbury] with quite other systems of values and customs and those who are developing new ways to meet the changed circumstances of their life and work.'[11] Nor can 'traditionalist' be equated with 'local', or 'non-traditional' with 'cosmopolitan', as Frankenberg has done.[12]

Merton defines locals and cosmopolitans by their orientation toward Rovere, the town in which the influentials who were so typed were studied: 'The localite largely confines his interests to this community. Rovere is essentially his world . . . to the virtual exclusion of the national and international scene.' The cosmopolitan, on the other hand, 'has some interest in Rovere and must of course maintain a minimum of relations within the community since he, too, exerts influence there. But he is also oriented significantly to the world outside Rovere, and regards himself as an integral part of that world. . . . If the local type is parochial, the cosmopolitan is ecumenical.'[13]

To what extent Banbury residents were parochial or ecumenical depended rather more on their social class than on their traditional or non-traditional orientations; for the traditional values of Banbury were part of a system of national traditional values associated with a traditional class system. There were traditional locals and traditional cosmopolitans as well as non-traditional locals and non-traditional cosmopolitans.

The second important source of social division and social tension which emerged in the first study was social stratification. The study concluded 'Social class divides traditional and non-traditional alike, although . . . the attitude of each group to these horizontal divisions and their impact on each is different. Each class has ways of life and values and attitudes so dissimilar that interaction between them, except in formal ways, is almost impossible, nor is it sought.'[14] The town was 'bisected two ways' vertically by the traditional/non-traditional division and horizontally by the middle-class/working class division.

The Banbury society was therefore seen as wide open to the challenge of change, but unlikely to experience open conflict because of the many cross-cutting ties. The social situation was seen as essentially fluid. The book concluded 'What is non-traditional today may well be traditional tomorrow and this new tradition itself open to the challenge of fresh change.'[15]

Certain predictions were made as to the changes that might be expected. It was predicted, for example, that the opposition of Labour and Conservative would replace the opposition of Liberal and Conservative.[16] It was also predicted that the ties of the traditional society were loosening and reducing the intensity of inturning social relationships and, at the same time, that demarcation between

3

the locality and the outside world was decreasing and the range of interests and relationships in the town widening.

The research team in 1948–51 had been as much concerned with how Banbury had changed and was changing as they were with what Banbury was like at that time. The notion of a restudy was therefore in their minds at the time they were analysing the results of the first study.

When, in the 1960s, a restudy became a serious possibility, the opportunity of testing the predictions of the first study was one focus of interest. Another most important focus was the fate of the traditional society. It had undoubtedly been under challenge around 1950; had it survived, in what form? In 'The Myth of Community Studies' Stacey outlined conditions under which a 'local social system' might develop and might be destroyed or changed.[17] Banbury in the sixties provided an interesting test case of these ideas. Not only had there been fifteen or so more years for the internal and external changes to which Banbury was subject at the time of the first study to have their effect, but also a new immigration was in hand, for Banbury was now an expanding town.

Application was therefore made to the Nuffield Foundation, who made a grant of £20,000 for three years from October 1966. One of the main aims of the research was 'to assess the social systems present in Banbury particularly those associated with class and tradition and to assess the social changes which have taken place in these systems since 1950'. The possibility, therefore, that the changes were of a kind which would have led to the disappearance of the 'traditional society' was conceived from the outset. Certainly there was no expectation that the local social system would be found as it had been left. In the event we have found that outside the political arena there is no local social system any longer definable. The demarcation between the locality and the outside world has indeed decreased, such that identifiable local social relations are not discernible in any local holistic sense.

There had been enough technical changes and upward movement in the national standard of life for some change in the stratification system to have been expected, although the findings of the Luton studies,[18] studies of the distribution of wealth and income[19] and the poverty surveys[20] had not led one to expect radical changes in resource distribution or life style. Since the first study had not found a unitary stratification system in the town, we were not altogether surprised not to find one in 1966–8. We were perhaps not prepared for the inappropriateness of contemporary concepts about social class and social status which we experienced when trying to analyse the data. Around 1950 the contemporary concepts had also been found wanting. In a sense we have now found that the inequalities of power, wealth, income, occupation, education and other resources are surprisingly formless. There is a pattern, but there are no sharp divisions in the pattern of stratification as there were around 1950.

It is perhaps in the area of power and self-determination, of formal politics and of administration that we have found evidence of the most interesting changes. Thus in religious, industrial and commercial organization as well as in central and local government we find increasing tendencies to centralization and removal of power from the town. We also find that some people are combining in new ways in response to these changes. At the same time much social life, in the family and the neighbourhood, continues with the participants little concerned with and not at all involved in these activities, which from time to time so much affect their daily lives.

This restudy of Banbury has been the first of its kind in Britain. Middletown was studied a second time by the Lynds;[21] Art Gallaher went back to Plainville, which James West had studied;[22] Oscar Lewis restudied Redfield's Tepoztlan.[23] In the Banbury restudy the field-workers were different, but the research director was the same. The restudy is unique in this regard, we think.

The nature of the data and the research tools limits comparability in studies of this kind. Time has affected the status and perspectives of the original researchers. The field staff belong to a different generation and have been brought up in a different sociological world.

Much had changed in sociology between the two studies. First, in the fifties there was the movement away from a holistic study of society and the necessary development of important specialisms, in industrial and educational sociology, for example. The works of Merton, which were not published when the first team was in the field, now have an established place in the training of all sociologists. The importance and relevance of Cooley, Mead, and Simmel and of Goffman, Wright Mills, and Lévi-Strauss have become plain. Grounded theory and ethnomethodology have emerged as topics of lively concern, and from a fashion of 'value-free', sociology has swung to one of commitment.

By the mid-sixties sociology as a discipline was much more experienced both in theory and in field-work than it had been in the late forties. Any aspect of social relations studied in Banbury in the second half of the sixties had to take account of a specialist sub-discipline; in the forties and early fifties it had been hard to find any comparable British data or relevant theory at all.

The context of the second study was therefore different from the first in a number of important ways. What has emerged is consequently a rather different kind of research report. Rather than

5

B

reporting on all aspects of the structure, culture, and process which were studied, the book concentrates on those aspects where there is something particular to contribute to sociology as a whole or to a sub-discipline. Changes or persistences in the substantive areas previously studied are briefly reported, and material is discussed in each of these areas only when it provides evidence relating to the main themes which were mentioned above.

In the study attention is paid to groups and quasi-groups, the formation and collapse of groups, the joining, leaving, and leading of groups by individuals. Some of these groups are small, informal, and recreational, others are large, formal and occupational, and there are many others of intermediate type and some, like the family, based upon a unique cluster of institutions. In so far as these groups are articulated to each other, i.e. in so far as there is any social structure or social system, it is through individuals who hold common memberships in a number of groups, that is, through the variety of roles individuals play. Groups were found to be most likely to form where individuals have a number of social attributes or social statuses in common, for example, not just manual workers but manual workers in a particular occupation, industry or workshop. In some events, for example, the expansion decision,[24] certain people appear to be particularly important. This is because of their structured positions, i.e. their statuses, and because of the constraints placed upon them by others in complementary or similar statuses. Their power derives from their individual characteristics and the cluster of statuses they occupy; the constraints upon them limit the way in which they use this power and also the way they exercise the powers of their offices.[25] The totality of social relations is conceived as made up of the actions of many individuals who are constrained by their many statuses to behave in particular ways. The relationship of the statuses to each other comes about through the action of individuals. The study thus attempts to use a structural-action frame of reference.

The field research was undertaken by Colin Bell, Eric Batstone and Anne Murcott between 1966 and 1968 under Margaret Stacey's direction. The field-workers lived in Banbury for those two years. One of the methods of study was participant observation, each field-worker participating in a different sector of the town.

A 6 per cent sample survey of individuals drawn at random from the electoral register was undertaken in the summer of 1967.[26] Three sub-samples were later drawn from the main sample to provide data on the extended family, sex roles, and social-class images.[26] Data were systematically collected about voluntary associations, their members and committee members, and their links with each other.

Progress papers were read during the field-work period to seminars at Swansea University College and other universities, to the British Sociological Association and the International Sociological Association. The analysis and writing of the final report began in 1968 while Batstone and Murcott were in Swansea for a year. Bell was then lecturing at Essex. It has been completed while all the workers have been scattered about the country in other jobs.

Initially each research worker wrote up the substantive areas where he had been responsible for the data collection. There was then a draft–discuss–redraft process and finally the total work was re-written by Margaret Stacey to ensure continuity of style. She therefore gratefully acknowledges the major contribution of each of her co-authors but readily accepts responsibility for all those aspects of the report which are different from the way her co-authors might have done it.

1 The changing face of Banbury: 1951–66

The first field-work team left Banbury before the end of the age of austerity which followed the 1939–45 war: food was still rationed, hardly any post-war private houses had been built. In the period between the two studies the 'affluent society', the 'permissive society', the age of the pop group and youth culture all emerged. Communications were radically altered: television was in widespread use by the time of the restudy and the once-empty Oxfordshire lanes filled with cars faster than most that were on the road when the first study was made. These, of course, were technical and cultural changes that affected the whole nation. They have undoubtedly reduced the relative isolation of Banbury in a number of ways. Once distant neighbouring towns, already nearer by road in 1950 than they had been in 1900, were now nearer still. Furthermore, the improved communications, both TV and motor car, were shared by large sections of the population. They were not the privilege of the few. At the same time rail 'improvements' have reduced the connections of Banbury with the outside world.

The town itself now sprawls over a much wider area. Its cattle market, under cover and discreetly hidden, bears little resemblance to the old cattle market in the open streets about which people still talked in the late forties. Highly capitalized and organized, the market has progressed from being the 'largest in southern England' to the 'largest in England' and now, they claim, is the 'largest in Europe'. Despite this, and the twice-weekly street market, Banbury by 1966 had much more the air of an industrial town than of a market town. Along the road north out of Banbury there is a complex of factories where once the aluminium factory stood in splendid isolation among the fields.

Dominant among these new industries is Birds, the custard factory, which had moved from a crowded site near Birmingham's Bull Ring.

Now a part of American-owned General Foods, the Birds factory prepares instant coffee and other foods. The aluminium factory is invisible from most parts of town. In contrast, the new Birds factory can be seen from many places. It dominates the skyline and dwarfs the famous 'pepper-pot' spire of the parish church. Inhabitants are reminded of the presence of the factory in other ways, for when the wind is in the right direction, the smell of instant coffee manufacture wafts over the town and occasional rumours are heard of coffee-coloured 'fall-out' on washing hanging out to dry. This is an unwelcome change for all those who so valued Banbury as a clean town. The food factory was followed by others, including Automotive Products, a large car-parts company. Indeed the northern area of the town has increasingly become the centre of the town's industry, whereas, with the obvious exception of the aluminium rolling mill, industry had earlier been concentrated in the town centre.[1]

Birds has come to town as part of an overspill agreement with Birmingham City Council, for Banbury by 1966 was formally designated an expanding town. It also had overspill agreements with the Greater London Council. Its population, 19,000 during the first survey, was now 25,000 and the signed agreements would push it up to 40,000.

Indian and Chinese restaurants, launderettes, and 'coin-op' dry-cleaners, a Fine Fare Supermarket, a couple of boutiques played their part in the impression that Banbury is now an industrial town much like any other. Between 1966 and 1968 a large 'old-fashioned' family grocer's closed, taken over by a nationally-owned dairy, and Brown's, the 'original Banbury cake' shop, which claimed to have been making and selling Banbury cakes for two hundred years or so, closed. The shop was pulled down, not without a fight, although mounted too late since demolition had already started, by conservationists concerned for its historic interest to inhabitants and tourists; it was replaced by a block of new shops and offices.[2] But some shops are still family concerns. There is a cobbler in one of the main streets and a successful cake-shop and tea room.[3]

Housing changes

To a field-worker returning from the first study the most dramatic visual change is the many acres of erstwhile fields now covered in new housing estates. The land between the main roads has been progressively filled in: the Council Estate between the Broughton and Warwick roads, the superior private housing between the Broughton and Bloxham roads, and the less expensive housing between the Bloxham and Oxford roads. All the country walks, at one time so close to the town centre, seem to have disappeared and with their disappearance the character of the town seems to have changed. There are no longer tongues of open country penetrating wedge-shaped behind the ribbon development which fronted each main road in the thirties, forties and early fifties.

The largest of the new housing areas is the new Council estate. It is large enough to warrant its own purpose-built community centre donated by a local philanthropist, to have new daughter churches, new schools and, some time after many of the houses were already occupied, a new shopping centre. So, where once a farmhouse over-looked surrounding fields, now it is encircled by streets of 'semis'. One farmhouse has been replaced by Council flats. At the same time, whole streets of small Victorian terraced houses near the river and canal (the 'little slum houses' of 1950)[4] in the centre of the town have been demolished, and two churches have closed as their congregations moved away.

Some inhabitants express a mixture of awe, horror and pride as they point out to those returning on a visit to the town the 'acres' of new houses. One elderly Banburian, talking with nostalgia of the pre-war days, said, 'One thing I regret is the growth of Banbury; life in old Banbury made people terribly matey.' Another, having stated her disapproval of the rapid growth of the town which had already taken place, retorted with regard to the proposals for further expansion of the town, 'They might as well build a New Town, it won't be Banbury any more.'

In this study no systematic ranking of houses was attempted,[5] because such a ranking would lack social reality. There are those who prefer new houses and, while many wish for a house, cottage, or bungalow in the country, this is not true of everybody. Some still prefer a town house. We have therefore used the politico-economic ranking by rateable value which is the district valuer's assessment modified by appeals. Figure 1.1 illustrates the ecological division of the town in 1966 on this basis. As with the earlier chart,[6] this Figure oversimplifies the geographic housing distribution. While there are now in Banbury many more areas of houses that are 'all the same', there still remains a mixture in many places and old houses tucked in among the new.

The first phase of the new housing development was to house the immigrants and new households of 1931–51, during which period the population increased from 13,000 to 19,000. At the time of the first Banbury study there was a severe housing shortage in the town. By the time war broke out in 1939 not enough houses had been built to accommodate the immigration of the thirties, and migrants continued to come into the town during the war. The shortage of dwellings, the extended family households, the overcrowding, the lack of bathrooms and indoor lavatories in 1950 were reported previously.[7]

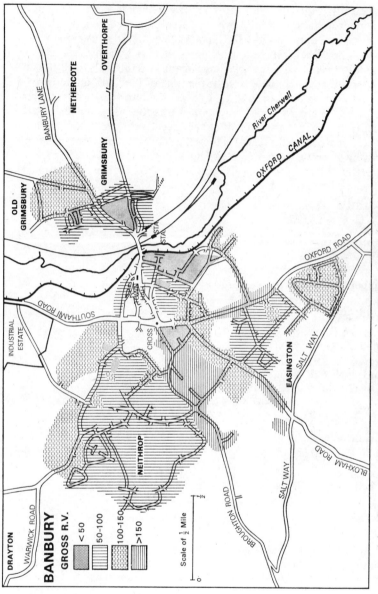

FIGURE 1.1 *Geographical distribution of dwellings by rateable value 1966*

Already at that time the local authority had large building programmes in hand, but little private development was taking place.

Tables 1.1 and 1.2 show the remarkable increase in dwellings since 1951. The visual impression of 'acres of new housing' is accurate. There were half as many dwellings again in Banbury by the time of the second study as there were at the time of the first: an increase of 55 per cent in the Borough and 48 per cent in the rural area surveyed.[8] In the early fifties the Council was the main builder of new houses, but by the second half of that decade private house building predominated. In the early sixties the Council was again building actively to house the new wave of immigrants, the 'overspill' population. Private house building also began to respond to this development.

TABLE 1.1   *Numbers of structurally separate dwellings: Banbury and District*

Area	1951	1961	1966
Banbury M.B.	5,213	6,526	8,080
Bloxham and Milton	493	507	590
Bodicote	263	347	640
Bourton, Cropredy, Wardington, Chacombe	552	555	630
Broughton, Drayton, Hanwell, Horley, N. Newington, Wroxton, Shotteswell	556	599	740
E. and W. Adderbury	450	591	700
King's Sutton	357	464	480
Middleton Cheney, Warkworth	417	538	800
Total Rural Area	3,088	3,601	4,580
Totals	8,301	10,127	12,660

Source: Censuses.

By 1966 there was therefore a greater variety of dwellings in Banbury than there had been in 1950. The rented Council house, which was then noted as representing a marked change in house ownership, had become even more important. Added to this there was now a wide price range of private houses available for purchase, both in the town and in the villages nearby. Furthermore, many of the new private house developments are in the rural district outside the Borough. Around 1950, although a number of people who lived

TABLE 1.2   *Increase in numbers of structurally separate dwellings: Banbury and District (%)*

Area	1951–1961	1961–1966	1951–1966
Banbury M.B.	125·2	123·8	155·0
Bloxham and Milton	102·8	116·4	119·7
Bodicote	131·9	184·4	243·3
Bourton, Cropredy, Wardington, Chacombe	100·5	113·5	114·1
Broughton, Drayton, Hanwell Horley, N. Newington, Wroxton, Shotteswell	107·7	123·5	133·1
E. and W. Adderbury	131·3	118·4	155·5
King's Sutton	130·0	103·4	134·5
Middleton Cheney, Warkworth	129·0	148·7	191·8
Total Rural Area	116·0	127·2	148·3

Source: Censuses.

in the rural area worked in Banbury, the built-up area of the town was for the most part reasonably well defined by the Municipal Borough boundaries. Bodicote, a parish to the south of the town, was the only area outside the Borough boundary which could in the late forties be described as a suburb of the town. By 1966 it was clear that the amount of building in parishes immediately surrounding the town was so great that 'the town' was no longer confined to the Municipal Borough.

Survey area

In the first study the survey area was defined as the area of the Municipal Borough. In 1966 this was not appropriate. Neighbouring parishes were therefore included in the 6 per cent sample survey[9] and are shown in Fig. 1.2 and in Tables 1.1 and 1.2 which set out the housing expansion.

The immigrants

Rather more than half (54 per cent) of the 25,000 people living in Banbury at the time of survey were immigrants, while not much more than a third (36 per cent) were born Banburians.[10] Around 16 or 17

1. *CASTLE*   2. *RUSCOTE*   3. *NEITHROP*   4. *EASINGTON*   5. *CALTHORPE*   6. *GRIMSBURY*

FIGURE 1.2   *Sketch map to show Banbury and survey area*

per cent of the immigrants now living in the survey area arrived in each of the decades of the thirties, forties and fifties. Over 40 per cent have arrived during the first seven years of the sixties. The English Midlands were still the most important source of immigrants to Banbury, but by 1960 London was the second most important source of migrants, replacing the rural area 10–25 miles around Banbury.[11]

Very few immigrants from overseas lived in Banbury. One semi-official estimate suggested there might be 100–150 Pakistanis and Indians living in town. These few were highly visible (in Merton's sense),[12] as were the American staff of a U.S. air base near Banbury. Despite their small numbers, these foreigners undoubtedly add to the more 'cosmopolitan feeling' experienced when walking around Banbury streets in the sixties compared with the forties.

On being an immigrant

The difficulties of adjusting to life in the town experienced by immigrants before the war[13] are echoed in the sixties. This is so despite conscious attempts by the Council, who exhorted the inhabitants of Banbury to see that newcomers were made welcome 'so that they quickly feel they belong here'. One immigrant said, 'When I first moved to Banbury I talked to someone in the street, who retorted "I don't know you", I went home and cried. . . .'; and another, '. . . they're a bit stand-offish here.' Also, despite the wish of the Council that 'there should be no colony of new residents in the town', a year after the first overspill family had arrived in Banbury, one area of the town was being called 'Little London', while another was called 'The Aviary' after the numbers of Birds workers living there. Many of the ex-Londoners appear to have felt that Banbury was 'lovely and lifeless'. The main attractions for immigrants were a house and the countryside, 'good for the kiddies', but in other respects they were often unhappy: 'There's no private life. My husband and I would go back if we could take the house with us.' Other comments, however, reveal a process of adaptation: '. . . when I first came here I thought the place Mediaeval—now I really quite like it; perhaps [as an afterthought] I am getting more Mediaeval!' Another, who hated Banbury at first, was heard to say after she had been to visit kin in London: 'This time, I was really glad to come back to dear old Banbury.'

Some of these feelings of the immigrants can be attributed to the views of those already established in the town, who sometimes characterized Londoners in a specific, frequently derogatory, way. Shopkeepers and some officials whose jobs brought them into contact with the public were particularly likely to be heard making such remarks. This stereotyping emerged, for example, in the common belief that the marked increase in crimes known to the police was due to 'the overspill'. We were unable to establish whether this view may have been justified, because of the well-known difficulties of interpreting criminal statistics.

The derogatory use of 'overspill' did not indicate the presence of open conflict between those already in the town and immigrants, either specifically from one part of the country or in general. 'Overspill', when used to denote a category of people, was an attempt to explain observed deviant behaviour. It was a scapegoating process, but the logic behind it was that while all deviants are probably 'overspill' not all 'overspill' are deviants. So, when he was talking of the declining membership of voluntary associations in the town, a Banburian remarked, '. . . we don't get support for societies' events . . . it's the telly . . . nor do we get the new people, the *hoi polloi* from Birds or the Estates . . .' Here he was using the name of the food manufacturer to denote a category of people recently arrived, but doing so in a way no more, nor less, derogatory than he might name others who fail to support such activities. In other contexts, Banburians would admit that there were also other old Banburians who were miscreants of one kind or another.

Communications

Although the town's bus station is new and the town so much more spread out, the buses into the centre from the estates still run only every twenty minutes and for many the town is still the main focus for shopping, entertainment and commerce.[14] There is also a new railway station. This is ironic, for the number of trains running through Banbury has decreased, especially since the electrification of one of the two main London-to-Birmingham railway lines, both of which bypass the town altogether. In this sense the town is now more isolated than it was at the time of the first survey.[15] But other forms of communication have kept pace with the growth of the town; the number of telephones and the ownership of private cars have increased spectacularly here as elsewhere.

Industry

Around 1950 the aluminium rolling mill was still the most recently arrived large-scale industry and still dominated the town's economy, employing about a third of the town's labour force in 1951. At that time town leaders were already worried about the heavy dependence on a single major industry, all the more so because aluminium was one of the basic industries and thought to be vulnerable.

Many of those who had come to Banbury in the thirties had come from areas where unemployment was particularly high as a consequence of local reliance on one industry. They had come from the 'depressed areas'. Some of these were among the town's leaders by the early fifties and were particularly anxious to see a wider range of industry in the town. This view was shared by those without personal experience of 'one-industry towns', and thus, as the fifties progressed, town councillors and leaders came to see Banbury's future prosperity as inextricably linked with greater diversification of her industry.

Diversification and expansion

At this time a new town clerk discovered a 'legal loophole' namely that planning permission for industrial development had already been granted on 86 acres along the Southam Road north of the town near the aluminium plant. Permission for industrial development had been given to a firm which ultimately went elsewhere. Permission once having been given, no Industrial Development Certificate was needed for this land.[16] It was felt, and later shown, that this 'freedom from control' would be an incentive for industry to come to town. The Borough, for the time being under a Labour-controlled Council, bought the land, feeling that otherwise they would have no means of controlling the type of industry that came. A leading Conservative, a member of the Council at the time has said that if the Conservatives had been in control they would have done the same.[17]

By 1956 the Borough began actively to consider the Town Development legislation as a way of increasing its chances of diversifying industry and of providing the people to man them. This legislation which made town expansion possible was passed in 1952 by a Conservative central government whose Prime Minister at the time made it plain that no local authority should be expanded against its will. Immediately after the war the policy of building new towns had been developed and implemented by the Labour government under the 1946 New Towns Act. The notion of Expanded Towns was an additional way of trying to provide accommodation for the increasing population in London and the large conurbations, i.e. for the 'overspill'. In practice an Expanded Town may start from a smaller population than that of many New Towns. The Expanded Towns were expected to develop rapidly without the benefit of a new administrative structure and with less generous financial arrangements than the New Towns had. The expansion of a town under the 1952 Town Development Act was therefore a considerable burden upon rates, i.e. upon the existing residents, in that longish period, perhaps fifteen years, when the costs of expansion were inevitably considerably greater than the returns that could be expected.[18]

Nevertheless, in the early sixties the Council decided to expand the

17

population, then about 20,000 and not much bigger than it had been in 1951, to 40,000 by 1974, by signing 'overspill' agreements with the London County Council and Birmingham County Borough Council. That is, they agreed to accept and house population from these two cities under the 1952 Town Development Act. The agreement with Birmingham was a limited one and was associated with the removal to Banbury in the early sixties of the one plant, Birds. The new factory was built in the early sixties on a large proportion of the I.D.C.-free land.

Table 1.3 shows the results of the diversification moves. The leading industries of 1950, metal manufacture, distribution, and transport, have all declined relatively, while employment in govern-

TABLE 1.3   *Employment by Industry[a]* (%): *Persons over 21 only*

S.I.C.[d]	1950[b] Banbury M.B.	1967[c] Banbury M.B.	District	Total
Metal manufacture	25·6	11·0	9·0	10·0
Distribution	12·2	11·8	13·1	12·3
Transport	12·2	9·3	6·4	8·3
Clothing	5·6	2·5	2·2	2·4
Government	3·1	3·9	6·7	5·1
Building	5·6	12·0	8·3	10·7
Services except professional	6·4	7·9	10·9	8·7
Professional and commercial services	8·3	14·5	10·3	13·0
Food and drink	3·8	10·4	8·7	9·7
Woodworking	2·7	0·5	0·6	0·6
Electrical machinery,[e] engineering	2·4	7·0	8·0	7·5
Printing	2·1	2·7	2·6	2·7
Agriculture	2·0	0·5	8·7	3·4
Gas, water, electricity	1·7	1·1	1·3	1·2
All other	6·4	4·7	3·2	4·4
	100·1	99·8	100·0	100·0

[a] The industries in which Banbury residents work, *not* the distribution by industry of workers in Banbury.
[b] 20 per cent sample of Banbury Borough.
[c] 6 per cent of Banbury Borough and District. (Banbury residential area now extends beyond the borough boundary. This addition, however, accounts for the apparent increase in agriculture.)
[d] Standard Industrial Classification.
[e] Includes mechanical engineering.

18

ment, professional and commercial and other services, food manufacture and engineering have all increased. Associated with the expansion, the proportion of people working in the building industry has roughly doubled.

Further expansion?

In the fifties the leaders of Banbury wanted diversification of industry and therefore accepted expansion. By the sixties pressure for expansion came from central government. The most outstanding example was the report of the South-East Study, on the edge of whose area Banbury lay. This study proposed a new town near Banbury, which was then faced with the alternative of expanding further or being dwarfed by a new town nearby.

In this climate Oxfordshire County Council drew up a plan, which received Ministerial approval in 1965, to expand Banbury beyond the projected 40,000 to 70,000. This proposal the town ultimately rejected soon after the field-work started.[19] The earlier decision to expand from 20,000 to 40,000 therefore still stood, and expansion to this target was proceeding visibly.

The indecision surrounding the several new proposals and the final rejection of the 'Banbury 70,000' plan had its own visible effects upon the town. Land which had fallen into disuse, some of it right in the centre of the town, remained derelict for many years. No decision had been taken about the development of the area, whether to use the land for a new road, for car parks, or shops, so no rebuilding could be started. Businesses wishing to develop claimed, no doubt with reason, that they had had development applications waiting a long time for a decision.

Power, persistence and change

The themes of this book are epitomized in the events surrounding the expansion issue: much has changed, but much also persists. The unequal distribution of power and influence and the opaqueness of their exercise remain. But the foci of power have shifted in a number of ways, and, in response, so have the efforts of people to gain or retain for themselves some small influence or control over their lives. The face of the town has perhaps altered more than the pattern of social relations, although these have also changed.

In one sense the prediction of the local civic society, when the restudy was announced, that we should find 'just as much tradition, and a bit more change'[20] is also our verdict. But we have also found that the tradition itself has been subtly changed to meet the new

19

situation and to justify the new kinds of action needed. We have also found that there is even less which is unique to Banbury nowadays than there was in 1948–50. More factories, more houses, more people, more like any other town in Britain: these were the obvious changes on the face of Banbury when the 1966 restudy began.

2 Banburians, immigrants and work

Industrial ownership and control

In the first study, traditional industries were defined as those which were locally owned and controlled. Length of establishment and size were two further criteria used to classify firms. Some tendency was observed for these variables to cluster, so that old-established industries tended to be also locally owned and controlled and of small scale. But, as was then observed, there were major exceptions: the banks and the railways were notable examples of old-established but large-scale enterprises owned and controlled from outside Banbury.[1]

In this context the aluminium factory represented the 'acme of non-traditionalism'[2] because it was newly established, large-scale, and owned and controlled from overseas. By the time of the restudy the aluminium factory no longer fitted this description. It has now been in the town for over thirty years and has, in the words of a native Banburian returning after twenty years away, 'become more like belonging'. Whereas in 1950 immigrants to the town were over-represented among aluminium workers,[3] the 1967 survey suggests that the ratio of Banburians to immigrants in Alcan reflects the ratio in the total labour force. The average age of its workers is now relatively high compared with other industries. Its managers used to play little part in the political life of the Borough but by now some have served on the Borough Council. Furthermore, the aluminium factory is less unusual in its scale nowadays, for all the major Banbury industries, with the exception of the construction industry, are now dominated by large companies.

But many small firms remain: the 1967 survey showed that over 42 per cent of employed respondents were working in establishments of less than 100 people. Few of these small establishments are found

21

in manufacturing; most are in non-manual service industries, i.e. professional and commercial services and the like. Those firms where the owner is actively involved in day-to-day management tend to be small establishments (half of the small-size firms have owner-managers compared with only 5 per cent of those employing over 100 people).

In 1950, firms where owners were actively involved in day-to-day management accounted for a third of the employment of male household heads.[4] In 1967 they accounted for only just over a fifth of the employment of males over 21 years of age. In addition, the 1950 tendency for employees in owner-manager industries to be Banburians has also declined.

In the thirties, a period of high unemployment in many parts of Britain, men came to Banbury to work in the new aluminium plant and brought their families with them. Thus at that time, and continuing into the war years when aluminium was in high demand, more immigrants and younger people tended to work there. Many of the children of the earlier immigrants have been born or brought up in the town and thus are Banburians by our definition. In so far as the sons of immigrants now work in the 'Alley', they have increased the proportion of Banburians working there.

This effect is increased by the recently established Birds factory which, along with Automotive Products, has taken the place of the 'Alley' in employing a high proportion of immigrants. The tendency for newly established firms in an expanding town to employ newcomers to the town is reinforced in the case of Birds because the firm brought so many of its own employees with it from Birmingham.[5]

Around 1950 there was some tendency for the industrial life of the town to be divided. There was a non-traditional sector with large-scale industry controlled and directed from outside the town and tending to employ more immigrants than Banburians and a traditional sector of smaller owner-manager concerns tending to employ a majority of natives. Some of the local owner-managers were also town leaders and stood in other leadership roles to their workers in addition to that of employer. These multiple leadership roles played by the élite were unquestioned by many of their employees, who had been brought up in the locality to accept the right of such people to lead in many aspects of the town's life. By contrast, the non-traditional sector lacked any cohesion and in no way constituted a social system. The relationship of managers to workers was confined to the work place and, furthermore, managers took little part in the life of the town.

This pattern has now been broken in so far as the small employers no longer have a majority of Banburians in their work force and many Banburians now work in the Alley. In addition, some of the

22

Alcan managers are now involved in town affairs. These, with some of the owner-managers, are in positions of authority over their employees in situations other than the work place.

There is less economic power in Banbury than there was in 1950, in so far as a larger proportion of industrial firms are now owned and controlled from outside the town. Managers in these firms have limited amounts of freedom, working within a policy laid down elsewhere, ultimately perhaps abroad, in America or Canada. The remaining owner-managers can, of course, determine their own policies and in this sense have more independence. They also work within constraints, however, for their power is quite limited. What policies they can decide on must depend upon the markets, and sometimes the world markets. Their continued self-determination at work depends upon the skill of their judgements and the size of their resources to combat market fluctuations. The persistence of a sector of small-scale owner-managers suggests that small men can still operate in such circumstances, despite the increasing dominance of the large firms.

The owner-managers are also subject to the decisions of town planners, and these owners, along with other small proprietors, combined in various ways to protect their interests. This they were able to do with more success where the relevant power lay within the Borough. When it lay outside they could be less effective.

Although at the mercy of economic and political movements, nevertheless there is still a real sense in which the owner-manager is his own master when contrasted with the manager in the large-scale industries. On the other hand, the latter, within the authority delegated to them, may wield much greater resources with more widespread effects than those of the owner-managers. The power may not belong to the employee-managers, but they have more of it.[6]

The workers in industries of all sorts are even more subject to constraints upon their activities than are the owners and managers. The Birds employees had a forced choice of moving to Banbury with the firm, or losing their jobs. Although unemployment was not high in Birmingham in the sixties, many preferred to risk the move rather than the unemployment. They were, after all, sure of a house. To find a house rather than a job was one of the reasons why others immigrated to Banbury. Nevertheless, nearly 60 per cent of the men interviewed in 1967 and who had come to town since 1960 gave work as their main reason for moving to Banbury.

Workers' preferences for plants of various sizes

It is clear that some workers prefer to work in a small-scale plant while others prefer a larger work place.[7] To some extent workers sort themselves out according to their preferences for large or small firms. But it is also clear that workers cannot always find a job in the kind of firm they prefer. Their chances depend upon the availability of jobs at the time they come to town or enter the labour market: hence the large number of migrants in the aluminium factory in the thirties. Analysis of workers now employed in Banbury shows that three-quarters of the Banburians who are likely to have started work before 1945 are employed in firms which were already established then, compared with a half of the Banburians who started work after 1945. A similar picture is found for immigrants.

Within the constraints imposed by employment opportunities it would appear that workers selected the firm which fitted their values. Nearly three-quarters of the small plant respondents in Banbury said that, given the choice, they would choose to work in a small rather than a large firm. As in 1950, those working in small firms were less likely to support the Labour party. They also perceived a lower level of hostility between classes. Indeed a significant proportion did not even believe that classes existed.[8]

Many of the owner-managers learned their business on the shop floor. Of one it was said that at that time he could be recognized because 'he worked harder, was dirtier and swore louder than the rest of the men'. Men respect the knowledge of gaffers such as he because 'he knows what he's talking about'. Furthermore he learnt from some of his own employees, who therefore have certain claims to superiority over him. Such bosses often give personal help and guidance to their men: financial help, a loan of equipment, housing advice and so on. Gaffer and men know each other as individuals rather than as members of relatively anonymous categories.[9]

Control in small firms also tends to be personal, the men being trusted to work to a satisfactory standard in required time limits with little supervision,[10] i.e. the compliance structure appears to be more normative than in a large plant.[11] Associated with this, evidence was found in Banbury of Gouldner's 'indulgency pattern', that is, managers and workers with mutual expectations of each other based on standards more commonly relevant among family members, friends and neighbours than in business or industry.[12] The personal nature of work in a small firm was the main reason given by survey respondents for preferring it.

It is consistent with this pattern of authority and legitimacy that trade-union membership should be lower in small firms than large. Three out of 38 small firm manual workers in the sub-sample claimed to belong to a trade union, compared with 35 out of 41 in large plants.[13] Fifty-two per cent of the men working in large plants who responded to the main survey claimed union membership. In firms with owner-managers only 13 per cent said they were union members, but the proportion rose to 35 per cent in small firms with employee-managers. The greater difficulties of organizing unions in small plants does not therefore appear to be the whole explanation for the low union membership in small owner-manager firms. Earnings were generally lower in small firms than in large, which also provides no explanation for the low level of unionism. Acceptance of lower incomes seems to be one price those who choose the small firm pay for their preference for its style of management.

Some workers in large plants envied the more personal relations in small plants, evidence of one cost to them of the jobs they had. Some also envied the possibility of seeing the work of a small firm as a whole. As one aluminium worker put it: 'I make something, but I just don't see what happens to it.' But others who worked in large plants preferred it there, enjoying the impersonality of the large organization, 'there isn't someone breathing down your neck all the time'; and the companionship of workmates: 'in a large firm there's no favouritism, everybody's equal'. Rather than good relations with management, those who preferred large firms stressed the security or the good working conditions the firm provided.

Economic constraints have led to a certain amount of mis-match for some workers between their preferences for large or small plants, although a majority prefer, or have become reconciled to, the styles of management in the place where they work. There is no doubt, however, that two quite distinct styles of accepting managerial authority emerge. One is that of the large plant employee who does not see much of management and does not want to: 'they don't bother me and I don't bother them'. The second is that of the small plant employee who enjoys involvement with managers and owners in the work place, accepts their help and advice in his private life and their leadership in social and political affairs. The former is more likely to be a trade unionist and a Labour voter and the latter to be a Conservative and not belong to a union. But this difference is not one between Banburian and immigrant. Place of origin and date of migration may affect place of employment, but are not related to preferences for management styles or plant size.

Occupational status in Banbury

Along with its increasing industrialization, Banbury has become less of a 'middle-class town' than it was in 1950. Less than 10 per cent of those in the survey area and only 7 per cent of those in the Borough are now in Hall–Jones classes 1, 2, and 3 compared with 13·5 per cent in 1950. It is also less 'middle class' than England and Wales and has more semi-skilled and unskilled workers (see Table 2.1).

25

TABLE 2.1 *Socio-economic groups of economically active males in Banbury and England and Wales compared (%)*

Socio-economic group	Banbury M.B.	England & Wales
Managerial and self-employed (SEGs, 1, 2, 3, 4, 12, 13, 14)	15·1	19·9
Other non-manual (SEGs 5, 6, 7)	18·2	18·2
Foreman and skilled manual (SEGs 8, 9)	33·9	35·0
Semi-skilled, unskilled manual and agricultural workers (SEGs 10, 11, 15)	30·5	24·9
Armed forces and misc.	2·2	2·0

Source: Census 1966.

Immigrants are still over-represented in the higher-occupational and higher-paid categories, as they were in 1950. Over a quarter (28 per cent) of immigrant men had occupations in Registrar-General Classes I and II compared with 12 per cent of Banburians, nearly three-quarters of whom are in manual occupations compared with just over half (55 per cent) of the employed immigrants.

These differences derive from constraints upon workers, in this case the more highly trained non-manual workers. Banburians with the appropriate education, training and skill are unlikely to find an executive, professional or managerial job available in Banbury when they are looking for work. They therefore have to look elsewhere. In addition the policies of large corporations with plants in many places, in Britain and abroad, demand mobile managers. Only 14 per cent of non-manual workers in owner-manager firms came to Banbury after 1960 compared with 40 per cent of those in employee-manager firms (i.e. overwhelmingly the large corporations). In the large firms in Banbury two in five of those in social classes I and II had left school after 17 years of age and more of these were Banburians. By contrast Banburians in higher managerial positions are more likely to have inherited their status and are less likely to have been educated to 17 years old or beyond. The more highly educated Banburians have left town for work elsewhere (see also pp. 127–8).

Economic status, place of origin and local involvement

Many authors have commented on the geographically and/or socially mobile non-manual workers, although each author has tended to stress a different aspect of the phenomenon. Frankenberg[14] appears to consider Stacey's non-traditionalists,[15] Watson's spiralists,[16] and Merton's cosmopolitans[17] as different names for the same category of people. Yet this is not so. Some of Stacey's 'middle-class non-traditionalists' were spiralists in Watson's sense, but her term covered more than these.[18] Merton was concerned primarily with orientations when he used the terms local and cosmopolitan and he made it quite plain that social structure could not be inferred from the orientations of residents.[19] In 1950 the local owners of small businesses still remained important local leaders, despite the presence of large-scale employers such as the railway and the aluminium works. Little challenge to the local leadership was offered by the new managers of large-scale enterprises.[20]

As the field-work continued we became increasingly aware of the complexity of the relationship between economic position and local social behaviour and realized that no simple and close association could be assumed between social and geographic mobility and particular sets of attitudes and behaviour. Stacey had already warned for the Banbury of 1950 that not all Banburians were members of the traditional social system while some immigrants were.[21] Perhaps even less in the sixties was any close association between employment, status, place of origin, social relations and attitudes found. In one respect a person might be locality-oriented, in other respects he might be quite the reverse, as Stacey had also noted.[22] Not all persons in the same economic statuses have the same local involvement, for many other factors are also relevant. Some local businessmen are more active in the affairs of the town than others because of long family traditions of 'public service'. These men are akin to Watson's 'burgesses'. It is probably true that Banbury businessmen frequently have a local orientation, but not all of them, even those actively involved in local affairs. Moreover in Banbury, as elsewhere, orientations may vary on particular issues.[23] In our view, therefore, economic structural position should be seen as predisposing but not determining the amount of local involvement of the incumbent.

The pattern of business contacts of the small businessman is frequently of a purely local kind, often the contacts could not be transferred elsewhere. He has no conflict between locality and business, his business tends to enmesh him in the locality. The extent to which this is true varies, of course, from one business to another. Some of the local businessmen are natives and come from families which have long been established in business in Banbury. Some joined the family business, but others have set up in businesses of their own. Some of the latter have rejected the style of business of their forebears. Some have moved into occupations where they could usefully combine formal or professional qualifications with the local knowledge and contacts which they 'inherited' from the position of their kin in the town and their place among their kin. Yet other sons left the town to work as managers or in other types of employment in other places.

But not all local businessmen come from business families. Some have been upwardly mobile within the town: the son of a railway workman was now an established and successful businessman and an important figure in the political and associational life of the town; he had been relatively successful at school, and had thus been able to work his way up through various office jobs to his position of relative eminence. Other natives had started their working life on the shop floor, and through their own efforts (some, according to local gossip, of a dubious kind) had managed to set themselves up in business and had become successful. Others remained self-employed, while the less fortunate found themselves back in the ranks of employees.

Furthermore, many local businessmen are not natives. Some have been socially as well as geographically mobile, others have not. A few were only recently arrived in Banbury, persuaded to come to the town under the overspill agreement with London, but these were fewer than the Council hoped. Others had come almost by chance. One, for example, had moved his firm to the town because he happened to have a country cottage nearby and had thus become aware of the possibilities of setting up in the town.

Thus, local employers in Banbury came from a wide variety of backgrounds, and in many respects their attitudes and behaviour varied widely. Some, and not only the natives, were actively involved in the affairs of the town, while others were not. Some were scarcely known in the social, associational and political life of the town, and among these were numbered many native-born businessmen.

In contrast to the businessmen whose economic interests are almost entirely in Banbury are the managers of the large international corporations whose business interests and contacts tend to pull them away from the locality. For example, in the food factory, raw materials come from outside the locality, often from outside the country, and Banbury makes up a minute part of the market for their products. Moreover, directives on policy frequently originate from elsewhere, and promotion may involve movement out of the town, to other plants or other companies; there is little opportunity of alternative employment in the town. The situation is much the same as in the aluminium factory in 1950.[24] In such cases, commitment to the locality would conflict with career interests. Most have little local commitment. Managers tend to come to the town because career considerations dictate it, rather than for any attractions of Banbury.

There is, however, a category of immigrants in firms run from outside Banbury whose work requires local knowledge. Many of these take a more active part in the locality. Personnel managers, bank managers, clergy and some government officials fall into this category. They are, for the time being at least, locally-oriented immigrants: they may perhaps be referred to as spiralist-locals. Some become so involved in the locality, or members of their families do, that they prefer to reject promotion rather than uproot themselves. If their spiralism is 'blocked'[25] it is at their own wish, not because of their lack of skill or failure to be selected.

TABLE 2.2 *Economic status, place of origin and local involvement*

	Place of origin	*Work involve- ment*	*Local social and political involvement*	*Orientation*	*Watson's categories*
Local businessmen; Owner-managers	Banbury or elsewhere	mainly local	may be local	probably local, but some more cos- mopolitan	assorted burgesses
		some cosmo- politan	may be		
Large corporation managers	outside Banbury	mainly local	may be	local/cos- mopolitan	spiralist- locals
		almost entirely cosmo- politan	unlikely to be	cosmopolitan	spiralists and blocked spiralists

Table 2.2 summarizes this discussion and shows that we have identified local businessmen and large corporation managers. The former may be native or immigrant and may or may not have been upwardly mobile. A minority is involved as leaders in local affairs. In many cases their business requires a good deal of local knowledge and thus involves them in local affairs. Their orientations may be local, but in some cases are more cosmopolitan. The large corporation managers are almost all immigrants. In some cases their work attach- ments are cosmopolitan and they have little local involvement. These are the spiralists. In some cases the work of these managers requires local knowledge and involvement: these are the spiralist-locals, some of whom move on but others of whom stay voluntarily, becoming settlers rather than blocked spiralists. Thus place of origin, demands of the occupation, personal orientation and interest all interact to determine the extent to which businessmen are involved in local affairs: it is no simple matter of natives and immigrants, nor of burgesses and spiralists.

3 Religion in Banbury

Contrary to some expectations, religious adherence and religious activity have not changed much in Banbury between the two surveys, whether judged by the numbers of denominational adherents or of church members (see Table 3.1). Nor is there any increase in the numbers without religion or denomination. Around one in seven adults in the Borough belongs to a religious body, about the same as in 1950, and significantly more than the members of any other voluntary organization or association, including political parties.[1] The majority of people in Banbury are married in a religious ceremony and non-religious burials are almost unknown.

The religious message also reaches many people through television and radio. There is a religious press and major events in the religious world are reported by all media. An ATV study of religion and television, in London, the Midlands and North of England, found that 45 per cent of those interviewed 'make a point of listening to or watching religious services on television', and 60 per cent of all those interviewed in fact saw religious programmes.[2] While religious activists see or hear religious programmes more than others, some people look on television services as a legitimate substitute for church attendance. Many children in Banbury attend Sunday-school; there are Anglican and Roman Catholic denominational day schools, and all state schools include some religious instruction.

There appear to have been some slight changes in denominational adherence between the two surveys. It seems that the Church of England and the Baptists have proportionately gained adherents and the Methodists, Salvation Army and Roman Catholics have lost compared with 1950. But the Anglicans as well as the Methodists have lost in the number and proportion of their church members (see Table 3.1). A number of sects new to the town are actively campaigning, notably the Mormons and Christadelphians, as well as

TABLE 3.1 *Distribution of denominational adherents and church members: 1950ᵃ and 1967ᵇ*

Denomination	Adherents					Members (Banbury Borough Only)							
	Banbury Borough				Englandᶜ %	No. of members		Denominational % of members		Members as % of pop.		Members as % of adherents	
	No.	%	No.	%									
	1950	1950	1967	1967	1964	1950	1967	1950	1967	1950	1967	1950	1967
Church of England	1,450	68·0	630	72·2	67	701	687	36·5	27·7	5·2	4·1	7·8	5·5
Methodist	252	11·7	73	8·5	} 13	448	527	23·3	21·1	3·4	3·1	28·4	36·0
Baptist	48	2·2	29	3·3		90	180	4·6	7·2	0·7	1·1	30·0	31·0
Salvation Army	36	1·7	9	1·0		72	120	3·7	4·8	0·5	0·7	32·0	67·0
Congregational	14	0·7	8	0·9		68	70	3·7	2·8	0·5	0·3		42·6
Roman Catholic	211	9·9	73	8·5	9	560	905	28·2	36·4	4·2	5·4	42·5	62·0
Other denominations	61	2·9	32	3·7	5	NA	(c.200)	NA	..	..	..		(36·0)
No denomination	49	2·3	8	0·9	} 6	..	..	..	..	..	..	..	..
Agnostic/atheist	13	0·6	13	1·5		..	..	..	..	..	..	..	..
Total excluding other denominations, none, etc.						1,939	2,489	100	100	14·5	14·7	15·5	15·1
Total in sample	2,134	100	875	100	100	..	..	..	..	..	..	..	..

ᵃ These data are taken from Table 14, p. 59, T. & C.

ᵇ 6 per cent sample, Banbury M.B. only.

ᶜ Social Surveys (Gallup Poll) Ltd for ABC TV, quoted J. Brothers, *Religious Institutions*, (Longman, 1971), pp. 11–12. The data cover London, Midland and North regions only.

31

older-established sects which have mounted evangelical campaigns. Roman Catholic membership cannot be established, but Roman Catholic congregations account for 44 per cent of all attendances compared with 16 per cent accounted for by Anglican congregations.

Except in the Roman Catholic church, women and those over 45 years old form a majority of activists. This is true of church attendance, where, in a survey taken, 60 per cent were found to be women and over 55 per cent were thought to be over 45.[3] Eight per cent of survey respondents[4] claimed membership of a religious organization: two-thirds were women and a quarter of these were widows or spinsters. Five per cent of respondents under 45 claimed membership compared with 13 per cent of those over 60 years old. This pattern is as it was in 1950.

Members of religious organizations are more likely to belong to the Registrar-General's social classes I and II (where 16 per cent belonged to religious organizations) than to IIIa and IVa (4 per cent) or to IIIb, IV and V (7 per cent). It is still true, as it was in the late forties, that within a denomination there are occupational class differences between churches.

In the late forties the social significance of religious organization and belief centred upon the variations in the beliefs of the denominations and sects and the relation of these to variations in the form of organization and of service. The Free Churches indicated a closer relationship of man to God than did the Church of England or the Roman Catholic Church, where the role of priest as mediator was stressed more strongly. None of the churches or sects was particular to Banbury, all being part of larger national and sometimes international organizations. But the amount of local control of religious affairs in Banbury varied, as did the power of the congregations. The Anglican and the Roman Catholic churches were hierarchical, the priest being appointed to, not chosen by, the congregation. The priest himself was subject to higher ecclesiastical authority. The Free Churches on the other hand, although all part of national and international movements, were more decentralized and democratic. The congregation often chose the minister and in some cases did not have a minister at all.

These variations were associated with beliefs and relationships which adherents exhibited in other social relations in the town. Free Church adherents tended to be Liberal and more interested in 'cultural' matters than the Anglicans, who tended to be Conservative and involved in a variety of sporting activities. The Roman Catholics, on the other hand, tended to be rather apart from the social and political life of the town, interacting for the most part with their fellow believers.

There was little co-operation among the denominations in the late forties. Although clergy and ministers met in a fraternal and there was some co-operation among the Free Churches, joint activities had little success. Indeed, it was not until 1965, just before the restudy, that a Council of Churches was formed.

At the time of the first study, the Free Churchmen and the Anglicans, despite their differences, shared certain beliefs about the importance of charity, although Free Churchmen emphasized self-help and mutual aid more strongly, as befitted their stress upon brotherhood and fellowship. Only one of the religious activists and leaders associated himself with the beliefs of the Labour party, which in Banbury at that time appeared secular and without overt religious connections. This may have been connected with an observed tendency for immigrants to be less religiously active than Banburians. Nevertheless, the town was not irreligious: rather, its religion was passive.

While these variations in belief and organization are still to be found among the churches, denominations and sects in Banbury, they were not the aspects of religion which seemed most important in 1966–8. The political division between the Liberals and Conservatives had been muted by the decline in the Liberal party and the disappearance of its leaders from positions of influence in the town. Although Free Church adherents still tend to vote Liberal more often than others and Anglicans are still more likely to vote Conservative, the opposition of Labour and Conservative has replaced, as predicted, the Conservative–Liberal conflict. The majority of leading lay Christians who are also active in politics are now associated with the Conservative party and politically opposed to the Labour party. Committees of both Anglican and Methodist churches have links with the Conservative party, although the Methodists also link indirectly with the Labour party. (A link is said to exist when one person sits on two committees.) Figures 3.1, 3.2 and 3.3 show the links of voluntary association committees with the committees of the Anglican churches, the Free Churches and the Roman Catholic church respectively. Although 'sharing' certain associations, the Anglican and the Free Church territories are somewhat different. The full analysis of links among the voluntary associations, which in 1950 yielded three territories, Anglican/Conservative/Bowling,[5] Free Church/Liberal and Labour, now yields only two major territories: Anglican/Free Church/Conservative and Labour.[6] The lack of Roman Catholic links has to be remarked.

Although on balance the Free Churches must be said to fall within the Conservative territory, nevertheless the Free Churches are on a frontier between the two major parties. The Free Church committees yield direct links with both Labour and Conservative territories, and Free Church committee-men are more likely than

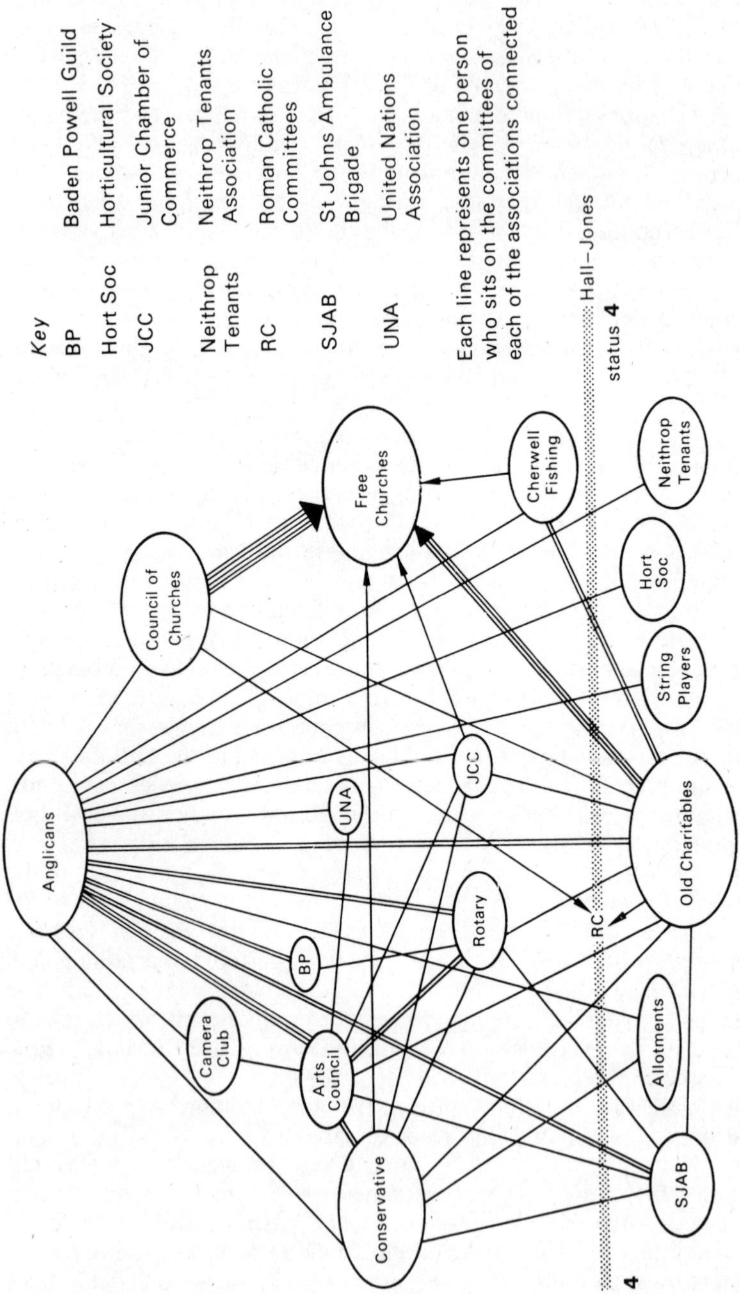
Key
BP Baden Powell Guild
Hort Soc Horticultural Society
JCC Junior Chamber of Commerce
Neithrop Tenants Neithrop Tenants Association
RC Roman Catholic Committees
SJAB St Johns Ambulance Brigade
UNA United Nations Association
Each line represents one person who sits on the committees of each of the associations connected
Hall–Jones status 4
4
Anglicans
Council of Churches
Free Churches
Cherwell Fishing
Neithrop Tenants
Hort Soc
String Players
JCC
UNA
Old Charitables
Rotary
BP
RC
Camera Club
Arts Council
Allotments
Conservative
SJAB

FIGURE 3.1 *Anglican territory*

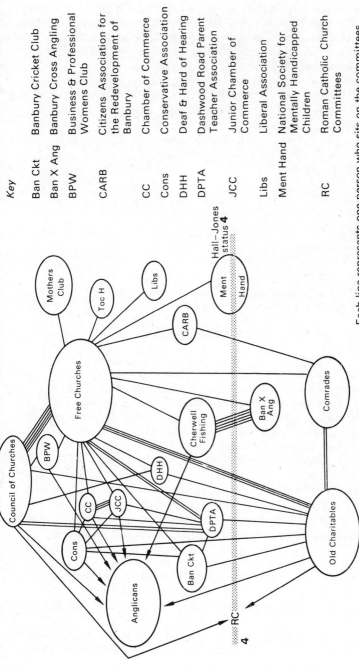

Key

Ban Ckt	Banbury Cricket Club
Ban X Ang	Banbury Cross Angling
BPW	Business & Professional Womens Club
CARB	Citizens Association for the Redevelopment of Banbury
CC	Chamber of Commerce
Cons	Conservative Association
DHH	Deaf & Hard of Hearing
DPTA	Dashwood Road Parent Teacher Association
JCC	Junior Chamber of Commerce
Libs	Liberal Association
Ment Hand	National Society for Mentally Handicapped Children
RC	Roman Catholic Church Committees

Each line represents one person who sits on the committees of each of the associations connected.

FIGURE 3.2 *Free Church territory*

Anglican committee-men to serve in both territories. This is not surprising as the notions of brotherhood and mutual aid are closely associated with some socialist values, while the occupational status of most active Free Churchmen has more in common with that of Conservative than that of Labour supporters.

Religious divisions in Banbury therefore no longer reinforce party political divisions as they once did. At the same time active religious adherents were attempting to reduce the differences between the denominations.

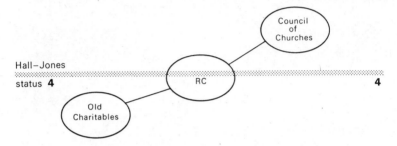

Each line represents one person who sits on the committees of each of the associations connected.

FIGURE 3.3   *Roman Catholic voluntary association links*

The younger lay members, especially non-manual workers, were the leaders of the ecumenical movement in Banbury. The clergy, although they showed sympathy with the movement, were dubious about it. Each of them had been socialized through a long period of training into a particular denominational tradition. They therefore were not only fully aware of doctrinal differences, but were highly committed to their own doctrines. In this they were unlike many members of the laity for whom denominational attachment was social rather than doctrinal. Lay members in conversation with a researcher often found they did not know the unique aspects of their own denominational doctrine and/or accepted those of other denominations. Their attachment was to a particular form of service. Some when persuaded by advocates of the ecumenical movement to attend the service of another denomination found that they had had mistaken ideas about what the service would be like. Some enjoyed the service, rather to their own surprise, an important discovery for those for whom the expressive role of religion is of outstanding importance.

The clergy, as individuals, have more at risk, of course, than their congregations, which also partly explains their hesitation about unity. Wilson has suggested that the unity movement is a product of the professional considerations of the clergy, because they have the greatest investment in the continuation of the Church.[7] The long-term decline in religious observance leads many to feel the future of the Church is threatened.[8] But the Banbury priests and ministers did not take this long-term view, although Wilson may be right for the higher levels of the clergy outside Banbury.

There is some analogy here with the position of the managers of some large corporations in Banbury described in the last chapter. The priest or minister is a spiralist-local (see p. 29). Few expect to stay in Banbury for the rest of their lives. Many hope for promotion, and some denominations encourage a rotation of ministers from one congregation to another. At the same time the work of the priest or minister requires that he should be involved in the locality to further the Christian message (on the success of which his career prospects may be expected to depend). Thus, on the one hand the clergy and ministers have a status in the town which derives from their responsibilities for and to a particular church. On the other hand, they have a much wider religious and organizational commitment which is the essence of their vocation. The first leads them to involvement in a particular pattern of social relationships in the town and encourages them to accept the *status quo* and make what they can of it. The second may lead them to attitudes in conflict with the local laity. The tensions, deriving from their spiralist-local status go some way to explaining the ambivalent and generally unenthusiastic attitudes of many clergymen towards the ecumenical movement. Although some laymen were the leaders of the ecumenical movement, many lay church activists were at least as hesitant as their clergy about the movement, thus reinforcing the latter's hesitation. Such laymen guard their own churches jealously. Many are attached to particular buildings where for many years their families have prayed and been graved. The laity too might well lose their official positions in the church or chapel, since after unity there would be fewer offices to go round.[9]

The ecumenical movement does not include the 'uninstitutionalized sects',[10] which in Banbury include the Mormons and the Elim Four Square, who have not softened their opposition to the denominations and churches. They have doctrinal objections to the ecumenical movement: they reject any compromise with the world or any 'watering down' of their faith,[11] emphasizing personal salvation and a personal relationship with the Saviour. These sects, unlike the churches and denominations (except the Roman Catholics), have many members who are manual workers. Furthermore they rarely have full-time ministers and are not represented on the bodies where priests and ministers meet. Occupational class, organization, and doctrine all set them apart and keep them outside the ecumenical movement. But all are active evangelists.

The ecumenical movement therefore is active in the Conservative/Anglican/Free Church territory, particularly among the young middle-class laity. It is active in that area where the socio-political divisions which used to reinforce the religious divisions have dissolved as a result of economic and political change. Furthermore, there are social similarities between Anglican and Free Church adherents.[12] The sample survey showed that 35 per cent of those claiming Anglican adherence and 36·5 per cent of Free Church adherents were in non-manual occupations. Those churches and sects which remained outside the ecumenical movement were also those with a major ity of adherents in manual occupations, namely the Roman Catholic Church (seven out of ten manual workers) and the smaller sects whose members seem predominantly to be manual workers. These two (quite different) religious groups share an aloofness from ecumenicalism and from many social and political activities in the town, a separateness reinforced by occupational status.

Charity was a value commonly expressed during the first study, especially in the Anglican/Conservative sector of the town. The value was expressed through various charitable organizations, some of which like the Old Charitable Society, were of ancient foundation. By the time of the second study, the way of offering charity was being redefined and the conception of the Church in the world revitalized.

Often the new welfare schemes were associated with the unity movement. The Welfare Sub-Committee of the Council of Churches is one example. The Fish Scheme is another. This scheme was organized by the combined efforts of a number of churches and was an attempt by Christians to give personal aid in the streets where they lived. Church members were to be ready to help anyone in their area who showed he needed help by getting in touch with a Fish Scheme official or by displaying the sign of a fish in his window. The Scheme met with some success, but this was limited by the fact that the helpers tended to be concentrated in the better-off residential areas, while those in need lived in quite other parts of the town. Thus residential segregation between occupational classes joined with the concentration of religious activists among higher occupational classes partially to defeat the latter's attempts at Christian charity.

In the Fish Scheme, as in the ecumenical movement, the laity played a prominent part. This was also true of a campaign, designed to increase church awareness of society and the need for unity, called 'The People Next Door'. In some of the Free Churches the laity have always been of equivalent status to the ordained clergy and some sects have no clergy. But in its present form the emphasis on the laity is new in the Anglican and Catholic churches.

The organizational centres and sources of ideas of all the denominations and sects lay outside Banbury, and in this they resembled the large-scale economic organizations. At the same time there was a movement to encourage greater initiative among the congregations, to decentralize. In some cases minority groups of laymen were pressing for reforms against the wishes of the majority and sometimes to the embarrassment of their clergy. There were, therefore, early signs of challenge to the centralized power of the church organizations.

Within the town religion does not reinforce other divisions as it once did. Religion creates its own divisions in the society, but where social, political and economic characteristics are common, denominations are increasingly co-operating. Some religious divisions remain important in their own right: the Roman Catholics, with representatives from all classes, are self-sufficient in charity as in their social life. The smaller sects are also separate, drawing together the poorer (but not the poorest) manual workers. This last religious division reinforces a class and status division. But religion nowadays in Banbury, except in the case of the Catholics, would seem to reflect economic and social divisions rather than itself causing division.

4 Political parties, voluntary associations and pressure groups

Banbury is a municipal borough in the County of Oxfordshire. Its inhabitants, at the time of the second survey, were therefore entitled, as they had been since the end of the nineteenth century, to vote for representatives at three levels of government: the borough council, the county council and the Parliament at Westminster. The Parliamentary constituency of North Oxfordshire, in which Banbury is the largest and most industrial town, has returned a Conservative member to Parliament since 1922. The County is also dominated by the Conservative party. Furthermore, the Municipal Borough Council (24 seats) has had a Conservative majority from the time of the first survey until 1956 and from 1959 to 1965. The Labour party has only had a clear majority on the Council for one year in the whole period between the two surveys, although there were years in the late fifties and early sixties when the parties were evenly divided on the Council.

Two main features dominated the pattern of politics in Banbury from the end of the war to 1950. One was the clear association between voting and occupational class and between party membership and occupational class. The second was the link between religion and politics. Neither of these sets of associations is as strong as it was, but associations between voting and religious adherence are of the same kind as previously. The tendency persists for women to vote Conservative more often than men. Women are also less likely to vote Labour.

As was mentioned in the last chapter, an Anglican/Free Church/Conservative territory has now replaced the former two territories, Anglican/Conservative/Bowling and Free Church/Liberal which were identified around 1950.[1] The new Anglican/Free Church/Conservative territory lacks the clear clustering which was found among

40

the town's leaders in 1950. This new territory is distinguishable from the Labour territory which by contrast is small and isolated, although somewhat less so than it used to be. (See Figs. 4.1 and 4.2.)

In 1950, after the links between the committees of all voluntary associations, religious associations and political associations had been charted, it was found that a clear occupational-status frontier divided the chart.[2] Those committees on one side of this 'frontier' had an occupational-status median of 1 or 2 (Hall–Jones scale) and those below it of 4 or 5. Only one link crossed this frontier. A picture emerged of a deeply divided town: there were even two distinct groups of sporting associations, one above and one below the occupational-status frontier.

In 1966–8 no such clear frontier emerged. Despite the undoubtedly higher average occupational status of joiners and committee members compared with the rest of the town, there is no longer a clear occupational-status frontier among the committees. Such division as there is appears to be lower, at Hall–Jones class 4, and not at 3 as formerly. This frontier runs through three voluntary associations (excluding religious and political organizations); 38 are above the line and 17 below.

In 1950 all the Labour territory fell under the line, i.e. the average occupational status of committee members was less than Hall–Jones 3. In 1966–8 not all the committees in the Labour territory had a median occupational-status of under 4, although most did. Furthermore, proportionately more of the Anglican/Free Church/Conservative territory falls below the occupational-status frontier than was the case in 1948–50. This is so despite the fact that the frontier has now been drawn an occupational class lower. This finding might suggest not only that Conservatism among manual workers remains strong, but also that such workers are becoming more actively involved in running affairs in the town.

It is still true to say of Banbury in 1967 as it was of Banbury in 1950 that 'the principal difference between supporters of the Labour and Conservative Parties . . . lies along social class lines. Almost all members of the middle class are Conservative (or if Liberal, at least anti-Labour) and almost all supporters of the Labour Party are working class.'[3] But the relationship is weaker than it was.

Property ownership, including domestic property, and work situation have, since Marx and Weber, been thought of as bases for class formation and for political action. Voting at the last election may be taken as one indicator of political belief and action. Table 4.1 suggests that there does appear to be a relationship between property ownership, higher occupational status and Conservative voting. The table displays the percentage of Conservative voters in a two-party vote, i.e. of the total of Conservative and Labour votes.

41

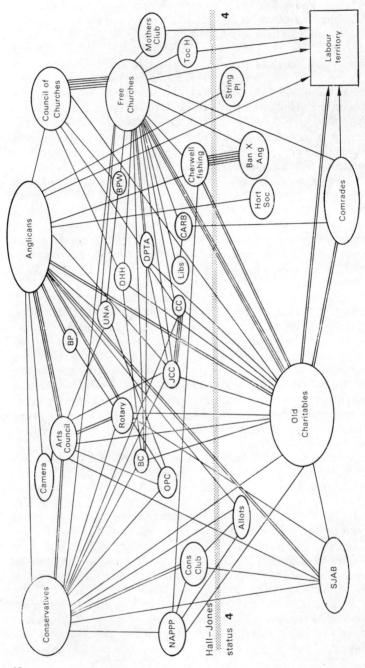

Key

Allots	Allotment Society
Ban X Ang	Banbury Cross Angling
BC	Banbury Cross Players
BP	Baden Powell Guild
BPW	Business & Professional Womens Club
CC	Chamber of Commerce
Cons Club	Conservative Club
CARB	Citizens Association for the Redevelopment of Banbury
DHH	Deaf & Hard of Hearing
DPTA	Dashwood Road Parent Teacher Association
Hort Soc	Horticultural Society
JCC	Junior Chamber of Commerce
Libs	Liberal Association
NAPPP	Neithrop Association for the Protection of Persons & Property
OPC	Old Peoples Club
SJAB	St Johns Ambulance Brigade
String Pl	Banbury String Players
UNA	United Nations Association

Source: Associations Survey

Each line represents one person who sits on the committees of each of the associations connected.

FIGURE 4.1 *Anglican/Free Church/Conservative territory*

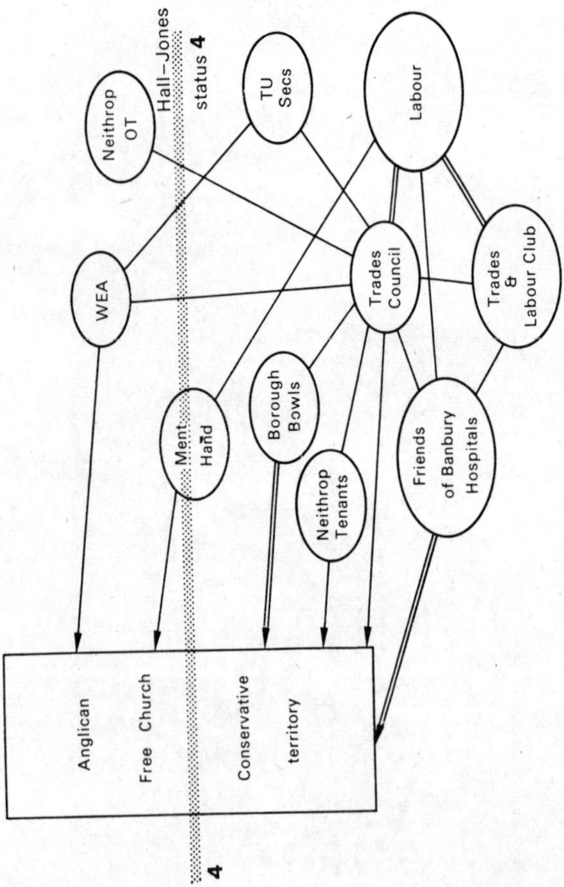

44

Key

Ment Hand — National Society for Mentally Handicapped Children

WEA — Workers Educational Association

TU Secs — Secretaries of Trade Unions

Neithrop OT — Neithrop Old Tyme Dancing

Neithrop Tenants — Neithrop Tenants Association

Source: Associations Survey

Each line represents one person who sits on the committees of each of the associations connected.

FIGURE 4.2 *Labour territory*

Those who own outright are the most Conservative category and include over 80 per cent in all classes from skilled manual and above. Among those who rent privately or who own subject to mortgage it is only in the non-manual categories that there is a large Conservative majority. Those who rent from the Council are most inclined to vote Labour, and this is true even if they are in non-manual occupational categories. It seems, therefore, that house tenure and occupational status combined can account for more of the variation in voting than either taken separately. An increase in property ownership has been one of the changes between the two surveys.

TABLE 4.1   *Occupational class, tenure and voting: Conservative vote as a percentage of a two-party vote* (*economically active married men*)

Reg.-Gen. Social Class	Own outright %	n	Own on mortgage %	n	Rent privately %	n	Rent from Council %	n	Other %	n	Total %
I and II	87·5	40	81·8	77	88·0	25	33·3	15	..	0	79·6
IIIa and IVa	81·8	22	76·3	38	81·8	22	53·3	30	..	0	72·3
IIIb	80·0	15	40·5	74	16·2	99	36·4	66	..	2	32·0
IVb	56·25	16	40·0	30	36·4	22	27·4	62	..	0	35·4
V	(5/5)	5	(1/3)	3	(5/10)	10	12·5	24	..	0	33·3

Source: 6 per cent sample, Banbury and District.

A combination of a non-manual occupation and education beyond the age of 16 is also highly associated with Conservative voting (see Table 4.2).

TABLE 4.2   *Occupation, education and voting: percentage voting Conservative of a two-party vote* (*economically active married men*)

| | Education completed at | | | |
| | 16 or over | | 15 or younger | |
	%	n	%	n
Non-manual	85·5	138	67·7	130
Manual	41·0	39	32·6	393

Source: 6 per cent sample, Banbury and District.

Immigrant manual workers were thought to have had a good deal of influence upon the rise of the Labour party in Banbury in the late forties. There was no significant difference in the proportion of Banburians and immigrants voting for the three parties in 1950 or 1967. However, there were, and still are, proportionately more immigrants among the Labour leaders.

In all other ways party leaders and activists exhibit, but more strongly, the same characteristics as their followers (see Appendix 7). There has been an increase in the number of salaried workers active in all parties compared with 1950. But the contrast remains between the Conservative and Liberal parties, which are largely non-manual, and the Labour party, where leading committee members and Borough Councillors are still predominantly wage-earning manual workers. As in 1950, none of the parties has any committee member of Hall–Jones occupational class 7.

Striking though the associations among voting, property owner-ship, occupational class, and terminal education age are, they are not reflected in clear divisions among the town's élite in 1967. Not only is the occupational-status frontier on the chart of committees' links lower than it used to be, the frontier does not indicate a break in social relations as the frontier of 1950 did. Then only one line crossed the frontier. In 1966–8, 44 links crossed the line (out of a total of 148 links). Occupational status does not seem to be having the same divisive consequences among the leadership as it had in 1950, yet paradoxically it remains important in the joining and running of associations.

The Anglican/Free Church/Conservative territory has absorbed almost all of the voluntary bodies within it, but by no means do all of these have committees with a median of over Hall–Jones 4. The Labour territory is below the line as before, where committees have a median of less than Hall–Jones 4, but there are many more links between this and the Anglican/Free Church/Conservative territory. The range of associations in the Labour territory is greater than it was.

Around 1950 it was noticeable that, while the Conservatives were much concerned with voluntary social service and charity, Labour activists were found only on officially sponsored social service agencies. This behaviour reflected the ideological position of the two parties. In 1967 Conservatives are still more involved with social service and charity than are the Labour people, as Fig. 4.1 and 4.2 suggest. But the presence of two charitable organizations within the Labour territory (the National Society for Mentally Handicapped Children and the Friends of Banbury Hospital) represents a major change in the behaviour of Labour activists. This reflects a new attitude, felt both locally and nationally, that there is a place for voluntary action in the welfare state. Such bodies as the National

Society for Mentally Handicapped Children also have a pressure-group character in their attempts to improve conditions of treatment.

The dominant position of the Conservatives in the government of the town is made plain in Fig. 4.3, which shows the links between committee members of the main parties and the governing and advisory bodies in the Borough. The Liberals are little involved. The Liberal links with statutory bodies reflect past rather than present political power.

Labour is now clearly articulated in the power structure. In 1950, although some Labour councillors were elected in the forties, the leaders of the Labour and trade-union movement had no recognized place in the political élite of the town. The process of their assimilation was just beginning. They still felt themselves to be, and with a few formal exceptions were, outside the local power structure. Their position is still weaker than that of the Conservatives, but Fig. 4.3 makes it plain that they are now clearly articulated in relation to local political executive bodies. They have, as predicted, replaced the Liberals.

Since a majority of Labour party leaders are employed manual workers and so are many of their supporters, in contrast to both Conservatives and Liberals, this change does mean that manual occupational classes are represented in the town's leadership and the town's affairs in a way in which they formerly were not. How much is their new involvement in charitable and voluntary service organization related to this change? Or should it be seen to be related to an opportunity, afforded by greater affluence, to be involved in individual charity?

People of a different kind are now involved in politics, but the number of political activists in the town is small compared to the total population. The large amount of overlapping in Fig. 4.3 testifies to this.[4] There are twenty-four members of the town council. All three parties have an agent/secretary. Conservative and Labour parties maintain ward organizations in five out of six wards; and these ward organizations tend to be dominated by councillors and ex-councillors. Labour party meetings rarely have an attendance of more than thirty in the town. Although the Conservatives can attract more for a major speaker, their normal meetings are no better attended than those of the Labour party. There are about another twenty people in each of the major parties who can be mobilized during local elections to help distribute literature and to man polling stations. The Liberal party does not maintain a separate ward organization, and the highest estimate for the number of active Liberals in the town would be between fifteen and twenty. It is difficult to argue that more than 150 people are in any way active in party politics in Banbury—low figures compared with those for

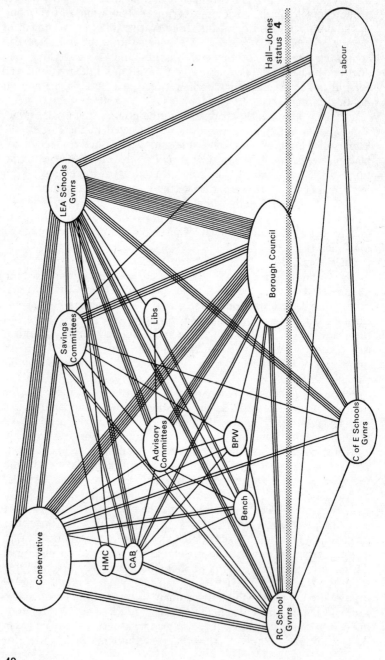

Key

Advisory Committees   Include Productivity, Road Safety, Home Safety

CAB   Citizens Advice Bureau

C of E Schools Gvnrs   Church of England Schools Governors

LEA Schools Gvnrs   Local Education Authority Schools Governors

HMC   Hospital Management Committee

OPWC   Old Peoples Welfare Committee

Source: Associations Survey

Each line represents one person who sits on the committees of each of the associations connected.

FIGURE 4.3   Governing and advisory bodies: links with Conservative and Labour parties

religious activists (see previous chapter). And yet many more vote, particularly in general elections, when around 80 per cent of the electorate turns out. At local elections it is unusual for more than 50 per cent to vote and perhaps less than 20 per cent, particularly in County Council elections.

It was difficult during the field-work to remember that the population of Banbury was not as fascinated by the local political system as we were and as the activists were. People in Banbury often had difficulty in naming two or three people on the Council. The names they did remember tended to be those of people who long ago ceased to be councillors. It seems that few people in Banbury felt themselves to be affected by what the town councillors, as opposed to the town officials, did. People were aware of the Municipal offices rather than the town Council. The fact that the officials were the servants of the Council made little difference to this view.

Many more people belong to voluntary associations in the town than are active in politics as such.[5] There is a long history of associations in Britain among all social levels.[6] In Banbury, in 1967, over half of the sample surveyed belonged to at least one association (57 per cent). Thirty per cent belonged to two or more.

Those who joined voluntary bodies, and even more those who served on their committees, were found in 1950 mostly to be male, middle-aged, and above average occupational status.[7] This was still true, with minor variations, in the sixties.

In 1967 only a third of men but just over a half of women belonged to no association at all. Nevertheless, there were by 1967 rather more all-women committees and more mixed-sex committees and more women on the mixed-sex committees than there had been around 1950 (see Appendix 3). The Townswomens Guild had started a new section which met in the evening, making the Guild available to more women. Two clubs for housebound wives had been started. Despite this, as in 1950, there remained a 'strong bias towards masculine management' and men still showed a greater range of interests outside the home than women.[8]

There seems to be also a slight trend to more youthful leadership of associations: 55 per cent of committees for which data are available had a median age of 45 or over in 1967 compared with three-quarters which had an average age of 45 or over in 1950. A branch of the Junior Chamber of Commerce had been set up since the first study, as had a branch of the Round Table, and its associated Ladies Circle, which had an upper age limit of 40. Nevertheless, although teenagers complained that 'there is nothing to do in the town', their clubs were still organized, as they had been in 1950, by those of nearly a generation older than the members.[9]

In 1966–8, as in 1948–50, the joiners tend to have above average occupational status.[10] This tendency is even more marked among committee members. Twenty-two out of sixty-seven committees for which data are available have a median occupational status of Hall–Jones 1 or 2 and a further twenty a median status of Hall–Jones 3.

People, of course, choose to join voluntary bodies for the enjoyment, interest or companionship which they hope to achieve. The overt objects of the associations show how varied their goals are. They still range, as they did in 1950, from 'a sweet pea society to a rugger club'.[11] There have been additions, for example, a Television Society, a branch of the National Society for Mentally Handicapped Children, a local Family Planning Association and a local branch of the Electrical Women.

At the same time, a process of consolidation is also visible. In 1950 there were a number of closely linked associations connected with music and the arts, referred to as the 'cultural connexion'. This has disappeared. An Arts Council was formed in 1962, later incorporating the old Arts and Crafts Festival which was a central feature of the cultural connexion around 1950. The Arts Council was formed as a liaison between cultural societies in the town to make the most efficient use of resources such as equipment, meeting-places and manpower. While individual clubs still exist, the close-knit cultural territory of 1950 now seems to have been institutionalized within a single association. Links made by individuals who choose to join and to accept committee membership of more than one association make clusterings which reinforce similarities and agreements. These links may provide a forum for people with similar views. Sometimes these may later be formalized into associations, as in the case of the Arts Council. This consolidation is also a process of differentiation.

At the same time formalized processes of unification are at work. Certain voluntary bodies draw members from others. These we have called delegate associations. The Old Charitable Association is one such (see Fig. 4.4). It not only links many voluntary associations together, it also has direct links with Labour and Conservative territories.

The statutory bodies make important formal links between many parts of the town, including politically opposed groups, as Fig. 4.3 shows. Figure 4.5 shows that these bodies also make links with a number of voluntary bodies. The number of voluntary association committee members who also serve on statutory and advisory bodies is relatively small: the 117 links in Fig. 4.5 are made by 65 people in 38 associations.[12] These can have an importance, as channels of communication and influence, out of all proportion to their numbers. Such individuals are 'gatekeepers'[13] and may play key roles, particularly when difficult decisions involving numbers of townspeople have to be made. Their presence or absence can be of some importance to

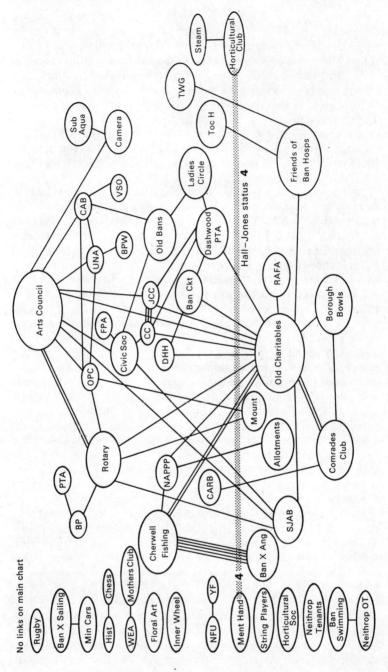

Hall—Jones status 4

No links on main chart

Key
BPW — Business & Professional Womens Club
Ban X Ang — Banbury Cross Angling
Ban Ckt — Banbury Cricket Club
BP — Baden Powell Guild
CC — Chamber of Commerce
CAB — Citizens Advice Bureau
CARB — Citizens Association for the Redevelopment of Banbury
DHH — Deaf & Hard of Hearing
Dashwood PTA — Dashwood Road Parent Teacher Association
FPA — Family Planning Association
Hist — Historical Society
Inner Wheel — Womens section of Rotary
JCC — Junior Chamber of Commerce
Ment Hand — National Society for Mentally Handicapped Children
Min Cars — Miniature Car Racing
Mount — Mountaineering Society
NAPPP — Neithrop Association for the Protection of Persons & Property
Neithrop OT — Neithrop Old Tyme Dancing
Neithrop Tenants — Neithrop Tenants Association
OPC — Old Peoples Club
RAFA — Royal Air Force Association
Rugby — Banbury Rugby Union FC
SJAB — St Johns Ambulance Brigade
Steam — Steam Society
TWG — Townswomens Guild
UNA — United Nations Association
VSO — Voluntary Service Overseas
YF — Young Farmers Club

Each line represents one person who sits on the committees of each of the associations connected.

FIGURE 4.4 *Links of voluntary bodies with each other*

E

53

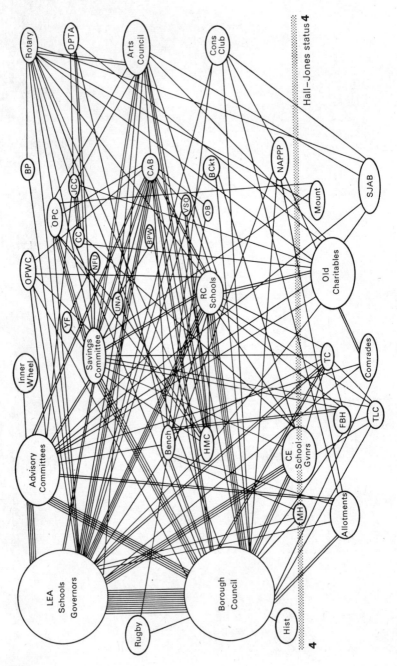

Key

Advisory Committees	Include Productivity, Road Safety, Home Safety
BPW	Business & Professional Womens Club
B Ckt	Banbury Cricket Club
BP	Baden Powell Guild
CC	Chamber of Commerce
CAB	Citizens Advice Bureau
DPTA	Dashwood Road Parent Teacher Association
FBH	Friends of Banbury Hospital
Hist	Historical Society
HMC	Hospital Management Committee
Inner Wheel	Womens section of Rotary
JCC	Junior Chamber of Commerce
MH	National Society for Mentally Handicapped Children
Mount	Mountaineering Society
NFU	National Farmers Union
NAPPP	Neithrop Association for the Protection of Persons & Property
OB	Old Banburians
OPC	Old Peoples Club
OPWC	Old Peoples Welfare Committee
Rugby	Banbury Rugby Union FC
SJAB	St Johns Ambulance Brigade
TC	Trades Council
TLC	Trades & Labour Clubs
UNA	United Nations Association
VSO	Voluntary Service Overseas
YF	Young Farmers Club

Each line represents one person who sits on the committees of each of the associations connected.

FIGURE 4.5 *Links of voluntary associations with governmental and advisory bodies*

pressure groups. It must be noted here that there were fifty-one voluntary associations about which full data were available but which had *no* links with any other voluntary or statutory committee analysed.

One of the most striking changes in the map of voluntary associations in 1967 compared with 1950 was the rise of local pressure groups. Some were specific to the town, for example, the Citizens Association for the Redevelopment of Banbury. Others were local branches of national associations, for example, the National Society for Mentally Handicapped Children. Such a change is not peculiar to Banbury.[14]

Groups which exerted, or attempted to exert, influence upon executive bodies in the town clearly existed in Banbury in the late forties. But such groups were not studied as pressure groups. Rather, as we have seen, the relationships of voluntary associations with each other and with centres of power and influence were examined. It was plain from this analysis that those associations which were most flourishing were those which had many links among their committees and with religious and political associations. Those with few links struggled on, some to disappear. It was as if the links gave access to a wider audience. People attending meetings could expect to meet friends there and also to find their attendance acceptable and understandable to those of their friends who did not themselves attend. The activity was part of their social world.

In addition it was clear that the Conservative party was surrounded by a well-organized connection of associations, sporting, charitable, occupational and other. The Labour party was not similarly surrounded. Furthermore, in 1950 such associations as were in the Labour territory had less potential influence, because the Labour territory was not yet well articulated into the local power structure.

Thus the Chamber of Commerce was well connected to political, economic, and religious centres of power and influence. The Trades Council was less well connected. Their relative positions in Banbury today are discussed in the following chapter. These associations can be said to be examples of old-established pressure groups. It is the newer groups which draw attention to the changing political scene in Banbury.

Bodies like the North Oxfordshire Association for the Advancement of State Education have recruited personnel, namely non-manual immigrants, who were rarely involved in politics in 1950. In addition, they address themselves, not to the Borough, which has no relevant powers, but to Oxfordshire County Council, which has, and to the Ministry in London which is ultimately responsible. Such activities are a reflection of the increasing removal of power from the locality, power which has an important impact on the daily lives of people living there.

In addition, there has been a multiplication of specialist pressure groups, such as tenants' associations, conservationist associations, associations for those specifically handicapped in some way. These would seem to be a response of people to the increased scale and complexity of the decision-making process on the one hand and of increased geographic mobility of sections of the population on the other. Already in 1950 the extent to which centres of economic and political decision-making were being moved from Banbury was a key to the social relations in the town. Similar profound consequences for a locality in the removal of local power were reported for Westrigg by Littlejohn.[15]

The Labour territory was largely still outside the power structure around 1950. It now has an established, if minority, place in that structure. Other groups now find themselves outside and are trying to establish methods of influence. Others again are outside and seem to accept that position, albeit fatalistically.

The process of government in Banbury seems therefore to result from the interaction of many groups. Some of these are linked with each other. Some links are provided by the status which people hold in the major institutional areas: economic, religious, political. Other links are established by voluntary associations. While the decisions that are reached appear to depend on the relative strengths of the groups involved, the way the decisions are reached by the relevant executive body is through the actions and interactions of people who link the groups or have formal or informal access to a number of groups.

5 Running the town: power, authority and influence in Banbury

In the economic, religious and political spheres an increasing number of decisions which affect the daily lives of people in Banbury appear to be taken outside the town. At the same time there is evidence of increased political control over certain aspects of economic institutions. This is true, for example, of the increased political control over the use and development of land. At the time of the survey this political control was shared among the borough, the county and the central government.

The process by which the expansion to 40,000 was decided upon in the early sixties, for example, contrasts markedly with the expansion of Banbury in the 1930s. Those developments were not referred to as town expansion, nor were they the result of a selfconscious decision on the part of the town or its Council. The Northern Aluminium Co., as it was then called, was looking for a site and considered Banbury appropriate in a number of ways. The origin of the expansion of the thirties was therefore the independent economic decision of a large firm, but the outcome involved more than this. The company were not willing to pay the price the owner was asking for the land, nor was he willing to reduce it to meet them. There were those in the town and surrounding area who were so actively in favour of the new industry coming to the town that they made up the difference in price. It is unclear to what extent they took this action because they perceived it to be in the town's interests and to what extent their own. At least they must have perceived the introduction of a large plant to be in the interest of the town or themselves and not against the interests of either. Thus the aluminium factory came to Banbury. There was no public meeting, no public inquiry, no new plan displayed, indeed no elaborate planning permission needed. The decision was taken by aluminium processors, who at that time had no links at all with Banbury, and by a few local businessmen, who were also active in local affairs.

The second influx of migrants was even less under any local control, being the result of evacuation from large towns, notably London and the Midland cities, caused by the 1939–45 war. Thus the two earlier population upheavals had been out of the hands, not only of the local citizenry, but also of the local Council. While the first was influenced by certain local men, there was no formal political process involved and nothing that could be described as a democratic process.

By the early 1950s central government legislation had greatly increased political power over industrial, commercial and residential development. While much of this increased power went to the County as local planning authority, the Town Development Act gave power of proposal to expand and power of vetoing a proposed expansion to the Municipal Borough. The discussion about expansion which went on in the fifties and the sixties took place in and out of the Council Chamber and in formal public inquiries. While to many people the events appeared simply to happen, as presumably did the events of the thirties, to those actively concerned with running the town a great deal of effort was involved.

The Borough Council is composed of elected representatives of opposed political parties. Nevertheless, in many ways the councillors are a united group. They have a common task to perform in running the town. It was interesting in the middle forties to observe the gradual change of attitude of the newly elected Labour councillors towards their opponents, whom they not only met face to face for the first time but in a situation in which they shared executive responsibility.[1] Over time councillors came to share experiences and traditions: both sides accept the legitimacy of the Council procedures. The jokes they share are often unintelligible to outsiders. Indeed, to a field-worker returning from the first study, the mutual joking between Labour and Conservative councillors was an important indicator of the changes since the forties in the relations between the leaders of the two main parties. Joking relationships had not been established by 1950: by 1965 they had.

In the Council Chamber, when councillors know they are being observed and recorded—when they are 'on stage',[2] they occasionally give expression to party political differences. Nevertheless there remains an observable air of unanimity. When they are 'back stage' this unity is even more observable.

At election counts, for example, all councillors are usually present and each candidate can appoint up to three scrutineers. The public and press are excluded. There is friendly and informal interaction between members of the opposing parties. Little groups earnestly discuss committee business, the dismissal of a car park attendant, for example. There is also a good deal of joking, each side assuring the other that they have won marginal wards by impossible majorities. Opponents join in a common condemnation of the electorate for its apathy. As the results gradually become known, the joking begins to develop an unkind edge.

The results are first declared inside the Town Hall to the candidates and their scrutineers. They all go downstairs for the formal declaration to the public and the press. The assembled public are supporters of the candidates. The politicians no longer speak to each other. Indeed they become partisan and expression is given to extreme differences of opinion. There is booing and cheering and occasional bursts of the 'Red Flag'. The change is notable. Councillors are public opponents but collaborators in running the town. In this they are friendly and co-operative, but the joking relationships cover, and also reveal, their awareness of their political differences.

Local politics in Banbury is partisan. The majority party tends to take a disproportionate share of aldermanic seats, chairmanships, and deputy chairmanships of Borough Council committees and of other forms of patronage. This goes a considerable way to explain the Conservative dominance shown in Fig. 4.3. Furthermore, policy is decided in meetings of party caucuses before the Council meets, rather than in the Council Chamber: and party members are subject to a 'whip' to maintain unity.[3]

The appointment of the Mayor follows a procedure agreed by both parties. This was also true of Aldermen until 1958 when, in a tense political atmosphere associated with the introduction of a ward system, the Conservatives broke with precedent. Much bitterness ensued, and a Labour councillor referred to 'a gratuitous insult to a local citizen of the highest possible reputation . . .' because he had been passed over for elevation to the aldermanic bench in favour of a Conservative.

For most of the time, however, the two political parties work together quite cordially: divisions on matters of principle are rare. Usually voting is on party lines without the formal application of the whip. Sometimes Labour and Conservative councillors vote with the opposite party. There has only been one expulsion from either political group since 1950 (from the Labour group).

The atmosphere of friendship and day-to-day comradeship conceals marked differences of emphasis. The Conservatives as 'guardians of the rates' tend to oppose increased public spending, while the Labour councillors are generally in favour of 'laying out money in the public interest'. These differences are kept alive by the party ideologies and the different socio-economic backgrounds of the councillors. Furthermore, councillors from opposing parties do not share each other's company in whatever spare time Council business may have left them.

The councillors act in concert in relation to outside bodies. Thus, when they initiated a public meeting in 1966, just after the field-work started, to discuss the proposal to expand the town to 70,000, councillors agreed that they would not take part in the discussion. They agreed to accept the Chairman of the Development Committee as their spokesman. In the event, one of the councillors broke the agreement and spoke strongly against expansion and in favour of a referendum on the issue. The Council spokesman had already rejected this notion. In this case it would seem that the councillor's loyalty to groups other than the Council overcame her loyalty to her fellow councillors, and also to a leader of her party. It is rare for councillors to show in public that other loyalties are more important than loyalty to the Council.

The old-established pressure groups in the town undoubtedly influence the councillors. The Chamber of Commerce and the Trades Council in a sense represent the interests of industry and commerce: the former from the side of proprietors and managers, and the latter from the side of the employees. Both bodies operate on a broad front and do not concern themselves exclusively with the interests of their members narrowly conceived, having in addition a concern for the 'good of the town'. This sometimes amounts to a concern for the citizen-consumer, as, for example, when the Trades Council made representations about bus stops or parking or when both bodies were bothered about the efficiency of the Borough Council's snow-clearing procedure. Both make quite frequent political interventions, but because they have members who are or have been councillors (both Borough and County) and who hold positions on other decision-making bodies, the Trades Council and the Chamber of Commerce rarely have to resort to public action to gain their ends. Many of the matters that concern them can be dealt with by a word with the appropriate official or by being raised in an appropriate committee. That is to say, their members are involved in decision-making or have easy access to decision-makers, although the Trades Council's connections are less close or extensive, since Banbury has almost always had a Conservative-controlled council.

Neither the Trades Council nor the Chamber of Commerce intervened publicly as organized bodies in the expansion issue. The Chamber of Commerce discussed the matter extensively and finally balloted its members, revealing an almost equal split: 57 per cent for and 43 per cent against. (Sixty-four per cent of the members voted.) It seems that not only did the perceived economic interests of members point in different directions, but that some members were concerned with values more general than straightforward business interests, for example, some did not want finally to lose the small-market-town character of Banbury. Because of this split, the public political intervention of the Chamber of Commerce was restricted to asking questions; many and telling were their questions at the public meeting called in 1966 to consider the proposals to expand to 70,000.

Interestingly, these written questions from the Chamber of Commerce were those which were taken first at the meeting. Once the expansion issue was settled, the Chamber again understood its task as expressed in the presidential address, to protect and further the interests of traders in the town during the expansion to 40,000. The Trades Council neither discussed nor acted on any discussions with regard to expansion. It did not discuss it because no trade-union delegate was asked by his union to raise the matter.

Although the Chamber of Commerce can usually work behind the scenes,[4] the Chamber nevertheless does from time to time have open conflicts with the Council. In the mid-fifties there was a conflict involving a lively public meeting over the letting of the Town Hall at preferential rates to traders from outside Banbury for trades exhibitions. Later there was another and more severe conflict over the re-rating of the central business district by a Conservative Council in advance of national reorganization and rating. Feelings in this case ran so high that Conservative votes were withheld: this is thought to be the explanation of the return of the first Labour majority. More recently there was a similar but less dramatic conflict over car-parking meters in the town centre. In this the Chamber had partial success.

It is possible that the Chamber is nowadays less effective than it once was because of the decreased power of the Borough. Certainly the Chamber still fears, as the members always have, the loss of the town's independence. They also fear officialdom. Many are the utterances against 'Whitehall', sometimes associated with hostility to the Borough Council itself.

In general the Trades Council appeared as a less effective pressure group than the Chamber of Commerce, but it attempts to influence a wider range of public bodies. This is partly because it has a greater interest in health and welfare matters than does the Chamber. These interests lead it into contact with a different range of public bodies.

A long-established and recognized pressure group, the Trades Council has members on a number of statutory and other public bodies in Banbury and District, for example the local Hospital Management Committee, the Banbury Productivity Committee, the Oxford and Banbury Disablement Advisory Committee, the Youth Employment Committee and the local Employment Committee, as well as having members who are or have been Borough councillors.

The Trades Council shares the concern of the Chamber of Commerce with traffic routes and with parking facilities in the town centre and their misuse (although the respective concerns of the two organizations have not always been from the same point of view). The Trades Council made representations about the bus services to the Borough Council, the Traffic Commissioners and the bus company concerned. But by the time the field-work finished there had been little success, the public bodies appeared to have no power to improve the situation and the bus company was unwilling to make the requested improvements which it said would be uneconomic.

Representations were made to the hospital authorities about a decision to reduce the number of beds in the hospital. The local Member of Parliament was also asked to lobby the Minister of Health. It is said that there was initial hesitation about asking the M.P., since the propriety of a Trades Council acting through a Conservative member was doubted by some.[5]

The General Nursing Council decided at about the same time to change the nurse training course at the hospital from a course leading to State Registered Nurse qualification to one for State Enrolled Nurses. Trades Council members feared this would mean that fewer nurses would come to Banbury to train, thus aggravating the staff shortage, but also that it would reduce the employment opportunities for young girls in the town. Their objections came too late. The decision to alter the course had been taken by a body outside Banbury and which judged its decision on considerations other than those of the Trades Council and to which the local Trades Council had no access.

The position which the Trades Council now occupies within the local power structure, recognized as representing a legitimate set of interests, with members who are or have been councillors, and others who are Justices of the Peace, is a result of the working through of changes in the local political structure which were only just beginning in 1950.

The Junior Chamber of Commerce (J.C.C.) was founded in 1958 and is closely linked with the senior Chamber, having representatives on the latter's executive committee. To some extent the Junior Chamber acts as a pressure group, although its primary concern is to train business and professional men not only for more responsible business positions but also as later full members of the Chamber itself. It intervenes in politics fairly frequently on a broad range of issues, although it is avowedly non-party political and non-sectarian. It has few direct links with those in power (but indirect links through the senior Chamber) and has representatives on advisory bodies such as the Home Safety Committee. Its members combine local shopkeepers, self-employed businessmen and executives, often professionals, working for large companies.

J.C.C. were much concerned about the expansion issue, but over this they felt relatively powerless. They had always sent someone to observe every Council meeting, but since committee meetings were held in secret and no J.C.C. members were councillors, J.C.C. had no direct links with the decision-makers. It is therefore not surprising that the J.C.C. were more often in public conflict with the Council than the senior Chamber.

In contrast to these old-established pressure groups is NOAASE, the North Oxfordshire Association for the Advancement of State Education.[6] While the Trades Council and the Chamber of Commerce could be said to be 'inside' the local power structure to some extent, new groups like NOAASE are outside it and have to create all their contacts from scratch. NOAASE at the time of survey had a narrow scope, starting as a self-conscious pressure group concerned specifically with state education. Consequently its political interventions were frequent and within four months it had begun to move from no involvement in decision-making to some involvement.

NOAASE arose in response to a specific crisis situation: the Oxfordshire Education Committee had plans for a rural comprehensive school. Formerly children from this area, if they passed the '11+', went to Banbury Grammar School, a school with a good academic reputation. This school was now being amalgamated with the town's secondary modern schools to form a new comprehensive Banbury school. Children from the surrounding rural area, instead of going into Banbury to school, were to have a comprehensive school of their own. This could not be built for some time. The Education Committee therefore planned to provide comprehensive education in existing school buildings in the rural area. This was not satisfactory to some North Oxfordshire people, some of whom began to discuss among themselves what could be done to change the plan. They were parents of the children involved and most of them were fairly recent immigrants to the area, working in professional or managerial jobs in large companies in Banbury. A number of others, most of whom worked in further and higher education, had for some time been trying to start a local branch of the Confederation for the Advancement of State Education (CASE). They suggested to the parents that, through CASE, pressure could be brought to bear upon the Oxfordshire Education Authority. After some hesitation the parents accepted this idea.

A widely publicized meeting, arranged to discuss ways of opposing the Education Authority, was well attended, mostly by men between 30 and 40, fathers of the children affected. The meeting heard a résumé of the County's proposals, and objections were raised to it. A branch of CASE was formally founded, a Midlands representative attending to explain the Confederation's aims.

After the public meeting, circulars were sent to the Oxfordshire Education Committee, head teachers of local schools and the Department of Education and Science (D.E.S.). Letters were also sent to individual members of the Education Committee. The local M.P. was approached and he agreed to help. When the Education Committee met, protests to the proposals, which included a number from parish councils, were acknowledged and an assurance was given that no final decisions would be taken until parents and governors had been fully consulted.

CASE held a further public meeting a fortnight later when these activities were reported. It was also reported that consultations had begun with the Director of Education. The constitution of NOAASE was ratified, formally linking it to CASE, and a committee elected including representatives from each of the localities involved. Within a month of starting their campaign not only had parish councils been contacted, but local County councillors had been seen, and the M.P. had asked a question in the House. The campaign continued and four months later membership was 200, with a strong recruiting drive continuing. Future plans included not only maintaining contact with elected representatives, but asking the CASE national executive to add weight to the NOAASE argument at the Department of Education and Science. A research sub-committee had been set up to define the changing needs of the Banbury rural area and to examine alternative proposals.

The members of NOAASE came from a social category hitherto uninvolved in local politics: they were mostly spiralists, not even spiralist-locals. Their involvement was as consumers of state education and ones who demanded and understood the meaning of high educational standards. The NOAASE founders were not concerned with the Borough Council or the Rural Districts, for these have no educational powers. They were concerned with the County Council as the local Education Authority, and also with the D.E.S. In the group that formed NOAASE there were those with considerable managerial talents, although initially having little special knowledge of the structure of educational administration or of the process of education provision. But there were also people who had access to the relevant information, others who were specially trained in how to collect it, and others again who had relevant higher education qualifications.

Thus by the time of the first public meeting the NOAASE founders had collected information which they presented diagrammatically and they had checked the dates of County Council committee meetings. Furthermore, they grasped the importance of getting allies among other organizations.[7] NOAASE also understood the importance of numbers, of the latent power of the voter, and hence paid attention to recruitment. They were aware of the complexity of the information needed, hence their appointment of a research sub-committee. Not only did they make themselves fully acquainted with the proposals and the reasons for them, but they also estimated the costs of schooling and the minimum school population required to make an economically viable school which would meet their requirements. In a short time and with encouragement from the national pressure group CASE, this group had developed the level of sophistication necessary to look after their interests in a complex situation.

NOAASE conducted a public campaign because they were outside the power structure, but they were aiming to move in and had already got closer to the decision-makers in the short months we observed their development. They seem to fit neither the typical American nor the older British models described by Newton and can be seen as a response to a new formal political situation.[8]

The Banbury and District Ratepayers Association, later renamed the Banbury (Oxfordshire) Ratepayers Association, was formed in June 1966, It was new to Banbury, but is of a type which has existed in various localities in Britain for many years. The long-term aim of the Association as mentioned at meetings in 1966 and 1968 was the abolition of the rates. Active members (i.e. those at meetings) appeared to be largely male and middle-aged or older. A few business-men and one or two professional people attended, although most participants seemed unlikely to have an education prolonged much beyond the statutory school-leaving age. Native Banburians, old and newer immigrants including a vocal group from Birds, were all represented. While the political affiliations of the members are not well known, there were both Labour and Conservative voters among them.

The Ratepayers were from the start a self-conscious pressure group. In 1968 they still seemed to feel outside the local power structure, and felt they should aim to get a representative of the Association on all possible committees 'so that they would be instrumental in decision-making as opposed to being presented with a *fait accompli*'. The Association was anxious not only to make contact with the local authority but to learn as much as possible of its working. It therefore held meetings to which experts, such as the Borough Treasurer, were invited to talk about matters of interest to them as ratepayers.

The Association started with a moderately broad scope only, for although it did act in other matters, such as the snow-clearing, which as we have seen also occasioned anger in other groups, the main concern was with the rates. The Association succeeded in some cases in getting rate reductions for members. Their concern with expansion to 70,000 largely derived from its implications for the rate burden, as their written questions to the public meeting on town expansion made plain. Nevertheless, this specific concern seems liable to lead the Ratepayers to political activity on a broader front, and of all the pressure groups we studied this is the one nearest to being or becoming a political party but, up to the end of the field-work, difficulties of finding personnel and funds had prevented the Ratepayers moving into more active politics.

It seems likely that the members were largely small owner-occupiers, although the Association was most anxious not to be closely linked with small property owners in this way. It was even proposed in 1968, although not carried, that the name be changed to Banbury and District Ratepayers and Residents Association to avoid the misapprehension that the Association was only for owner-occupiers, for tenants also paid rates. The Ratepayers Association was in fact quite keen to join forces with the Neithrop Tenants Association, a group of Council house tenants.

In contrast to the Ratepayers, which as a group might move towards becoming a political party, the Neithrop Tenants Association is an example of a pressure group which changed in the course of its existence away from being a pressure group; it became a social club and finally dissolved altogether soon after we left the field. It was formed in June 1965 on a large new Council estate where lived considerable numbers of new migrants to the town. In effect the Association was formed to fight short-term battles primarily with the Borough Council and mainly about physical aspects of the estate. The complaints at this time were about the condition the contractors had left the gardens in, the state of the pavements, the lack of shops, not only on the estate but also in the town (Marks and Spencer's and Sainsbury's being frequently mentioned), the lack of telephone kiosks and other services. Many of the complaints were justified objectively, but some, particularly those about shopping facilities, also seem to have symbolic significance, a situation similar to that reported by Cullingworth for Swindon.[9]

Initially the Tenants Association had contacts with the Conservative party through the local Member of Parliament and with the Labour party through two members who were Borough councillors, lived on the estate, and had themselves come from London on the overspill scheme. In addition to these contacts with elected representatives the Association had direct contacts with the town clerk, who, the chairman said, was always 'most helpful'. The chairman felt that the main problem with the town Council was not that they did the wrong thing but that they did not do anything. Since the Association's existence, the estate had been tidier, but as he realized 'many of our achievements are only so-called and are not really achievements of the association but are instances which [would have] happened anyway'.

67

After the first eighteen months, the energies of the Association were put less into pressure group activity and more into social activities. Sports days were organized in the summers of 1967 and 1968 and there were children's parties at Christmas. In the second winter Bingo started, at first fortnightly and then weekly. These changes in function led to a change in leadership. At the third A.G.M., in the summer of 1968, women outnumbered men for the first time. The original chairman resigned 'for personal reasons' and was replaced by a woman. Henceforth the Association concentrated on social activities. Its aims, from being quite specific in channelling complaints from tenants to members of the Council, became diffuse. In Dennis's terms the Association had failed to combine the functions of spokesman with those of sponsor of sociability.[10] Despite a tendency at the start for the Association to be largely composed of Londoners and in effect limited to Council house tenants, it had had a wide socio-economic range, including white-collar workers and 'roughs'.

The 'roughs' now tended to be dropped as 'frankly undesirable', as one Labour councillor said. The new chairman and a local clergyman both regretted the loss of 'middle class leadership', people 'with better jobs'. The membership now seemed to be almost entirely respectable manual workers who had come from London under the overspill agreement.

The Association changed from a pressure group to a social club as the initial physical needs, which estate residents of all kinds had in common, were satisfied. It may be that the social club met a need felt particularly by ex-Londoners. It may be that the club eventually wound up a year later because there came to be fewer factors that these people had in common and that held them together. The demise of tenants' associations, community associations and the like as new housing estates grow older has frequently been reported in the literature.[11] The Neithrop Tenants Association appears to have followed this pattern.

The Historical Society is really not a pressure group at all, but simply a group of local people interested in history. Their involvement was an interesting example of the way in which any organized group may get involved in politics, however reluctantly, when their chosen interests are threatened. To its embarrassment the Historical Society became involved in an ill-fated campaign to save the original Banbury cake shop from destruction. It joined the campaign at the instigation of the Council for the Preservation of Rural England (C.P.R.E.). The C.P.R.E. seems to have stronger connections with decision-makers outside the town than inside it. Its failure to preserve the Cake Shop shows its relative weakness in the town of Banbury.

The C.P.R.E. was extremely vocal at the public expansion meeting in 1966. It was acutely opposed to the loss of rural amenities implied by the ring of satellite villages round an expanded urban area which were an integral part of the 'Banbury 70,000' plan. It was one of the groups to whom the outspoken councillor who proposed a referendum appeared to feel, in this particular situation, more loyalty than to the Council itself.

There are, of course, many associations which have never become involved in politics and do not intend to become involved. Once organized, a group of people have some potential to influence others to their own advantage or in pursuit of their common interests. The range of organized groups discussed here have all been involved in government. They range from the Council, the 'best club in town', itself involved in governing, through special interest groups like the Chamber of Commerce and the Trades Council, to the Tenants Association turned social club and the Historical Society, fleetingly and uncharacteristically 'political'. But these groups are not distinct. They share members directly or indirectly: there are ties between them. These ties were demonstrated for the leadership in the last chapter. In the next chapter an example is discussed of the interaction of such formal organizations and also of other groups in coming to a decision which affected the whole town.

F

6 Making decisions: the example of expansion

In the previous chapters we have seen that some of the social group and social categories which are associated with the major economic religious and political institutions are also associated with each other. We have also seen that certain groups emerge from people's voluntary leisure-time activities and that these groups are associated in various ways with the major social institutions. Certain patterns related to the social structure and culture emerge from the relationships among the groups and networks discernible.

We have also seen that the links between the groups result from the behaviour of individuals who occupy a status in a variety of groups, formal or informal. It is through the playing of the associated multiple roles that interrelations are made among the major social institutions.

The extent to which groups which have formed in various parts of the social structure may influence each other must depend to a considerable extent upon whether they share personnel. A man is likely to have to account to his friends and associates for his actions, especially when the latter affect the former in some way. When members of a group (formal or informal) are making decisions within or on behalf of that group, they are likely to take into account the relationships they have in other groups and networks. That is to say, in making decisions individuals experience constraints deriving from the other statuses they occupy and the roles they have to play associated with them. The multiple roles which decision-makers occupy may modify the decisions they take in any one of those roles. Such individuals are particularly likely to experience difficulty when the influences from their other roles indicate contradictory courses of action. Sometimes particular individuals, either because of one leading status they hold or because of a combination of statuses, may have a key role to play. The way it is played will in some ways be idiosyncratic to each individual, but in fact the behaviour will be to some extent the consequence of acting within important constraints deriving from the multiple roles occupied.

The decision which the Banbury Council had to make in 1966, as to whether the town should expand to 70,000, provided a nice example of the interaction of groups with varying interests and the roles of particular individuals who had statuses in a number of the interested groups. The issue is also an interesting one because a decision in favour of this large expansion would affect everyone in town to some extent, as well as everyone in the country for several miles around town. A study of how the decision was reached therefore shows interactions among people and groups and their hierarchy of values in this connection. It also shows, by default, those who did not even attempt to defend or further their interests, whether as groups or individuals. The last is at least as interesting as the first for an understanding of the unequal distribution of power and influence and ways in which this might change.

A study of the feasibility of expanding Banbury beyond the already agreed 40,000 to 70,000 had been decided jointly by the Banbury Borough Council, the Oxfordshire County Council (O.C.C.), and the central government in 1963. It was inspired by the former (Conservative) government's study of the South-East Region. The plans had been drawn by a firm of consultants in association with the O.C.C. planning department. In the autumn of 1966 the time for decision was near. There were strong demands from some townspeople for further information. The booklet *Banbury 70,000* about the 'expansion' was published and maps and models were put on display in the town library. A public meeting was held. The audience, composed of those people who arrived in time to get into the Town Hall, was exceptionally enthusiastic about the meeting and noisy and almost entirely against expansion. British reserve and decorum were forgotten.[1]

On the platform were representatives of the public bodies who were concerned with the plan: the O.C.C., the Greater London Council (G.L.C.), the planning consultants, the Borough Council, the Ministry of Housing and Local Government (represented by an Under-Secretary). Representatives of these groups had been working together on the plans behind the scenes ever since the 'feasibility' study was agreed. By the mid-sixties officials of the Ministry, the G.L.C. and the O.C.C. were more interested that Banbury should expand further than was the Banbury Borough Council.

Whatever the officials on the platform may have felt personally about the plan, they attempted to present it neutrally, stressing the right and responsibility of the town to make up its own mind. The

G.L.C. representative also stressed that, while London had to export a million people by 1981, they 'did not want to go to any town where they are not welcome'. ('Good', and 'hear, hear', said the audience.) The G.L.C. probably meant this. Banbury, after all, was only one place among many they were negotiating with. The consultant also took the same neutral line.

Although the officials pretended to public neutrality, they nevertheless also had to say publicly that they believed the plan to be good, sound and satisfactory. It is likely that some of them, perhaps even more those behind the scenes, had a good deal of personal investment in the plan. Banbury town officials, who, as servants of the Council, had to appear neutral, were likely to gain from expansion, which would make better jobs and promotion opportunities available. Only those not equipped for larger-town administration or with non-work interests which ran counter to expansion and which were more important to them than their work interests would be likely to be against expansion. At least one councillor feared that the officials were over-persuading the Council to expand; he said he thought expansion was being used as a 'lever to inflate the Council staff'. This view was strongly rejected by the main body of councillors. It was 'not done' to say such a thing. When expansion was rejected, one senior official soon took a job elsewhere.

There were many conflicting interests to consider among the townspeople: the tradespeople, the workers, house occupiers or owners in places where development would take place, school children, motorists, and so on. The political parties also had to consider the likely effect of expansion on them. In the rural area there were residents and farmers who would see their green fields turn into urban areas if so large an expansion took place.

Many of these groups were present at the public meeting. The audience fell into two main categories: the businessmen and those from the rural area. A third miscellaneous category represented people interested in particular aspects of the plan. The businessmen, who were mainly but not entirely local, fell into three categories: those who had property and business in the town centre; those from outside who had or might in the future have financial interests in the town; those in professional or service occupations which give advice or other services to businessmen. Those from the rural area had become involved as the implications of the plan dawned on them: farmers; self-designated 'village dwellers'; and representatives of parish and rural district councils. The miscellaneous individual citizens were concerned with interests they felt were threatened: a house they had recently bought; children who had to travel across town to school; a wish to keep Banbury a small town because that was why they had moved in, and so on.

A good many of the local businessmen's questions were put to the platform as written questions from formal associations. The Chamber of Commerce, itself split about the desirability of expansion, posed eleven probing questions. The first asked who wanted expansion to 70,000, the government, the County Council, the Borough Council, or the people of Banbury (loud 'Noes' from the audience). Six other questions concerned shops, for example, the compensation for shops to be demolished and the rents of new shops. The Chamber was also concerned with capital funds for the expansion and with incentives to attract new population and industry.

The Citizens Association for the Redevelopment of Banbury (C.A.R.B.) put nineteen written questions. A new association, C.A.R.B. was apparently formed among businessmen, especially shopkeepers, who had premises in the new central business district and who were strongly opposed to expansion. Their opposition stemmed from a lack of assurances concerning the future of their businesses. Their questions reflected this, and they were not reassured. Requests for preferential allocation of premises for displaced traders, companies and developers were also refused. Their question about hospital facilities met with the reply that some assurances had been received from the Ministry of Health but the Borough Council was not satisfied and was pursuing the matter.

Many of the tradesmen faced real difficulties in deciding their attitude to expansion. It may be assumed that their aims, as tradesmen, were to maintain and if possible increase profits. But in the expansion issue the means to these ends were not clear. It was not known, nor could it be discovered, what the rents of premises in the rebuilt town central area would be. Many feared the rents would be so high that they would be put out of business. Other traders, entrepreneurs and small manufacturers were convinced that they could only gain business by expansion and were therefore in favour. While one may assume that all tradesmen wanted to maintain their profits and, other things being equal, to increase them, not all were willing to pay the same price for this. Thus, for some it would seem that they preferred merely to maintain their present profit level rather than achieving more, if the price to be paid for this more was losing the 'small town ethos'. Others, unwilling to take the risk, or unsure of the outcome for themselves, would find the certainty of maintaining their present economic and social holdings most easily expressed and justified in terms of value placed upon 'the town as it is'. The division of economic interest and of perception of economic interest (for both factors are involved) and the conflict between these and other perceived interests were reflected in the referendum taken in the Chamber of Commerce on the expansion issue. Sixty-four per cent of members replied, and of these 43 per cent were in favour of expansion, the rest being against. Their division on this issue contrasts with their solidarity in the late forties in the face of socialist successes.

The public meeting where these doubts were expressed and where strong anti-expansion feelings were also expressed had no power to take decisions. It was a public relations exercise. The decisive power lay with the Borough Council. Party politics were therefore involved in the decision and the opinions of the political parties important.

The Conservative party had a chequered history in regard to expansion, no doubt partly explained by the divisions of opinion among the businessmen. It was during a period when there was a clear Conservative majority on the Council that the first proposals for the development of the Borough and the diversification of its industry were made. One Mayor put what many saw as the overriding criteria plainly: 'We have to get the plans for a Borough which will become increasingly industrialized but does not lose its old world charm and become a replica of some of these Midland and Northern areas.' In 1960 the Council with a Conservative majority had accepted, although rather hesitantly, the idea of taking London overspill on the grounds that 'now we've got industry, we need labour to go with it'. At this time both parties were in favour of expansion. In 1966, however, the Conservatives voted against expansion to 70,000. By now expansion had become a party issue with the Conservatives ranged against it.[2]

Although the Labour party had all along supported expansion, there were those, notably two leading figures, who from the beginning were less than enthusiastic. They were persuaded to drop any public opposition when the issue became a clear party matter. For the Labour party the goals were clear: to increase job opportunities and improve wage levels in Banbury and to help the workers in London to get decent houses. They felt that an expanded town would be able to provide much better amenities for the ordinary people of Banbury. Social, educational and other services would be improved in an expanded borough and the shops would improve too. Marks and Spencer's and Sainsbury's, the popular chain stores, would come to town given a large enough population increase. Indeed 'Marks and Spencer's and Sainsbury's' became the symbol for the improved amenities which it was hoped expansion would bring. By the time the issue was well developed there was a Labour government at Westminster, which was actively implementing the Town Development Act and other dispersal measures. The Labour party was, therefore, also inclined to support the dispersal policies of a Labour government on grounds of party allegiance.

But there is no doubt that in the short run the Labour party were in some difficulty. The expansion to 40,000 when it was only at the 25,000 mark, as it was in 1966, had brought various discomforts such

74

as overcrowded schools and hospital, and air pollution from the coffee. Labour had been in control of the Council in 1955 when the I.D.C.-free land was bought. As a party they stuck to their pro-expansion line but were less successful in organizing support for 70,000 than they might have been. The short-run difficulties compared with the nebulous long-run advantages may have made their followers hesitant to come out and beat the pro-expansion drum, or made their leaders anxious about asking them so to do.

It may well also be that once expansion had become a party political issue the Labour party felt that they had lost the battle. In such circumstances they might have attempted to mobilize public opinion, for at that time the Council was equally divided between the parties. To change even one vote in the delicate balance on the Council would have led to a pro-expansion vote on Council. The Labour Party's own lack of unity and conviction may perhaps explain their failure to do this, or a feeling that only at election times does a party go out to organize public support. The small number of active Labour supporters is also highly relevant. There is a limit to what a few people can do. Certainly no champions for expansion spoke up at the public meeting. The Labour councillors kept faith with the Council's decision not to speak at the meeting.

The local aim of both parties was of course control of the Council. Each had to calculate whether expansion would be likely to bring this about. The Labour party were probably right in guessing that to industrialize the town further would increase the proportion of manual workers and of Labour-voting manual workers in the town, greatly increase the chances of achieving a Labour Council and make the North Oxfordshire parliamentary constituency at least marginal, if not Labour. The Conservative party were probably equally right to conclude that this process would tip against them a delicate balance which since the war had been slightly in their favour. The *status quo* did not give power to Labour. They had little to lose by change. The Conservatives had a good deal to lose in the long run. In the short run they might well alienate large sections of their present followers by supporting expansion, partly because the businessmen were afraid of losing their positions and partly because Conservative followers other than businessmen, like Labour followers, were inconvenienced by the bad phasing of the first expansion programme.

The largest local paper actively campaigned for expansion, although its rival took an opposite view. Arguing for expansion openly was therefore left to this one paper and a few committed individuals.

For local politicians successful expansion would mean increased honour and prestige and unsuccessful expansion the reverse. One of the difficulties for the local leaders was to know what would constitute successful expansion and which of their followers in the electorate would perceive any particular facet of expansion as successful. There were many areas where information was lacking; sensible guesses, quite apart from predictions, could not be made.

In these circumstances politicians would be sensitive to the opinions expressed in their networks. At the same time, as Bailey has pointed out, when uncertainty prevails, when it is hard to find rules to guide action, leadership is called for.[3] One man who provided this leadership was the Chairman of the Borough's Development Committee.

This chairman was a Banburian, the son of an immigrant who had been one of the local businessmen to facilitate the arrival of the aluminium factory in the thirties. He had high economic, political, and social status in Banbury: a J.P., a leading local industrialist and a leading Conservative councillor. On this account he was jocularly called the 'King of Banbury' by some people, although not by his close friends. We will use this nickname for him. His role as Chairman of the Development Committee had led him into many discussions with County and central government representatives. He played a sort of middleman role between local and external authorities. As Committee Chairman he also had to play a mediating role between officials and councillors, and he also mediated between the politicians and the businessmen, being a member of both groups.

The 'King's' most important overt goal was to serve the best interests of the town. No doubt he also had an unarticulated goal of maintaining and enhancing his honour, prestige and standing in town. This presented no contradiction, for he was closely identified with Banbury. As a local industrialist he undoubtedly also had the goal of maintaining and improving the profitability of his business. The evidence is that expansion would not have affected that either way: for his business it would have advantages and disadvantages. There is no doubt his concern for the town was genuine. In a situation in which his firm would clearly have benefited from expansion and in which he could have improved the lot of his work people and provided other services for the town, it might be imagined that the 'King' would have experienced a considerable conflict among normative themes associated with 'the good of my firm and my work people', 'my responsibility to provide as decent a life as I can for my wife and family' on the one hand and 'the losses of tradesmen who may be displaced from the town centre' and 'the good of the town as a whole' on the other. Since this conflict did not in fact arise, whether he supported expansion was likely to depend on how he read its consequences for the town, for those in all classes who voted for him and for his personal friends. A leader who does not in practice interpret 'good of the town' in this way will, in any situation with elements of democracy in it, soon become discredited and cease to lead.[4] In some such conflict situations a politician may prefer to resign.[5]

The 'King' was not concerned, however, with losing his seat on the Council. Indeed, he had already decided to resign before the expansion decision was reached. This was consistent with the normal patterns of Conservative businessmen who felt it their duty to serve on the Council for a period. He had served from the middle fifties. The work involved had imposed a considerable strain upon both his home and his business life. He was not, however, resigning from public life *in toto*, only this aspect of it. He had been Vice-Chairman of the constituency Conservative party for three years and was to take up its chairmanship on resignation from the Borough Council. He retained many other public offices including Justice of the Peace.

Along with his Conservative colleagues, the 'King' must have had a genuine difficulty in concluding what the best decision would be. The division of opinion among their friends in the Chamber of Commerce must have made the decision harder. The 'King' had tried but failed, to keep the issue out of the party arena. The Conservatives decided against expansion. The councillors were evenly divided between the parties. In these circumstances it was inevitable that Conservative councillors would vote against expansion and, with Labour voting in favour, that the count would be even. It was equally inevitable that in these circumstances the Conservative Mayor (an immigrant of the fifties and an executive of the aluminium factory) would use his second, casting, vote against expansion.[6] It is arguable that if the 'King' or other prominent leader of the Conservatives had made a strong pro-expansion bid, the issue would not have become so clearly a party one. Any move to pro-expansion commitment would, in the circumstances, have run the risk of splitting the party, something which in the British political system is strongly discouraged. Nevertheless, nobody, apparently not even his close friends, knew up to the last minute how the 'King' would vote. He had on a number of occasions voted against his party colleagues. In the situation of even balance one man voting against his party would, of course, change the whole outcome in Council.

It seems likely that Conservative opinion hardened against further expansion partly because of the difficulties in phasing the 40,000 expansion plan. On the development committee there had been struggles with the Ministry of Health in an effort to get the promise of a new hospital and with the Ministry of Transport about the roads, especially a by-pass, for the main North–South English traffic poured through the town centre. Indeed, one thing that was attractive about expansion was that it would increase the chances of getting something done quickly about the through traffic. But the

77

realities upon investigation appeared less encouraging. There were national economic difficulties and a national slow-down in road plans. The central government had not increased its credibility in the eyes of the town. The committee found the lack of co-ordination between Departments discouraging. It was known that the County would be in difficulties over schools provision, because the difficulties they were already in were known. Overspill populations always have a high family size, because it is those with housing difficulties who are particularly likely to be rehoused in expanding towns. There is therefore a considerable pressure on the schools. Many townspeople were reacting strongly against the difficulties the existing expansion was causing them.

The planning consultant had argued that expansion to 40,000 by 1974, to which the town was already committed, would, while not being uneconomic, only show a modest profit at the end of eight years when it was completed. The expansion to 70,000 by 1981, although it imposed a 'heavier rate burden' in the short run, would pay handsome dividends by 1981, i.e. fifteen years hence. He argued that this prospect could be used to reduce the rate burden even after five years. From the point of view of the 'King' and his colleagues, even if 70,000 would pay the Borough better in the long run and the possibility of larger profits for businessmen would be there with the increased population, in the short run the situation was different. There was the real possibility of loss to local businessmen in the course of the redevelopment of the town centre which would have to go along with expansion. There had been that previous occasion when the central area businessmen had suffered loss (see p. 62). This was when their premises had been re-rated by the Borough in advance of a national re-rating. They were angry with their own party, the Conservatives, who had done this. The next year the Borough had a clear Labour majority for the first and only time in the post-war period. This was thought to be because these offended businessmen at least withheld their Conservative votes, if they did not actually vote Labour. This was only eleven years before, when the 'King' and other Conservative councillors were members. They would not want to risk a repetition. Against this, they were in close contact with officials who were pressing for expansion. As for the 'King' himself, his closest personal friends, political and business associates were all applying pressure directly upon him to oppose expansion. So, on balance, the Conservative party decided against expansion and, when the decisive vote was taken in the Council Chamber, all the Conservative councillors voted against it. Labour voted for expansion. The count was equal. The Mayor cast his vote against, and so the decision was reached.

It would be tempting to suggest that the final decision was a triumph for 'tradition' against 'change', but such a conclusion would be far too simple. Conservative and Labour councillors alike were proud of the changes already taking place in the town. Rather, the decision should be seen as the outcome of tensions among a number of divergent groups, at the intersection of many of which the 'King' stood, so that a particular burden rested upon him. The outcome was one in which the strength of some groups (e.g. the strength of the economic interest of the tradespeople) are seen to persist despite other changes already taking place. Equally important to note is the largely quiescent majority, all of whose interests were very much at stake, but who played almost as little part in this expansion decision as they had in former decisions, despite the apparently democratic processes now involved.

There were many social categories quite unrepresented at the public meeting. There were very few manual workers, in particular there were very few semi-skilled or unskilled workers present: only three manual workers spoke during the meeting and few others were identified. Many, it appears, were unaware of the public meeting. While there were non-manual workers, including junior non-manual workers, present whose dwellings were threatened by the expansion plans, the poorer people living near the town centre whose homes would be wiped out by the expansion of the central business district did not speak at, or, as far as our three observers could judge, even come to the meeting.

One such town central area, clearly designated for demolition and replacement by a car park if the expansion plan came about, is discussed in Chapter 7. This was a cul-de-sac of small late-Victorian terraced houses, many with very little garden, most without bathrooms or inside lavatories, and described in the booklet on 70,000 as 'sub-standard'.

When the plan was first published, the field-worker had expected that there would be a good deal of discussion of it, of fears among the residents for their future, and perhaps even a move to co-operate in putting pressure on the authorities to protect their interest. To the field-worker's surprise, no one ever mentioned the subject, not even the 'king pins' of the road, who had, and liked to maintain, the reputation of being well informed. They were local 'gate-keepers' in Cauter and Downham's sense.[7]

The field-worker finally opened the subject, asking the 'king pins' what they thought of expansion. They responded by saying 'they' (those in authority) had been talking about expanding the town 'for years, on and off', and nothing had ever happened yet, nothing would come of it this time, and so it wasn't worth bothering about. Even if it did, there was nothing that could be done about it, but anyway it wouldn't. Another couple in the same cul-de-sac, but young, recently moved in and buying their house on a Council mortgage, thought that expansion plans would not affect them. When the field-worker pointed out that the street was designated for a car park, they said it would take ages for 'them' to get through 'all the red tape' and nothing would happen for years. The couple said they had paid no attention to the expansion issue until the field-worker had mentioned it. Other residents with whom the field-worker tried to discuss the subject mumbled, changed the subject, or simply looked blank, almost as if the field-worker were talking in a foreign language.

These data are of crucial significance. They accord with the account by Hilda Jennings[8] of the reactions of residents to the proposed demolition of Old Barton Hill and to comments in other studies about the disbelief that residents have that their property is to be demolished until the 'white death certificates' actually go up on the house doors.[9]

These citizens, the cul-de-sac residents and many others like them, so far from being themselves participants, did not appear even as observers of the expansion tussle, although their own personal lives, and often their economic as well as their domestic interest, were threatened by expansion. They had the formal political right to appear, they had the vote. They lacked the skill either to understand the situation or, having understood, to express their objections. They could not have mounted a campaign of the NOAASE type. No leader saw fit to rouse them or to show them the way to participation.

The other large category of persons who did not join the public fight was those in favour of expansion. Given that the parties were evenly balanced on the Council and the Mayor was Conservative, one might have expected that the Labour party would have rallied vocal town support for expansion at the public meeting. Possible reasons for their silence were discussed earlier in this chapter. Furthermore, at the public meeting there were no representations from or even questions asked by the Trades Council, which was concerned to look after 'working class interests' in the town. So far as the field-workers are aware the Trades Council never even discussed the issue.

Thus, while powers were unequally distributed among those involved in the expansion issue, power was also exercised more successfully by some than by others, in part independently of the unequal distribution. In particular, the powers of voters and associated rights of free speech were much more effectively used by some than others. The greatest variation was perhaps in Marshall's third type of power 'the use made of the capacity for successful action'.[10]

The notion of a disjunction in experience and meaning, in salience between the governors and certain sections of the governed seems to be a possible explanation of the failure of large categories of people either to recognize that their interests were threatened or to act to protect them: a type of alienation perhaps.

The non-participation appears partly to be the result of the acceptance of a division of labour: 'it's their business to run the town', i.e. it is the job of elected representatives and officials. This is not seen as the job or the calling of most ordinary folk. Such an attitude does not necessarily involve the notion of deference, rather of detachment. But the non-participation also relates to the experience of such people in attempting to enter into dialogue with officials or councillors: an experience which had led many people to believe that language and meanings were so different it was not worth trying.[11] In addition, for them 'talking' is not 'doing': 'they are always talking about it [expansion, for example] but nothing ever happens'. The terms of reference of councillors and officials tend to be quite different from those of everyday life. A similar disjunction could be observed at several levels.

At the public meeting the people present gave the impression, as one of us remarked at the time, that they were angry, that they felt they were being pushed around by authorities outside Banbury, and that nobody consulted them as to what they wanted.

Another disjunction appears to exist between the townsfolk who were politically active and aware, including the town leaders, and the representatives of the planning authority, the G.L.C. and the Ministries. There was a tendency on the part of the outsiders to see the decision to reject further expansion as 'small minded', 'narrow-minded small-town folk who can't look into the future, can't see beyond their own noses'.

The issue was relatively more important for people in Banbury than for the G.L.C. in the sense that other places might be persuaded to expand instead of Banbury and in any case Banbury was only a relatively small part of a much larger plan. This was also partly true for the O.C.C., but here the investment of the planning team (as opposed to the authority as a whole) was sizeable.

Thus at several points the way in which the decision was arrived at appears not to have been one of rational discussion on agreed premises, but much more a matter of people with different values, different interests and quite different frames of reference talking past each other. Often they seemed not to be talking about the same thing and, when they were, the issue meant something quite different to the parties involved. This is perhaps not uncommon, but the actors, non-participant and participant alike, seemed not to be aware that this was the case.

The formal decision to reject this large-scale expansion leaves Banbury to grow beyond 40,000 or not in future depending upon the decisions made by individuals, elementary family domestic groups and firms small or large. Some of their actions are constrained by planning legislation; there will be less privileged overspill housing when present agreements are satisfied. Whether and when Banbury reaches the already agreed 40,000, and by what date, also depends upon the many decisions of individuals in interaction with officials and with each other. Banbury had an estimated population of 31,000 and by the end of 1972 had built 1,311 of the projected 2,000 dwellings needed to honour its agreement with the G.L.C.[12]

7 Neighbours and neighbouring

Who the neighbours are depends on where the dwelling is. Increasingly in Banbury as elsewhere access to a dwelling is either through a building society for a mortgage or through the local authority housing committee for a Council house. Normally, long-established local authority residents are given preference, but in the case of Banbury, because of the overspill agreements, a migrant coming to town to work could gain ready access to a Council house. Access to a mortgage was most readily available to those young couples who had a salaried non-manual job and could find a house at a price where mortgage repayments would not exceed 25 per cent of the husband's income. The constraints imposed by the building society policy could be avoided by those who, although their incomes were lower than average, had acquired capital by some means. There are four ways in which this came about. Some manual workers or lower-income workers had inheritances or aid from kin and by making a larger down-payment were able to keep their mortgage repayments at a low enough level to be acceptable to the building society. Others had saved enough during their lifetime to make a sizeable down payment; these therefore tend to be older than the better-off home owner when they first buy. The third factor was provided by the older childless couple where the wife worked. In Banbury there was a fourth modification which resulted from the generous housing allowances provided by Birds for their employees who moved from Birmingham to Banbury. Birds employees were thus to be found on a number of estates, one which happened to be built just as Birds were moving to town being known as 'the Aviary'.[1]

These factors reduce the proportions of those on the new estates who are in family-cycle stages one and two, in at least junior non-manual occupations, and with an income at least of £1,000 to £1,500

83

per annum. They thus reduce the age, family-cycle stage, income and occupation homogeneity of many of the new estates.[2]

The interplay of the major institutions sets considerable limits on the choice of house and neighbourhood that any one individual, elementary family, or household may make and therefore also limits the social categories of the neighbours they have. The chapter on religion showed how in the 'Fish Scheme' neighbourly aid was offered to those in need, but some restriction was set upon the utility of the scheme[3] since the offerers were largely from middle social levels and those in need largely in lower social levels, each category tending to inhabit different parts of the town.

We see a two-stage process connecting the institutions of the larger society and any specific neighbour relation. First, the institutions filter the type of person who is likely to occupy a house in a particular location. In the case of new suburbs this often leads to homogeneity, but with the modifications outlined above. In zones of transition the process can lead to diversity.[4] Second, who is sociable with whom is associated with the sharing of roles in the larger society as well as sharing the neighbour role. Within these limiting factors, propinquity and idiosyncratic preference may play their part.

In this study, as in 1950, it is neighbouring, rather than neighbourhood, which forms the focus of study. No attempt has been made to examine a 'neighbourhood' in the sense that planners use that term: no study has been made of the social relations throughout any one Council housing or speculative builder's estate. Such areas are both too large and too small in sociological terms: too large to examine the face-to-face relations between neighbours, and too small in the sense that no formal organizations are based upon them or significant point of power or authority found within them. From time to time in such an estate there may be aspects of social relations of some importance involving people from the entire estate, but never all of them. One example of such neighbourhood interaction is discussed in Chapter 4.

Detailed studies of the social categories of people who lived near each other, of which neighbours interacted and in what way, showed that for the most part neighbouring still takes place on a small scale. The studies also suggested that the quality and quantity of neighbour relations is determined more by the institutions of the larger society and by the statuses held and roles played by residents associated with these institutions, often outside the locality, than by any physical characteristics of the locality itself or of propinquity within it.

Three streets and their immediate surrounding areas were examined in detail by the method of participant observation. The number is therefore fewer than in the first study when seven streets were studied. Furthermore, no Council houses were included, although aspects of a Council house neighbourhood are dealt with in Chapter 5.[5] In the first study most of the streets were observed only for some weeks; in the second study they were observed for periods varying from eighteen months to two years. This lack of comparability in the quality and quantity of data between the two studies is the inevitable result of the different social circumstances of the two generations of field-workers.

The three streets

Of the three streets[6] studied between 1966 and 1968, one is a street of Victorian workers' cottages near the town centre; the second is a private estate recently built in a village, fast becoming a dormitory suburb, on the outskirts of the town; the third is a very mixed area where an erstwhile village has long since been swallowed by the town and where still, as was reported for many parts of Banbury in 1950, houses and occupants of very different type and occupational status are to be found 'cheek by jowl'. Neighbour relations in the two physically homogeneous areas will be discussed first.

One End Street

The Victorian street, called for convenience here One End Street, has much the same appearance now as it had eighty years ago, and is officially described as 'sub-standard'. The twenty-odd houses are all terraced and back access is by a common alley. In 1967 only three houses had a bath and only two an inside lavatory. In most cases all hot water is heated on the stove. Many houses, particularly the rented ones, i.e. about two-thirds of the total, are in bad repair, with rotten woodwork, crumbling plaster and a shortage of paint. The gross rateable value for houses in the area is generally less than £50.

When compared with the streets studied in 1950, One End Street is most like Statham Terrace, from which it is not far distant both in number and type of houses, but Statham Terrace was a through road. One End Street is similar in terms of the age and origins of many of the inhabitants, but the social relations in the street perhaps appear more complex.

Seventeen of the twenty-seven elementary families who live in One End Street are in the final stage of the family cycle; seven are in the home-making or procreation phases. Twelve of the households have lived at their present address for fifteen or more years contrasted with eleven for five or less; only two households have been in the street from six to ten years and none between ten and fifteen years. There is thus a fairly sharp distinction, of a kind which is often found in streets as old as this one, between the older inhabitants and the newcomers. This dichotomy seems to emerge where a number of families have remained in the street throughout the greater part or all of their married life. As they die or perhaps move away in old age, so young couples take their place. In addition there seem also to be a number of houses which constantly change hands as people move in and out of the street. Either way the newcomers in the streets such as this, whether they will turn out to be transients or to settle, tend to be young and the long-established to be old.

Seven of the households are of one person only, eleven of two, seven of three or four, one of five and one of six. In 1968 there were sixty-four residents in the street altogether, including the children. As might be expected, two-thirds of the household heads were over fifty and nine of the twenty male household heads were retired.

All the male occupants whose jobs were known were manual workers with the exception of the field-worker's household. Most of the men were in semi-skilled or unskilled jobs. The women who were, or had been, gainfully occupied and whose occupations were known, included a telephonist, typist and clerk as well as domestic workers and cleaners.

Six of the households ran a car, a few had fridges or washing machines. Some of the women were often to be seen around the street in flowered overalls over a worn cardigan, with slippers on their feet and, not uncommonly, hairnets and curlers. 'Best' clothes were for church on Sundays for the few regular attenders, evenings at the Guild or Bingo, and Sunday afternoon outings. Three of the elderly male residents were to be seen, summer or winter, wearing cloth caps.

The residents of One End Street were observed to act as a collectivity on only one occasion during nearly two years. This was when a resident died and one person from each side of the street collected contributions for a wreath. At the same time, it should be noted that it was the kin rather than the neighbours who supported the bereaved.[7] Apart from this incident, neighbour relations were among selected groups of individuals in One End Street rather than among the street as a whole. Around 1950 the neighbour relations recorded were largely among the women.[8] In One End Street, and also in other streets studied in 1966–8, neighbour relations were observed among men as well as women. In One End Street this largely derived from the considerable proportion of the male residents who were retired and, like the housewives, were in a position to spend much of their time around their home. Indeed, the neighbour relations were perceived in One End Street as being between households rather than individuals, although there were ties between particular individuals within the household links.

One elderly couple dominated the neighbour relations, the husband being referred to by a new arrival as 'The Mayor of One End Street', a nickname by which he will be called here. Mr Mayor had been born in the street and his wife just around the corner. He owned his own house, had been a manual worker before he retired and still worked part time. All Mr Mayor's four children lived within five minutes' walk of their parents. Mrs Mayor had a widowed sister, apparently childless, who also lived in One End Street. There were frequent comings and goings between all these women. Cooked food covered by a white cloth was carried across the road between the sisters. Mr Mayor's grandchildren often came round for the afternoon to their 'gran' or great aunt. Both the older ladies helped the younger mothers with washing and other household tasks. The women all shared in shopping excursions and outings to Bingo. Mr Mayor's sons-in-law helped with his garden and decorating. Mr Mayor maintained his house well and this marked it off from other houses in the street. He was rumoured to own some land elsewhere in Banbury. In addition Mr Mayor ran a large car,[9] which he spent a good deal of time polishing outside the house, thus giving him ample opportunity to observe and interact with his neighbours. If anything was going on in the street, Mr Mayor and his wife were sure to know. She maintained close relations with a number of other residents, four women in particular. The number of households with which Mr and Mrs Mayor had contact was far and away the highest in the street.

These close relations were not always cordial. One of the four women mentioned to the field-worker that she did not know how Mr Mayor and his wife came to have so much and implied that they were not altogether straight. Another complained that Mrs Mayor was always poking her nose into other people's affairs. Certainly she used her position in the gossip networks to try and control the noise made by the children of a family of which she did not approve. The field-worker also observed that Mr Mayor and his wife did things for other people, but were not willing themselves to become obligated to others.[10] By inducing a sense of obligation in their neighbours, Mr and Mrs Mayor were able to get their own way in certain detailed matters connected with neighbour relations. Thus they were successful in resisting the erection of a gate across the communal back lane, although there was no legal objection they could raise, because the people who wished to put it up felt obligated to them.

The Mayors' house was in such a position that to reach it one had to go past almost every other house in the street, thus giving opportunity for observation, but once inside their own place, the Mayors were in a poor position to see what went on. This was no doubt more than compensated for by the news that was carried to them by their relatives and by the households with which they had close contact and which were scattered throughout the street. The Mayors at the same time reaped the benefits of not being observed by others.

The corner house in a cul-de-sac can be used as a strategic position from which to make social contacts and to exercise informal social control, for everyone must pass this house as they go in and out of the street. In One End Street the old man used the position in a quite contrary manner. He did not want to become involved in street relations and appreciated his physical situation because, as he said, 'I can come and go as I please and people won't see me . . . they're too gossipy down here . . . I can choose who I want to see when I want to . . .'[11]

Within the street generally, considerable informal social control was exercised. There was a strong norm of 'not being a nuisance to the neighbours', a norm entirely understandable in a situation where there were some sixty-four people, including children and shift workers, in so small an area. New arrivals were informed, for example, that the man next door was always in bed by ten at night since he had to be up for work at six. Children and dogs had to be kept under control, and trained not to stray beyond their own patch of garden. The common access path at the back had to be kept clean at all times. Sanctions exercised to maintain these norms included grumbling, gossip, complaints and ostentatious clearing up of alleged mess made by miscreants.

While children were not in practice confined to their own small patch of garden, they soon learned not to play near certain houses. When two elderly ladies living next door to each other came out and chased some children away, one father complained bitterly, 'It's only natural for children to want to run about a bit . . . and be a bit noisy.' He went on to say that those who had complained 'were children once too, I'll bet they made a noise then, but I suppose it was too long ago for them to remember . . .' Another old lady born and bred in the street had a longer memory and more sympathy, saying, 'They've always been like that down here, when I was a child I used to get it too . . .'[12]

The children who played in the street did not all come in for the same treatment, however. Mrs Mayor let her own grandchildren play in the street when they were visiting her. The grandchildren then got into trouble just as the street children did. This Mrs Mayor resented. Yet she chased away the children of certain families from her neighbours' garden as well as from her own. One of these families she chased off because they were 'rough and dirty', while the others, although she would admit they were 'kept very nicely', were nevertheless 'really rather rough . . . and a bit of a bad influence'.[13] Similarly in the control of pets: one miniature poodle's behaviour occasioned a lot of adverse comment. It was owned by a family of recent arrivals. The household head was frequently unemployed; his wife was said to be a bad housewife and mother. The fact that she rose late and had not washed or dressed her children by midday, although they were allowed on to the doorstep, was highly visible to all. The antics of their poodle might have been better tolerated if they themselves had conformed better to the local norms.

As opposed to those who had lived in the area from birth, there were a variety of reasons which had led newcomers to take houses in the street, and these added to the status differences. Thus one old lady, who had been a supervisor in an office for many years, sympathized with the fieldworkers' family, saying, 'I can see you are like me, educated people who have fallen on hard times.' A librarian had moved there when her daughter had an illegitimate baby: 'she had to give up her nice house . . . it's such a shame'. One worker and his family lived there because, with a Council mortgage, he could escape from the caravan he had been in for two years. Any more expensive dwelling would have been beyond his means, given the insecurity of his work in the building trade. Another couple were living together with their baby and came because the house was cheap and they did not want to live with relatives.

The divisions and groups in One End Street

Age, length of residence in the street, family-cycle stage, status differences and location were the underlying factors which led to divisions and to groupings in One End Street. A number of these factors vary together of course. Thus of the twelve who had lived in the street for more than fifteen years, eleven are in the final stage of the family cycle and all are over fifty. Between such groups of friends it was permissible to borrow the proverbial cup of sugar, or half a loaf on Sunday evening for a man's lunch pack the next day. In minor crises neighbour's aid was sought, for example, to mend a burst pipe on Christmas Day. Thus the neighbours took no part in the street death, mentioned earlier, except to collect for a wreath. The resident who was minded by neighbours when he had a heart attack had no kin.

While undoubtedly the physical layout of the street was such as to tend to maximize contact and, therefore, encourage interaction, and, as already indicated, there was a good deal of both co-operative and antagonistic interaction, it was also possible to opt out of any but the minimum interaction of acknowledging others when passing in the street. The lady in the corner house was not the only one to do this. One household maintained this distant relationship throughout the field-worker's stay and, according to the reports of the older neighbours, had successfully done so for all the nineteen-odd years that they had lived there.[14]

Availability for neighbourly contact has already been mentioned as a variable affecting interaction. Those who had fewer roles to play away from home, for example, the retired, semi-retired and the housewives, were available for gossip, baby-minding and the like. Those who worked, both men and women, were less often available. Thus for those who worked and those who did not, the work role, or its absence, affected the neighbour role, or at least set limits upon what neighbouring was possible. Other roles also affected the neighbour relations. Neighbours were called upon for aid on the basis of their own skills in other spheres, as decorators, nurses, clerks and so on. In at least one case neighbour relations were reinforced because both the neighbours were Roman Catholics.

When length of residence, stage of family cycle and number of households who have contact with each other are analysed, it appears that those in the final stage of the family cycle and with long residence score high, i.e. they have the highest number of contacts, but those in the final stage with short residence score low. Those in the procreation and dispersal phases score high, even if they have not lived in the street for long. The relevance of children in initiating neighbour relations was noted previously.[15] Those in the final phase who have lived long in the street, such as Mr Mayor, had in many cases reared their children there. It is impossible to say that the children 'caused' the high rate of interaction, but it would seem likely that this aspect of the residents' shared past was a contributory factor to present relationships among these older neighbours, old in years as well as length of residence.

Little Newton

This hypothesis could not be tested in Little Newton, the village outside Banbury which is the second subject of study here, for all the residents were new to the area. A large new housing estate was built by developers in Little Newton from the early sixties onwards. There was nothing at all comparable to Little Newton in the Banbury of 1950. Like much of the building in Banbury town and in other surrounding villages, this development was associated not only with the national increase in private house building in the sixties, but with the decision taken in Banbury itself to expand the population of the Borough to 40,000. The development could in some sense be seen as an unplanned overspill. A planned version of village development was included in the ill-fated 'Banbury 70,000' plan. Already in 1950 Little Newton was beginning to become a dormitory suburb for Banbury, but by 1967 the housing estate development all but dominated the previous village status, so that Little Newton had become effectively not only a commuter village, but, in fact if not in administrative arrangement, almost part of Banbury's urban development.

The data about Little Newton are derived from general knowledge of the housing market; observation of behaviour on the estate as a whole, about 200 households, mostly composed of domestic groups; from an examination of the returns of twenty-six interviews undertaken for the main sample; and from a detailed study of relations between neighbours in twenty adjacent houses in one corner of the estate.

A number of factors appear to have affected the type of people who went to live in Little Newton. There were those who were attracted by the notion of living in a village (for whom the 'village-in-mind', to use Pahl's phrase, has an appeal).[16] The notion seems to be that by living in a village one is living in a small stable community which constitutes a haven from the 'rat race' and other career stresses, a full-time rather than a weekend cottage. The advertising referred to attractive semi-detached chalet bungalows in a small estate on the edge of the village adjacent to open countryside. People attracted by such advertisements would no doubt prefer, if they could afford it, to live in a converted cottage or a detached house in a village, preferably not on an estate at all.[17] However, those who positively want to live in a village are constrained as much as others who come to live in Little Newton by economic considerations. These do seem to have been paramount in most people's decisions to live there.[18]

Most of the houses on the estate are semi-detached and cost between £3,000 and £4,000 in 1966. Thus these houses are distinguished from old village cottages, which if cheaper to buy are more expensive by the time the conversion is completed, and from detached houses, houses on smaller estates tucked in ones and twos among older village developments. It seems that the majority of people buy the most expensive house they can afford, partly to have as good a base for their home as they can and also because a house is of itself seen as 'status-giving'. Thus many who came to the estate did so because it was only here that they could find a house on which they could get a large enough mortgage from a building society and a down-payment that they could afford. They simply could not get an equivalently cheap house with such a large loan in town, for building societies are chary of lending on an older property. (It will be remembered that one at least of the One End Street residents had had the mortgage for his house from the Council; Councils offer loans to house buyers specifically in an attempt to counteract the consequences of the building societies' policy in this matter.) In addition, no building society will lend an amount of money upon which the

91

repayments total more than a quarter of the available income of the purchaser in any given period. It is this at least as much the constraints imposed by his own income and the building societies' policies which lead the house-seeker to buy a new house and to buy one in a village, as it is a positive wish for such property in such a location. Many, of course, make a virtue of necessity and praise both house and locality. In an expanding town, not only are there more new houses for sale than old ones, but, as everywhere, information about houses on new estates is much more readily come by than information about old houses for sale. This is especially true for newcomers to the town. New estates tend to be more visible both physically and in the advertising space devoted to them.[19] Time is saved also, not only in the search, but in the 'package deal' that the seller and the building society offer between them. These influences affected people who chose to live in Little Newton.

The combined consequences of all these factors are that the occupants of any one estate tend to be drawn from within a fairly narrow socio-economic range, and therefore tend to exhibit a good deal of homogeneity. Indeed, the expectation on the part of prospective buyers that the estate would be composed of 'much the same sort of people as us' apparently acted for many as a positive attraction. Many people perceive hazards in living in a 'mixed neighbourhood', as they call it, in town. Estate agents report that otherwise similar houses fetch less in a neighbourhood perceived as 'mixed' than they would in a neighbourhood where the houses and the people in them were perceived as being 'the same'.[20] The tensions found in a mixed neighbourhood are the subject of our third case study.

The importance of children in neighbour relations in One End Street was stressed. Those who have children seem to be particularly concerned about who the neighbours will be and, therefore, with whom their children will be likely to play. This seems to be an important reason for avoiding 'mixed neighbourhoods'. The private development of 'family' houses therefore attracts those in the home-making and procreation stages of the family cycle.

These expectations of social and economic homogeneity were to some extent fulfilled in the Little Newton estate. Most people had fairly low, but secure, incomes. Most were in junior non-manual occupations, many on the lower rungs of an occupational ladder, with expectations of promotion. The manual workers were mainly skilled. The majority of the residents were either in the home-making or child-rearing phases of the family cycle. About three-quarters of the adults were under forty-five and about half under thirty. Newcomers to the Banbury area were over-represented. But there were also the older manual workers and lower-income employees referred to earlier,[21] many in the dispersal or final stage of the family cycle, having at last achieved the bungalow of their lifelong ambition. These reduced the expected family-cycle/income-bracket homogeneity of the estate. It was also further reduced by the surprisingly large number of houses to rent on the estate at the time of survey. This was a function of the career mobility of many of those who bought the houses initially. Thus Mr A, who was a systems analyst for one of the large firms, was offered promotion which involved going abroad for three years. He decided to let his house rather than sell it, because at the time there was a credit squeeze which would have made the house hard to sell at a good price. By letting the house, he could not only get a return on it, but also its value would appreciate while he was away. Others had made similar decisions. Houses put up to let in this way were commonly rented by Americans from the nearby American Air Force base. There were in fact six American families at the time of survey living in the area around Mr A's house.[22]

Sociological determinants of neighbouring

Although the personnel of the Little Newton estate was in many ways so different from that of One End Street, particularly in being younger, non-Banburian and better-off, the sociological determinants of neighbour relations appeared to be essentially the same. Thus it was seen in One End Street that those neighbours who interacted with each other as neighbours were those who had other roles in common: kinship; common stage in the family cycle; having children at home; place of origin, especially residence in the area. So it was in Little Newton, although there was some variation in the roles which were held in common.

In One End Street long residence together and especially having been born in the street, tended to lead residents to be friends as well as neighbours. In Little Newton everyone was a relative newcomer. Common place of origin in a sense replaced long residence together as a basis for developing neighbour relations. Thus it was noticeable that Banburians were friendly with each other: some had been to the same school, others had been brought up in the same part of Banbury before they came to Little Newton. There were many non-Banburians on the estate. The Americans were perhaps the most alien and chose each other almost exclusively as neighbouring companions. They popped into each other's houses and frequently entertained each other, but their relations with their English neighbours rarely got past the stage of a chat over the garden fence or a nod in passing.[23]

The Americans, of course, not only had place of origin but work place in common. This latter factor tended to be associated with neighbour relations among the English also. Thus Mrs B and Mrs C had both come from Birmingham and had husbands who worked in Birds. They frequently had coffee together, went on shopping expeditions and to association functions together. They, like the Americans, had place of origin as well as husband's occupation in common.[24] Both the Americans and the Birds people had moved to Banbury at the behest of large-scale organizations. The large organization had led to the men moving, their wives came too and now lived near each other and found themselves 'in the same boat' on a new estate among people who were mostly strangers in every sense. As well as common place of origin and common work place, common membership of sports clubs and other associations tended to lead to the development of neighbour relations.

In Little Newton, as in One End Street, availability to neighbour, i.e. being about in the locality, was important. Thus those who were around the house for long periods of time were in a position to develop neighbour relations. As in One End Street, among domestic groups where the wife went out to work there were few neighbour relations compared with those where she was at home. In Little Newton the men were young and at work for the most part. Neighbouring for the men, as for the working wives, was thus largely confined to exchanges in the evening or at the weekends. The neighbour relations of working women and men were largely of the coincidental kind, superficial exchanges when working in the garden, hanging out the clothes, or cleaning the car. Without other overlapping roles, such exchanges seemed rarely to develop into any other form of interaction. In contrast, those women who did not work and more particularly those who were the mothers of young children (and these categories overlapped very largely) were not only available in the locality for a great many hours, but also had the mother-role in common and children who played together and/or went to school together. For them the chances of establishing interaction with neighbours were higher because availability and overlapping roles coincided.

To begin with there was no shopping centre on the estate, so that housewives had to travel away, often by car, to shop. However, during the course of the field-work a supermarket was built in the centre of the estate, and many residents walked there for their shopping. This not only increased their visibility to each other, but also the chances of their interacting: in this sense their availability for social interaction with their neighbours increased.

Frankenberg has contrasted the difficulties of establishing contact with the residents of a Welsh village, who for such long periods are shut up inside their houses, with the relative ease of doing so in a climate where much of the social life can take place out of doors.[25]

For similar reasons, the chances of coincidental neighbour relations taking place are greater in summer than in winter. That is to say, availability is effectively increased in the summer. This is, of course, proportionately more true in a street of 'semis' surrounded by gardens with fences and with separate access to each dwelling than it is in One End Street where physical proximity makes visibility fairly high in winter as well as summer. In One End Street too there was, of course, more interaction out of doors in summer than winter.

In Little Newton the importance of coincidental contact as a way of initiating neighbour relations between those who did not have any other roles in common was plain. Thus when Mr and Mrs E first moved into the estate they had no social contact with anyone living there. They started work on their garden and then they spoke to their neighbours and were also offered the use of various garden tools to help them. Acceptance of such offers resulted in the establishment of obligation to the neighbours and is a precondition for the neighbour relations to develop beyond the superficial level. When similar offers were refused it was noticeable that neighbour relations were minimal. But, as in One End Street, such exchanges also form part of a system of informal social control. The lending of garden tools in Little Newton was effectively a positive sanction tantamount to saying 'we value tidy gardens here'. Those who fail to keep their gardens tidy are perceived as 'anti-social'.

The Little Newton estate had passed through its early pioneer period just before the field-work started, but sufficiently recently for the field-worker to be given clear accounts of what the 'early days' were like. There were then many problems associated with its newness, numbers of them of a kind similar to those experienced in Neithrop and which had been one reason for the formation of the Tenants Association discussed in Chapter 5. The characteristics have been described for other estates, although more commonly for Council than for private developments.[26] Many of the problems are common to private and Council estates. The residents are all new and have a high degree of awareness of a common situation. Whereas Council residents tend to blame 'the Council' for their difficulties, to some extent the private estate residents have common complaints against the builder. The apocryphal story was retold of the resident who had a bad smell in his bathroom which was found to be caused, it was said, by a workman having left his packet of sandwiches under the bath. Stories were told of more serious allegations.

During this period the expertise of residents deriving from their work roles was often used, as it was in One End Street. Thus a resident with a knowledge of building was asked for advice on how to

95

deal with the builders, and the knowledge of the gardeners was often called upon by those who were making new gardens for the first time. It was felt to be a sign of prestige to have such skills available and advice was often proffered unasked.

It would seem that the helpful neighbouring behaviour which occurred in individual crises in One End Street was a frequent occurrence in the common crisis of living on a new estate. But after this period was over, such a pattern of neighbouring was far less frequent in Little Newton than in One End Street, perhaps because of the higher average income level in Little Newton.

In the twenty adjoining houses where an intensive study of neighbour relations was made, it was observed that there was a high turnover of residents, ten houses having a change of resident in two years. Two houses in fact changed hands twice in this period. The most common reason for moving was connected with work: American servicemen were posted; promotion in the firm meant moving to a plant elsewhere. Several families moved away to 'better' houses elsewhere. One manual worker moved back into Banbury because his wife 'couldn't get on with the people round here' and wanted to be back closer to her mother and other relatives.

Among the houses where the first occupants still lived, contacts were more frequent than among others, as one would expect. This was particularly true of two men living six doors apart who exchanged visits and garden tools. However, both moved away before· the field-work finished. Given the high mobility and the newness of the estate it was perhaps surprising to find that there had already developed a quasi-kinship role in one case. Thus Mr and Mrs J were much older than the rest and had at one time been jokingly called 'Mum' and 'Dad' by one of their neighbours. They did in fact play something of this role.

Most of the neighbour contacts in these houses were limited to next-door neighbours unless there were also overlapping roles played outside the neighbourhood. Only among the Americans was there much lending and borrowing of household items. Help with major tasks was commonly received from kin or friends from outside the estate and not from neighbours. Thus the only help Mr O had in laying his drive was from his younger brother. Mr P was helped by friends, not neighbours, to lay his lawn, while Mr B, who had neither kin nor friends in the Banbury area, laid his lawn entirely unaided. These neighbours got to know each other while doing these tasks, but did not share them. Because the men were available and visible when doing these tasks, some neighbouring took place among them, thus supporting the hypothesis that availability and visibility in the locality are necessary but not sufficient conditions for the development of neighbour relations. In so far as neighbouring tends to be among women, it is only because in some circumstances, especially during child rearing, the women are about the locality more. It has been stressed that where roles are shared among neighbours interaction is increased. This was as true of the twenty Little Newton houses as it was of One End Street: housewives and mothers interacted more than most. Nevertheless, for the majority of residents in Little Newton neighbours were a relatively unimportant form of social contact, although most considered that 'everyone round here is very friendly'.[27] For locally born or locally brought-up residents kin members did the baby-sitting and came visiting regularly. In major family crises such as the birth of a baby, in Little Newton in 1966/8 as in Banbury in 1950, it is the kin, especially the mother's mother, who comes.[28] Mrs D's mother came from fifty miles away when Mys D's baby was born.

In Little Newton, as in One End Street, it would seem that while major social institutions, especially economic and administrative institutions, determine the type of neighbour one is likely to have, it is also one's position in other institutions, familial, associational, and work, which determine whom among one's neighbours one will be friendly with. Layout and proximity only have any significant effect upon those who are 'about the place a lot', notably the mothers of young children, other housewives who do not work and the retired. Neighbour relations are more determined by other social relations than they determine them.

Generally speaking, as has been shown, the high mobility rates in Little Newton reduced the chances of long-lasting relationships between neighbours developing. In the twenty houses studied it seemed in some cases people had moved away before the neighbours had got to know them at all.

The Village

Let us now see what the evidence from the mixed neighbourhood in Banbury has to add. Although it is many years since The Village was swallowed by the nineteenth-century expansion of Banbury, it is still known as The Village. In 1950 fields and pleasant country walks almost reached The Village, but by 1966 it was quite engulfed by new development. It is a bus ride from the country now. No area like The Village was studied in 1950.

Nowadays The Village contains houses which are a mixture both of tenure and of age, being characterized by the estate agent to the field-worker who was thinking of living there as 'not one of the best areas of the town' and having 'Council houses further down the street'. It was to avoid areas like The Village that many people bought houses in Little Newton.

97

A slightly winding street runs through The Village. The houses one side are connected at the back by allotments, garages and alley-ways. The main part of this street, Wychtree Road itself, contains twenty-two houses and is the most mixed, both in housing type and socially. In Wychtree Road there are examples of all the types of housing to be found in The Village except Council houses. Wychtree Road has the oldest houses in The Village: eighteenth-century dwellings built in the local Hornton stone, converted into 'town houses' for socially mobile immigrants. It also has the four most modern of The Village houses, built in the early 1960s, although half their occupants are Village residents of at least four generations' standing. Among these very old and very new dwellings are inter-war 'semis' and Victorian villas (some divided) and a row of nineteenth-century terraced cottages. The heterogeneity of Wychtree Road is most marked and in no sense could it be said to be a self-conscious whole; indeed, there is little interaction among the residents from different parts of the street. The owner of one of the Victorian villas, a retired maiden lady, spoke to no one else except one of the immigrant families who lived in an eighteenth-century house, because, as she said, she could see they were 'nice people'. There are three other parts of Wychtree Road: Wychtree Terrace, ten late nineteenth-century terraced houses similar to the row in Wychtree Road itself; Mayfair Drive, ten houses built soon after the First World War and originally privately rented, but now all owner-occupied; and Upper Wychtree Road, composed entirely of late-1940 Council houses, about forty in number.

The route to the town is from the Council houses through Wychtree Road, past Wychtree Terrace and Mayfair Drive. The corner shop and the pub which are just round the corner from Wychtree Road are used almost exclusively by the Council house tenants from Upper Wychtree Road and serve as foci for the interaction of these neighbours. The allotments that lie at the back are held by residents of central Wychtree Road, Wychtree Terrace and part of Mayfair Drive. The adjacent garages are used by the Wychtree Terrace and Mayfair Drive residents. The allotments and the garages both afford centres for gossip among the men: here the men, having their roles as neighbours reinforced by the roles of allotment- or garage-holders, develop social relations. The women from these streets meet to gossip in the shops across the busy main road at the bottom of Wychtree Road.

The Village has long had a reputation for being 'rough', Wychtree Road being at one time as bad as the rest.[29] Today Wychtree Road is relatively respectable and its residents decry the residents of Upper Wychtree Road. Interaction among neighbours occurs within Mayfair Drive, within Wychtree Terrace and within Upper Wychtree Road.

The numbering of the houses in this area is illogical and confusing, relating to their date of building and not to their position in the road. Numbers 'jump' across the street, and each of the four parts has its own numbering system. To ease the difficulties of the postmen and other officials, the Council decided to renumber the houses 'rationally'. This met with fierce resistance because the distinct names and numbers in the four parts of what is physically one street symbolize important perceived differences of social rank.

These sharply felt differences are largely between people who might broadly be called 'working class', i.e. all were of one social level. There were certain objective criteria related to the felt differences. Out of eighty household heads, only three in all the Wychtree area were in higher non-manual occupations and all these lived in Wychtree Road proper. There were twenty-one unskilled household heads. All but two of these lived in Upper Wychtree Road. Mayfair Drive and Wychtree Terrace had none in either of these categories, Mayfair Drive being almost equally divided between routine non-manual and skilled manual workers, all owner-occupiers. Wychtree Terrace, all privately rented houses, had twice as many skilled manual as routine non-manual workers. In Upper Wychtree Road there lived some routine non-manual workers and some skilled manual workers, but the street was characterized for the rest of the villagers by the unskilled workers, and by the less law-abiding who lived there.

In The Village there is a higher proportion of people born and/or brought up in Banbury than there is in the town as a whole. Forty-seven of the sixty-six household heads whose origins are known are Banburians. Banburians predominate in all the four sections. Upper Wychtree Road, being an older Council house development, has no London overspill nor any Birds people from Birmingham. In Wychtree Road and Upper Wychtree Road just over half the household heads were under 50, but in Mayfair Drive and Wychtree Terrace nearly all were over 50.

When in The Village one has the impression that there are many more children in Upper Wychtree Road than elsewhere. But this is not altogether true: certainly the distinction between Wychtree Road and Upper Wychtree Road in terms of family-cycle stage is not marked. It is true that a few of the families in the Upper Wychtree Road are very large (two have thirteen children and one has ten children), but it is the visibility of these children as much as their actual numbers which is important. Upper Wychtree Road children played in the street, so that their dress and behaviour were visible. Mayfair Drive children did not play in the street, nor did Wychtree Road or Wychtree Terrace children. Children from these streets, when they were seen, were smartly and 'respectably' dressed and usually accompanied by a parent. This was not true of Upper Wychtree Road children, who constantly 'played out' and were rarely 'dressed up'. Their parents also used the street as a social arena, especially during the summer, behaviour unacceptable in the rest of The Village. Upper Wychtree Road mothers during summer evenings often sat in their front doorways gossiping loudly across the road. At all times and all seasons people were to be seen about in the street. This confirmed the views of the rest of The Village that the Upper Wychtree men never did an honest day's work. Furthermore, their gardens were not cultivated.

Upper Wychtree Road was one of the earlier of the post-war Council house developments. Among those who were rehoused there were families who have kinship links with families who still live in caravans. Three of the Upper Wychtree Road families have themselves been caravan dwellers. One family is the first generation to live in a house and is part of a kin group well known in Banbury before any of them lived in a house. They are dealers in a small way, their womenfolk collecting other people's discarded items in old prams. When the matriarchal head of the kin group died, the so-called 'Queen of the Gipsies', her death was reported in the national press. She was given one of the largest funerals that occurred during the field-work (attended by respectable town leaders as well as by her own kin and friends). Her caravan was burned and other traditional gipsy rites followed. This family may have been particularly outstanding, but there are other families in Upper Wychtree Road who are also placed socially by links they have outside the street. There are a number of 'Banbury Irish', a derogatory term used to describe a low-ranked group similar to the didicoys, who live there. The Banbury Irish are held to be recognizable by their surnames and include the few large families in the street.

Upper Wychtree Road is well known to the social and legal services and to the Council housing department. The latter look upon the street as one of 'bad tenants' who do not dig their gardens and fall behind with the rent. During the two years' field-work there were two evictions for rent arrears and two threatened evictions prevented by the O.C.C. Children's Department. The probation officer's car is frequently in Upper Wychtree Road. At one time he had nine clients in the road, six from two families. At the same time, two household heads were in prison. Police and magistrates alike know some of these families well. When one of the residents was before the magistrates for climbing the Cross and other offences when drunk on New Year's Eve, he claimed it was not him, but his brother. To this the magistrate replied, 'Very likely, but we've got you here.'

The rest of The Village label Upper Wychtree Road, like Zone III in Winston Parva, by the behaviour of its most outstanding residents.[30] Not all are rough or unruly, but all are assumed to be by the respectable workers of other parts of The Village.

Wychtree Terrace residents, nearest in occupational status and tenure to Upper Wychtree Road residents, are perhaps those who keep their distance most carefully from the Council house people. The Terrace residents are particularly annoyed by the Saturday-night drunks who ring their doorbells after the inhabitants are asleep and those who send their children to steal milk from the doorsteps early in the morning. Wychtree Terrace is in some ways similar to One End Street. Both have a high proportion of elderly and old-established residents. Quite strong social norms are enforced in the Terrace. When an old man died, all the curtains were drawn on the day of the funeral, a custom not observed in other parts of The Village. Wychtree Terrace also has a leading couple 'Mr and Mrs Kingpin' who occupy a house in a strategic position at the corner of the alley. Mr Kingpin is important beyond the neighbourhood, providing links between a number of voluntary associations. Mrs Kingpin has two daughters who live in the same street and these, along with a number of old friends, mean that she has strong links with many households in Wychtree Road as well as Wychtree Terrace and is the centre of an extensive gossip network. She distinguishes sharply between the Upper Wychtree Road people who 'live like pigs', 'drag up' their children and are a 'thieving lot' for whom she has no time, and the Mayfair Drive residents who are 'a cut above themselves' and 'a bit snobby'.

Certainly the reaction of the residents of Mayfair Drive to being renumbered and renamed part of Wychtree Road would seem to confirm this judgement. The residents got up a petition, claiming that to have the name Wychtree would lower the value of their property. A past Mayor, brought up in the area, suggested the whole street, which was locally referred to as 'Muck Bottom', be renamed Mayfair Street, Wychtree being dropped altogether, but he lost his case.

Groups and quasi-groups

The renaming and renumbering issue, imposed from outside, in fact turned quasi-groups into groups between which conflict flared. The quasi-groups were based on a combination of tenure, occupation and behaviour in the street. Within each of these quasi-groups there were some social groups and some wider networks. What emerged on One End Street as disputes between individual families is seen in Wychtree Village as conflict between social-status groups. There are twenty houses in One End Street and eighty in the Wychtree area. The importance of underscoring social distance when the neighbours are physically proximate applies here as in One End Street. Know-

101

H

ledge and a shared history in both these cases lead to a type of social relation among neighbours, whether hostile or co-operative, which was hardly reported at all for the residents of Little Newton.

Neighbourhood pubs

Where there are facilities, notably pubs, in a neighbourhood, groups or networks which fall between the formal association and the informal neighbour relation may develop. Appendix 4 reports on Thrift Clubs, some of which have a neighbourhood basis. Other groups, such as darts or dominoes clubs, are also found in neighbourhood pubs. The social consequences of this commercially provided and usually profitable activity can therefore be considerable. Because there is a pub in the neighbourhood it does not follow that neighbours will take their recreation together. But it is *possible* for them to do so. They may of course use the 'local' as a way of marking their separateness as much as their togetherness, as happened in Wychtree where, since it was much used by the despised residents of Upper Wychtree Road, the local was eschewed by other residents of The Village. They went to another pub a little further away if they drank in the locality at all.

Propinquity and neighbouring

Thus it is clear that while physical layout does have some effect on neighbour relations and neighbouring norms, this effect is by no means a deterministic one. Certain positions, for example, corner houses, are strategic for making friendly relations with neighbours if the occupants so wish, but equally they may be used to avoid such relations, as in One End Street. Close proximity may make coincidental contact hard to avoid and is likely to lead, whatever persons may wish, to levels of interaction which can more easily be avoided in less dense developments. These relationships may be either friendly or hostile. The neighbour relations in the 'banjos' described by Willmott for Dagenham parallel those found in cul-de-sacs in Banbury around 1950.[31]

The part played by high physical visibility in encouraging neighbouring patterns of a particular kind has often been pointed out and is well described by Hilda Jennings for Old Barton Hill.[32] Nevertheless, even in this neighbourhood where there were high interaction rates there were those, Jennings reports, who kept their front doors closed and did not join in the social life of the street. We have reported similarly for One End Street. When people feel they have a good social reason to ignore their neighbours, they will do so whatever the proximity. In the first study the case was recorded of a child

102

being made to play in a ten-by-six-foot back yard because the street children were not thought to be fit companions.[33] In another of the streets studied there were two distinct children's play groups differentiated on social-status grounds as indicated by their dress and the behaviour their parents expected from them.[34] This tendency went so far in the case of the gentry that they did not define as their neighbours those who lived physically next door to them, but only those of a similar social status living in other parts of the County.[35] In all these cases, however high physical visibility might have been, neighbours were able to render each other socially invisible. The anger about the drunken doorbell-ringing and the stolen milk in The Village was no doubt increased beyond the actual annoyance caused because such actions made it impossible to ignore the neighbours one wished not to know. Although the physical layout may make it easier or more difficult for people either to get to know or to avoid their neighbours, it is clear to us that planners and architects cannot create particular neighbouring patterns by their plans. These patterns are determined by a complex of social factors.

In the sixties, as in Banbury in 1950, the items in the transactions between neighbours also varied by economic class. Those with fewer resources tended to exchange basic commodities such as sugar, salt or tea, while those of the middle classes who were more independent economically exchanged advice or garden plants and tools. Some services were exchanged in most neighbour relations, but again the nature and frequency of these varied with class.[36]

Relations between neighbours do not often impinge upon persons in power, nor do they appear to have any significant effect upon the macro-structure. These facts may help to explain the neglect of the neighbour relations in British and American textbooks, despite the considerable amounts of field data on both sides of the Atlantic. There are, of course, the circumstances in which disputes between neighbours come to court, and those when residents of a particular area unite for common action. The group formation which took place in The Village over the threatened renumbering has already been discussed. An example of more formal group formation among neighbours, the rise and fall of the Neithrop Tenants Association, is discussed in Chapter 5.

Generally speaking, however, rather than neighbour relations having any effect upon the larger society, our evidence suggests that neighbour relations are themselves determined by social groups, relations and institutions in the wider society. Sometimes the wider society in this context means other parts of Banbury, or the town as a whole, often it refers to institutions which are at least national.

8 Women and the family

There are no signs that the form of the elementary family in Banbury is changing in any major way. The institution of marriage seems as popular as ever it was: in 1966 as in 1950 just over half of the total population was married.

During the discussions preparatory to the second study, informants told us that one of the major changes since the first study was the increase in the number of married women working.[1] This is true: in 1950, 18 per cent of married women worked,[2] in 1967, 42 per cent (the U.K. figure is 38·5 per cent).[3] But upon closer investigation we found that the family is still the central life interest for women and women still tend to undertake different work from men and for lower pay.

Over 80 per cent of men over 21 years are working full time; just under 45 per cent of the women work and half of these are part time. This is not of course to say that the 52 per cent of housewives are inactive, merely that they are not gainfully occupied. The work that men and women do is also markedly different, although the division is not rigid. Thus, all, those tasks which involve more skill and the supervision of others tend to be weighted heavily to men. Women outnumber men in the lower non-manual occupations, especially junior non-manual, in personal service (an almost exclusively female category) and in unskilled manual work. Men predominate as employers, managers, professional workers, foremen, supervisors, skilled manual workers and farmers (see Appendix 5).

Women also tend to earn a good deal less than men: they tend to have lower-paid jobs anyway and when they are in similar jobs they tend to be paid less for them. Seventy-six per cent of women in full-time non-manual employment say they earn less than £15 a week compared to only 28 per cent of men. Similarly among manual

104

workers, most women receive less than £10 a week compared to less than one in ten of unskilled men (see Appendix 5).

But the lower rewards and lower occupational status accorded to women have not led them to be well organized. On the contrary, their rates of membership of occupational associations are much lower than those of men (see Appendix 5). All these data taken together suggest the relative lack of commitment of women compared to men to gainful employment. It is as true of Banbury in 1967 as it was in 1950 that the world of work is largely a man's world.[4]

Men who are not economically active do not describe themselves as 'housewives'. 'House-husbands' has not yet become a word in English usage, although there are a few men in this role. Women who are not economically active do not find it necessary to legitimate this by describing themselves as 'chronic sick' or 'unemployed'. Few women, and most of them single, describe themselves as retired (see Table 8.1). Single women in their work relations tend in this and other ways to be more like men than married women. Even so almost 10 per cent are housewives despite their single state.

Notions about what roles it is thought appropriate for women to play are not confined to their roles in the family. But it is still true that women are largely employed in tasks which involve following, helping and serving men and minding and teaching children. Except for religious activity, women are also less active in formally organized voluntary associations than men, as we have seen.[5]

There are some small indications that a redefinition of sex roles may be taking place, or at least some loosening of the cluster of activities it is thought appropriate for a woman to undertake. There are now 14 per cent of women in Banbury who have or have had jobs in the Registrar-General's classes I and II. At the same time there is also a good deal of evidence that there has been little fundamental change since the nineteenth century. Most women are still wives and mothers first. The most active arena for women is still the family.

Banbury women in 1950 saw themselves as part of a family unit,[6] their lives followed a pattern dictated by the family cycle.[7] For them work was regarded as filling in time before marriage, or as an 'unfortunate necessity in a bad or broken marriage'.[8]

The marked increase in married women working might reasonably be thought, and usually is thought, to indicate a notable change in the status of women and in the social arrangements of their families and thus perhaps in the institution of the family itself. While it can be argued that over time the employment of married women must have an effect in other areas of their lives and in social institutions other than the family, no such effects can yet be recorded.

A detailed study of a sub-sample of women[9] showed that the family cycle still dictates the pattern of a woman's life. Of 64 cases in the

105

TABLE 8.1 Economic activity, by sex and marital state (%) (Population over 21 yrs., Banbury and District)

	Males				Females			
	Married	Single	Widowed, Separated, Divorced	Total	Married	Single	Widowed, Separated, Divorced	Total
Housewife	0	0	0	0	57·0	9·5	52·3	51·9
Working: full time	82·4	87·5	25·7	80·2	17·2	68·2	19·8	22·3
Working: part time	2·2	1·2	5·7	2·3	24·9	4·8	18·6	22·2
Retired	13·8	5·0	62·9	15·3	0·9	17·5	9·3	3·6
Chronic sick	0·9	2·5	2·8	1·1	0	0	0	0
Unemployed	0·7	3·8	2·8	1·1	0	0	0	0
N	586	80	35	701	523	63	86	672

Source: 6 per cent sample.

sub-sample (N = 139) where the wife was not working at the time of interview, 17 had stopped working on marriage and 27 stopped when the first child was expected. 'The pattern today is work until marriage, work after marriage until the children arrive and a return to work when the children grow older.'[10] Only 17 of the 75 working wives had a pre-school child. Of the 64 who were not working, 42 had at least one pre-school child. By 1967, the time when the youngest child starts school had become important in the work pattern of married women.

Respondents themselves frequently said 'the children are too young' to explain why they were not working. The family is therefore still crucial in determining the pattern of most women's lives. The change is that a different stage, or indeed stages, of the family cycle are now the determining factor: it is not now simply that married women do not go out to work, but rather that married women with young children do not go out to work.

In the late forties and early fifties it was noted that from 'middle life onwards, the housewife has much less to occupy her time and attention, a period which is also being prolonged at the other end by the increased expectation of life'.[11] These years were not then filled by a return to work, but by the sixties many middle-aged women were returning to work. Although work for women was still in 1967 regarded by many as filling in time before marriage, or as an unfortunate necessity in a bad or broken marriage, twenty-five out of the sixty-four wives who were not working at the time of interview expected they would return to work when 'the children were old enough'.

The family cycle itself has changed its shape since 1950. The proportion of elementary family domestic groups[12] which have reached the phase of dispersal or the final phase (i.e. some or all of the children have left home) while the husband and wife are both alive has increased noticeably. In 1950 only 19 per cent of couples were in this phase compared with 32 per cent in 1967.[13] The earlier age of marriage (of parents and their children) and the relatively small contemporary families mean that women have completed child-bearing and child-rearing at an earlier age than formerly. There is now a small but measurable proportion of women whose children have all left home before they are 45 years old (see Table 8.2). This truncating of the two central phases of the elementary family domestic group makes more women available for work. Economic changes in Banbury and an increasing demand for labour have made vacancies available. These two trends together seem to have contributed to the increased employment of married women.

Despite these changes in their pattern of employment, wives still see themselves primarily as part of the family unit. Overwhelmingly,

TABLE 8.2   *Stages of the elementary family domestic group* (%)

		1950[a]	1967[b]
Young couples (wife less than 45 yrs)	No children	7	6
	All children at home	36	38
	Some children left home	1	2
	All children left home	0	1
	Total	44	47
Old couples (wife more than 45 yrs)	No children	5	6
	All children at home	11	7
	Some children at home	9	11
	All children left home	9	18
	Total	34	42
The widowed, divorced and separated	No children	3	2
	All children at home	7	2
	Some children at home	7	2
	All children left home	5	5
	Total	22	11

[a] T. & C., p. 134.
[b] 6 per cent sample, Banbury and District.

the reasons that were given for wives working related to the benefit of the family: to provide extra material goods, a holiday, a new three-piece suite, better clothes for the children.[14] This change in female activity has, of course, materially contributed to the higher living standards, compared with 1950, of many families. Conversely, the reasons given for a wife not going out to work related to the effect it was felt that her employment would have on the family rather than to anything intrinsic to a job.[15] Home-making and child-rearing remain the 'central life interest' of the majority of women in Banbury.

Husbands and wives still tend to share the same religion and the same politics. We do not have data as to whether this is a consequence of selection before marriage or conversion afterwards. The tendency to politico-religious consensus between spouses is clear from Tables 8.3 and 8.4. The smaller the denomination or party the greater is the probability that the partners will be of the same mind. This is true, for example, of Liberals and of Methodists.

It is still the custom in Banbury that each elementary family should form a domestic group of its own, The custom that a couple

TABLE 8.3   *Index of denominational intermarriage[a] (Male and female respondents combined[b])*

	Ego's denomination			
Spouse's denomination	R.C.	C. of E.	Meth.	Other NC
Roman Catholic	8·2	0·45	0·14	0·33
Church of England	0·45	1·2	0·46	0·35
Methodist	0·14	0·46	7·7	0·63
Other Nonconformist	0·33	0·35	0·63	14·2
N	79	873	84	55

Source: 6 per cent sample, Banbury and District.

[a] The index is calculated on the following formula: the proportion of X denominational adherents married to Y denominational spouses divided by the proportion of all respondents married to Y denominational spouses. A figure of more than one indicates that the probability of X marrying Y is greater than chance; a figure of less than one indicates a probability lower than chance.
[b] Refusals, others, D.K. excluded for both respondents and spouses.

TABLE 8.4   *Index of association for voting of respondents and spouses[a] (male and female respondents combined[b])*

	Ego's denomination			
Spouse's voting	Cons.	Labour	Liberal	Did not vote
Conservative	2·04	0·18	0·32	0·32
Labour	0·18	2·26	0·46	0·38
Liberal	0·33	0·33	10·1	0·66
Did not vote	0·33	0·24	0·46	4·74

Source: 6 per cent sample, Banbury and District.

[a] The index is calculated on the following formula: the proportion of X voters married to Y voters divided by the proportion of all voters married to Y voters. A figure of more than one indicates that the probability of voter X marrying voter Y is greater than chance; a figure of less than one indicates the probability is less than chance.
[b] Refusals, others, D.K. excluded for both respondents and spouses.

on marriage should 'set up on their own' is one that was much more possible to comply with in 1967 than it was in 1950. At that time, this custom was often more honoured in the breach than the observance because of the national housing shortage, which was acutely felt in Banbury, as was explained above (p. 10). Many couples were lucky if they could leave the parental roof when their first child was born, customarily the latest possible time to do so. In 1950, 12 per cent of married men were not household heads, most of them being young married men.[16] In 1967 less than 3 per cent of married men were living in the households of others, and they were evenly distributed among all the age groups.

This customary preference for each elementary family to have its own house, even if this means that the older generation stay behind in an old or sub-standard house, or the young family occupy a caravan or an old dwelling because it is all they can afford, is one which Banbury shares with most other parts of Britain.[17] Where there were additions to the elementary family in the domestic group, the additions were usually members of the family of origin of the household head or his wife, or of the family of marriage of their children.[18] In 1967 the older generation was brought into a household almost twice as often as the younger generation remained at home after marriage.

The additional kin are still more often the wife's than the husband's and more often the daughter's than the son's, but this tendency is perhaps less strong than it was.[19] Respondents to the 1967 sample as a whole show some tendency to be somewhat more matrilocal than patrilocal. (See Table 8.5.)

Data were not collected in 1967 about the extent of knowledge kin had of each other, so it is not possible to say whether women still exhibit greater knowledge of their kin than men. In all other respects the sex differences in kinship matters still appear to suggest that kin links are maintained more by women than men, although, in some respects, the sex differences are now slightly less marked.

The field-workers of 1966-8 were struck, as had been those of 1948-50, by the number of surnames that they had not come across before, but which were frequently met in Banbury. Six surnames which were not recorded as being numerically important nationally were frequent in Banbury. Several more had been common in Banbury for at least four centuries. Some Banbury 'families' are conscious of having had representatives in the town for some time. Not much stress is laid on counting generations, but families which have been in town and economically successful for more than one generation may still be thought of as relative newcomers by 'real' Banburians.

Whether they are accorded high or low prestige, the notable kin

TABLE 8.5 Proximity to parents: married and once-married people (%)

Where parents live	Banbury[a] Men[b] Mother	Banbury[a] Men[b] Father	Banbury[a] Women[b] Mother	Banbury[a] Women[b] Father	Where parents live	Swansea[a] Married sons	Swansea[a] Married daughters	Where parents live	Bethnal Green[e] Married persons	Where parents live	Woodford[f] Married men	Woodford[f] Married women
In Banbury[c]	29	27	34	34	Same locality of Swansea	26	42	Within 5[g] min's walk	41		14	19
Banbury District	14	13	13	13	Other locality of Swansea	45	38	Elsewhere in borough	13		16	14
Up to 10 miles	9	7	6	8	Region and up to 12 miles	9	5	Outside borough	46		70	67
Elsewhere	48	53	47	45	Elsewhere	20	15					
N	274	235	293	240	N	383	408	N	369		201	193

[a] Source: 6 per cent sample, Banbury.
[b] All ever married.
[c] Including those in household.
[d] C. Rosser and C. Harris, op. cit., Table 6.1, p. 212.
[e] P. Willmott and M. Young, Family and Class in a London Suburb (Routledge & Kegan Paul, 1960), Table XI, p. 78.
[f] Ibid., Table IX, p. 69.
[g] Including those in same house.

groups are less those which have been in town for generations (although they may have been) than those who have many representatives at present living in town: brothers or cousins in business, for example. In 1967, as around 1950, there were notable local families who were judged by their worst members, the whole kin group being therefore accorded low prestige. Examples have already been quoted in the discussion of neighbour relations in The Village (see pp. 100–1) where there were Banburians of prosperous old families and of poor and deviant families.

There are still interlocking kinship networks in Banbury, but they are proportionately less important than they were. A knowledge of the 'social map' of Banbury depends less than it did even in 1950 on understanding the pattern of kinship.

Furthermore, it is now no longer possible to say that the extended family or the kin is more important for Banburians than for immigrants.[20] Although they are still not 'Banburians', the 'settlers' among the immigrants of the 1930s have now been in town for a generation. They, along with born and bred Banburians, form a stable population among whom closely interacting kin groups can be found. In many cases the children of immigrants and Banburians have married each other.

The groups which form among kin for mutual assistance and recreation tend to be formed from among members of the family of origin and the family of marriage. The relationships are based upon common membership of elementary families. Kin groups with such a basis can form in a generation: they do not depend on ancestors beyond parents or at most grandparents, or on a long lineage. The kinship circumstances of the older immigrants are therefore not much different from those of the native born.

There is no doubt that now, as in 1950, the elementary family is of paramount importance. The extended family is still important at all social levels here as elsewhere,[21] but it derives from the elementary family.[22] The extended family provides some of the most important social ties an individual has. These ties differ by social level in their content, but the processes of social and geographic mobility do not necessarily or even usually break the ties.

Just over half of the ever-married members of our sample have their parents (where they are still alive) living in or near Banbury. The remainder are scattered all over Britain, with a few abroad (see Table 8.6). Nevertheless, over 80 per cent of those married or once married had had contact with their mothers (face to face, by phone or letter) in the week before they were interviewed (86 per cent of the women, 82 per cent of the men). Furthermore, over half of the ever-married in the main sample who had parents alive had seen them both within the last week.

TABLE 8.6 *Frequency of face-to-face contact with parents of those ever married*

| | Banbury[a] | | | | Bethnal Green[b] | Woodford[c] | Swansea[d] |
| | Men | | Women | | | | |
	Mother	Father	Mother	Father	Mother	Mother	Mother
Within last 24 hours	22	19	28	23	43	30	42·5
Within last week	30	33	28	30	31	33	33·5
Week–month ago	17	19	20	20	26	37	24
Longer	31	29	24	27			
Total	100	100	100	100	100	100	100
N	274	235	293	240	290	346	693

[a] 6 per cent sample, Banbury.

[b] P. Willmott and M. Young, op. cit., p. 38.

[c] Ibid.

[d] Combined columns 1 and 2, Table 6.3, Rosser and Harris, op. cit., p. 219: Contact with mothers; married daughters with mothers alive.

Almost without exception all of the respondents claimed that they would do all they could for their relatives, especially for their parents. This was particularly true for those who had been in the same occupational class over two generations. Twice as many of the latter as of the mobile thought they would do more for relatives than for neighbours. On the other hand, half of those who had been occupationally mobile thought they would do as much for neighbours and friends as they would for relatives. Similar responses were given by both Banburians and immigrants. But it would seem that geographic distance does not reduce the feelings of obligation to kin or increase those to neighbours. Practice, of course, may differ from intention, although the evidence from Little Newton suggests that this is not so (see Chapter 7).

Over half of the sample think that relatives do less for each other nowadays, a belief that is particularly prevalent among those who have had manual occupations over at least two generations and amongst those downwardly mobile from parents with non-manual occupations. Those who feel most strongly that relatives do the same now as they always have done or even more than they used to do come from families which have had non-manual occupations over at least two generations. It is interesting to note that all those who said that they did not know the answer to this question had been occupationally mobile, most of them upward. There were no differences in the responses of Banburians and immigrants to this question. But immigrants more often said that they would like to see more of their relatives than Banburians did. It seems that migration in itself does not lead to any lessening of affectual ties between relatives. The only two respondents who wanted to see less of their relatives were Banburians who had been upwardly occupationally mobile in the locality. All five of those who wanted to see more of some relatives but less of others had been occupationally mobile.

While the differences in family patterns and behaviour between social levels appear to be limited, the family as a social institution appears still to play a not insignificant part in the maintenance of social inequalities. This perpetuation seems, however, to be mediated through financial aid rather than in other ways.

It is true there were still some shops and small businesses in Banbury in 1966–8, as there had been around 1950, that were run as family firms and passed on from father to son. Now, as then, there were also examples of such businesses closing because there was no willing heir. The closure of the Banbury cake shop, already mentioned, comes in this category. At the same time few of the sub-sample respondents had ever worked for or with a relative,[23] or had help from a relative in getting a job.[24]

Only four of the seventy-two respondents who were house-owners (outright or on mortgage) were living in houses previously owned by a relative. None of the twenty-five Council house tenants was in a Council house previously occupied by a relative, although the Council allows 'passing on' to a relative. Of seventeen respondents who rented privately, two were related to the previous tenant and one had been helped by a relative to get the tenancy.

But this is not to say that parents did not help their children at the start of a marriage and to set up house. A quarter of the Banburians and 47 per cent of immigrants had received financial help with housing. Thirty-seven per cent of the total sample had initially lived with relatives (mostly parents), although none was now doing so. Immigrants received more financial help with housing because of their higher occupational status and that of their parents.

Forty-five per cent of the sample (nineteen Banburians and thirty-two immigrants) said they would turn to their relatives in a sudden financial crisis. All those who said they had no one to turn to had been either upwardly or downwardly occupationally mobile.

Banburians, while receiving less financial aid, had received more personal aid than immigrants.[25] The differences which underlie these differences between Banburians and immigrants are in fact differences of social level. Whether Banburian or immigrant, those parents who can afford it give financial aid to their children. Those who cannot, offer house room or personal service when necessary.

It is clear from these data that not only does the economic position of the household head affect the social circumstances and life style of an elementary family domestic group, but that these are also affected by the economic position of the family of origin of the household head and his wife. These factors are more important for social differentiation than is place of origin. The family of origin mediates the economic system so that the succeeding family of marriage can maintain the position of the former or improve upon it. The socioeconomic differentiation is thus maintained from one generation to the next and children continue to be born into families which can give them markedly different initial material and cultural opportunities.

9 Inequality and order: social class, social status and power

The full conspectus of social levels in Britain is not to be found in Banbury: the most wealthy and those with most power and authority do not live there. Although isolated representatives of this category, Parkin's dominant class,[1] are found in the surrounding areas, the higher social levels are not part of the social interaction system itself.

But these 'absentees' are not without influence upon the daily lives of people in Banbury. Decision-makers in industry, commerce, religion and politics are increasingly outside Banbury, sometimes abroad. Their vital influence is felt as social constraint rather than taking the form of social interaction. Part of the object of some of the newer pressure groups was to try and initiate some sort of dialogue with such decision-makers.

Only the more sophisticated in Banbury, themselves of higher-than-average occupational or political status, had any appreciation of the complex nature of the absent authority that was being exercised. For many, as in the cul-de-sac example,[2] those with authority and power constituted an undifferentiated 'they' occasionally personified as town council officials or bosses at work. It is a socio-logical truism to say that people interact on terms of social ease which indicate equality with people whom they define as 'their own sort', 'people like us'. In the expanded and increasingly complex society that is contemporary Banbury, it is difficult to see what are the bases of such definitions. Characteristics which appear to link people in one situation seem to divide them (or people apparently like them) in another. There are multi-bonded groups visible, but it is less certain that they are social-status groups.[3] Nor is there consensus among the people living in and around Banbury, the actors involved, about social status. Much depends not only on who they are, but the situation they find (perceive) themselves in at the time they make a comment.

116

This is not surprising. How can one say that there is a system of social status in a universe in which large numbers of people are quite unaware of the existence of others and of their life-styles? A system of social status, as Marshall has pointed out, implies not only total knowledge of the individual, but the existence of a community.[4] Before there can be consensus as to ranking, there must be knowledge of what there is to rank, both persons and their attributes. It seems unlikely that in Banbury there was any such consensus or such knowledge. Furthermore, the field-workers' knowledge of the beliefs and values of numbers of people in town led them to believe that such a consensus could not exist. There did not even seem to be a clear pattern discernible among the élites.

It was possible among the better off to isolate certain sets, groups, or networks of people, members of each of which had certain characteristics in common. But these could not be said to constitute a social-status system, because all were not necessarily articulated to each other.

The set of which the 'King' was a member is found within the category of 'locals' and 'spiralist-locals'.[5] The group is of particular importance and might be called 'the King's set'. Through its members it is closely linked to Rotary, the Conservative party and the Masons. Not only do members of this set meet in a wide range of associations and through their businesses, but they also have other links, for example, a number of them live in one particular street in west Banbury. Several go on holiday together. The set does include others who live further away, and has, as do most such informal groups, a number of fringe members. Thus it shades off vaguely. Members of this set interact on a basis of social ease which, despite fine distinctions made among themselves, gives the impression that members treat each other as peers, as equals in some sense. There is among them a certain consensus about values, for example, those which lead them all to have similar sorts of houses in a particular part of town. They also share certain values about politics and sport. But within the area of consensus there are also considerable areas of dissensus: there is in particular a considerable variation about how much difference of opinion and behaviour it is reasonable to tolerate in the society at large. There is, one could say, a range from right-wing to left-wing Conservatism among them. But all of them think of themselves as 'middle-class businessmen' and therefore Conservative. They are businessmen and believe in the importance of usefulness. What is useful is valuable because it will increase output and profits and living standards. Many of them are therefore anti-intellectual in so far as they are inclined to judge intellectuals as 'useless'. This is not to say they are against academic training if it can be shown to be useful, to be valuable in industry. Members of this group pride

117

themselves on being hard-headed and practical. In this they can be distinguished from two other sets.

One is made up of those who tend to live in the country and includes professional people, some industrialists, some gentry and retired army officers. This set is also Conservative in party allegiance and general orientation, but includes those people, referred to in Chapter 5, who are concerned to maintain and improve certain values associated with the British countryside which have expression in the formal organization of the C.P.R.E.[6] People in this set are 'preservationists' and could be said to be more 'tender-minded' and somewhat more 'intellectual' than the 'King's' set.

The other set from which the 'King's' set can be distinguished is more clearly intellectual and not necessarily Conservative. They could be called the 'Banbury intelligentsia'. One particular set is composed mainly of school-teachers and lecturers at the technical college. Many of them, being mostly in their thirties, are younger than the 'King's' set, which is largely made up of people in their forties. Of this particular set most are Labour party supporters. But again there are disagreements among them within this general consensus. Thus one field-worker recorded a bitter dispute about the desirability of expansion of the town between two members at a party in one of their houses. These people would also call themselves middle class. They generally only meet members of the 'King's' set and other businessmen in cultural associations in the town.

It would do violence to the evidence to put these three sets of people on a vertical scale above and below each other, except as measured by particular criteria such as wealth or income or amount of education, and then there would be overlaps. The sets are distinct but not discrete. The people who interact within the sets have a number of attributes in common. This seems likely to be a cause of the group formation. These sets are unusual in the number of multiplex role relations they have. This is particularly true of the 'King's' set. It has been noted elsewhere that it is a characteristic of élites to have such multiplex role relations.[7]

While sets or groups of this kind cannot be ranked on a vertical scale, they do appear most often to develop within a social level,[8] where individuals have a number of characteristics in common. These characteristics perhaps most often derive from occupation. The members of the group are likely to refer to the social level concerned by such phrases as 'middle class', 'ordinary people'. Individuals within the set or group are likely to be invidiously ranked on the basis of their reputations by other members, i.e. their social standing,[9] their honour and prestige, may be ranked in relation to others. It may be that there is some similar ranking of one group by another. This, however, rapidly merges into some form of stereotyping. That is to say the categoric characteristics of one or two people in the group, such as 'insurance man' or 'bank clerk' (which is all members of the second group know about them), are attributed to the group as a whole. In addition the informality of the group and its structure means that it has no clear boundary. Even among the business and professional men of the town, not all such groups or clusters of people know each other. Neither did the field-workers know all the clusters, although their collective knowledge may range more widely than that of any single inhabitant.

Among business people and professional people there is some likelihood in a town of the size of Banbury that a number of them will get to know each other. Away from occupations of this kind such knowledge is less likely. Workers in one part of the town are not aware of those in another, although notions associated with the common lot of 'workers' remain fairly widespread at an abstract level. There are a variety of bases for interaction: work, associations, residence, and other shared characteristics. These cannot, however, be charted on to one social-status map of the town. The lack of common knowledge, not surprising among 25,000 people, makes it impossible to 'do a Gosforth' for Banbury.[10]

Within particular social contexts, however, groups or quasi-groups form, and these can be seen in interaction. Sometimes the ranking of the groups by each other can also be discerned. This was true of most of the residents in The Village. The three categories of people living in different parts of Wychtree Road in their different types of houses could perhaps accurately be called social-status groups. They were aware of and could observe each other. They could and did rank each other and were in some state of tension towards each other, i.e. there were some reciprocal attitudes and actions. The evidence is stronger for the group of elderly and long-established residents in Wychtree Terrace. They shared certain norms (e.g. drawing the curtains on the day of a funeral) which were not held by others.

Generally speaking, persons of widely differing social levels did not interact with each other, except in chance encounters or in certain defined, simplex relations, shopkeeper and client, doctor and patient, for example. One club in Banbury, however, provided an opportunity to observe interaction between people from different economic and social levels.

The club was started around 1950 to provide a meeting-place for the retired and is now run by three committees: a management committee, most of whose members are delegates from other associations in the town; an executive committee, which is a sub-committee of the management committee; and a house committee,

119

which is elected by the old people themselves. Representatives of this house committee sit, in turn, as delegates to the management committee.

In comparison with all other committees of associations in Banbury, the management committee of this club contains a notable concentration of élite members (arbitrarily defined here as people holding three or more committee positions). These management committee members attend few club meetings. Some only attend the Annual General Meeting. Others enlist the help of associations which they represent and organize a stall for the annual fair. It is the executive committee which organizes and attends the Christmas dinner.

Only one member of the management committee is involved in the weekly running of the club. Those who help every week are rank-and-file members of women's organizations and individuals recruited personally by the exceptional management committee member. Participant observation shows that the weekly helpers see their duties in terms of a 'good deed for the day' and think of the club members as different from themselves, although on grounds of age the helpers are themselves eligible for club membership.

This we/they conceptualization is reflected again in the relations between management committee and club members. While the Annual General Meeting is one of the few occasions attended by the management committee members, only a handful of the 230 club members attends. In general, it was noticeable that the more involved committee members became in the affairs of the town, the less time they had to help at the club.

It would be wrong to imagine that the interaction (and the places where it is absent) observed in this club typified those among similar people throughout the town. The club's existence depends on the value attached by some of the better off in the town to 'doing good' and 'offering service', and their associated definition of 'the old' as those worthy to be done good to. The leadership is therefore self-selected and representative of many, but not all, similar people. The followers are also self-selected; they are those among the elderly who are willing to accept the service offered and the form of its offering. The club is a model of the interactions among social levels and age categories for some people in the town, but not for all.

Whereas around 1950 the committee members of voluntary associations were clearly divided by an 'occupational-status frontier', a line which few crossed, this was no longer so around 1967. The frontier is lower than it was, is blurred and many lines cross it.[11] This means that many more people nowadays than around 1950 sit on committees with those of both higher and lower occupational status than themselves. For a number of those who join associations, therefore, the economic and the relational aspects do not correlate closely.[12] There are cross-cutting ties between groups in the middle sixties where there appeared to be a major fracture in the network of social relationships at the end of the forties.

Interaction between kin and friends also suggests certain over-all tendencies but no clear fractures (see Table 9.1). A simple count of persons encountered in the last week comparing their occupational class (Reg.-Gen. social class) with that of the respondent showed that contacts were widespread throughout all the occupational classes, although in two of the sub-samples the range was narrower as far as friends were concerned than it was for kin. The number of contacts between those in manual and non-manual occupations was not great, particularly few for contacts with friends. It seems that friends tend to be chosen more often, but by no means exclusively, within the same broad occupational category or social level. It also seems that maintaining contact with kin is not prevented by differences of occupational class.

While people behaved in certain contexts as if they were ranking others invidiously and also made remarks that could be interpreted as part of the same behaviour, they talked about social class very little. The few people, a vicar, a curate, a probation officer, for example, whom the field-workers heard spontaneously talking of 'social class' were people whose work brought them into touch with others from all social levels. Perhaps their frequent encounters with widely different kinds of people forced them into such categorization. (They are also among those most likely to have read some sociology.)

When specific attempts were made to tap the social images which Banbury people had in their minds, weak and confused conceptions of social class emerged.[13] A limited range of class awareness was exhibited and little class conflict was perceived. Those working in small plants were even less likely than those in large plants to perceive any class conflict and also less likely to see conflict in occupational or economic terms.

The small plant workers held a consensual model, i.e. they emphasized the value of personal social relations with their superiors at work and they lacked any sense of class identification, perceiving class conflict as unimportant and not politically relevant. In contrast, the workers in large plants tended to hold an accommodative model. These respondents identified with 'the working class', perceived class conflict as fairly important and/or perceived class as politically relevant, emphasizing economic aspects of class. But they were accommodative rather than radical or revolutionary. Neither category of respondents was deferential. Those with consensual and accommodative models both indicated an equivalent absence of deference to an aristocratic élite.

TABLE 9.1 Registrar-General social class of kin and friends seen in the last week (male subjects only)

Kin

Reg.-Gen. social class of kin seen	Sub-sample 1 (social class images) Subject's social class								Sub-sample 2 (status and roles of sexes) Subject's social class								Sub-sample 3 (family) Subject's social class							
	I	II	IIIa	IIIb	IVa	IVb	V	ALL	I	II	IIIa	IIIb	IVa	IVb	V	ALL	I	II	IIIa	IIIb	IVa	IVb	V	ALL
I	1	1	0	0	0	0	0	2	0	2	0	0	0	0	1	3	7	2	0	1	0	0	0	10
II	2	1	3	0	0	1	0	7	2	6	0	1	0	2	0	11	1	6	1	0	0	1	0	9
IIIa	0	0	3	7	0	4	3	17	0	1	2	3	0	1	1	8	1	3	5	0	0	0	3	12
IIIb	1	4	3	18	0	11	2	39	1	2	4	16	0	9	0	32	1	2	5	2	0	5	3	18
IVa	0	0	0	0	0	1	0	1	0	0	0	1	0	0	1	2	1	0	0	1	0	1	1	4
IVb	0	1	2	7	4	2	3	19	1	1	6	14	0	12	1	35	0	0	0	1	0	2	2	5
V	0	0	0	2	0	6	2	10	0	1	2	1	0	2	1	7	0	0	0	1	0	1	2	4
ALL	4	7	11	34	4	25	10	95	4	13	14	36	0	27	4	98	11	13	11	6	0	10	11	62

Friends

Reg.-Gen. social class of friends seen	Sub-sample 1 (social class images) Subject's social class								Sub-sample 2 (status and roles of sexes) Subject's social class								Sub-sample 3 (family) Subject's social class							
	I	II	IIIa	IIIb	IVa	IVb	V	ALL	I	II	IIIa	IIIb	IVa	IVb	V	ALL	I	II	IIIa	IIIb	IVa	IVb	V	ALL
I	2	0	0	0	0	0	0	2	1	0	0	0	0	0	0	1	7	2	0	1	0	0	0	10
II	6	5	2	1	0	0	1	15	1	11	2	1	0	1	0	16	1	6	1	0	0	1	0	9
IIIa	4	0	9	2	0	1	0	16	0	8	8	3	0	0	0	19	1	3	5	0	0	0	3	12
IIIb	0	2	1	25	0	8	6	42	0	2	2	12	0	4	1	21	1	2	5	2	0	5	3	18
IVa	0	0	0	0	0	0	0	3	0	0	0	0	0	0	0	0	1	0	0	1	0	1	1	4
IVb	0	0	2	3	0	2	2	9	0	0	2	6	0	5	2	15	0	0	0	1	0	2	2	5
V	0	0	0	2	0	1	2	7	0	0	0	1	0	0	3	4	0	0	0	1	0	1	2	4
ALL	12	7	14	33	5	12	11	94	2	21	14	23	0	10	6	76	11	13	11	6	0	10	11	62

Source: sub-samples.

Our evidence to date, therefore, is that, while people tend to interact in conditions of social ease with people from the same social level, there are many discrete groups of that kind within any one level. Furthermore, kinship, friendship and common social interests may lead to a loose interpretation of 'people like us'. In addition the groups within any one level are not ranked on a vertical scale in relation to each other. Finally, people do not accord a major place in their perceptions to differences in social levels and associated life chances.

These findings are consistent with the 'objective' data derived from an examination of various economic and social categories. Occupation, ranked as in the Registrar-General's social classes or the Hall–Jones scale, for example, has often been taken as an indicator of 'social class' or as the single most important stratification factor. Indeed, many writers have slipped into using a dichotomous stratification model with manual and non-manual occupations as indicators of 'working class' and 'middle class'. This is perhaps more meaningful when only men are ranked by occupation in this way. For the reasons indicated in Chapter 8, it is rather meaningless to put men and women together on one scale.

In Banbury we have certainly found that, while occupational-status rankings may be associated with other attributes, social, economic, or political, the relevant point of division in the occupational scale is variable. It is not always between manual and non-manual, but sometimes within the manual and sometimes within the non-manual categories. At a minimum this suggests that Parkin's 'buffer zone'[14] is wider than his argument appears to assume. Further, it is commonly occupational status in association with other statuses[15] (e.g. house tenure, geographic mobility) that suggests a social category of individuals with certain common attributes.

Rex has recently argued that, in addition to being divided into classes based on economic position, the population is divided into classes based on position in the housing market.[16] Undoubtedly freedom of action to determine domestic living conditions is greatly affected by position in the housing market, just as position in the economic market increases or decreases self-determination in the work situation. If positions of greater freedom or self-determination in the work situation went with positions of greater freedom and self-determination in the housing situation, sharp divisions of the society into economic levels might be expected to result.

Table 9.2 suggests that this is not so. Occupational status and housing status do not run together so closely as to produce sharp divisions between economic levels. House tenure has been taken as an indication of position in the housing market (although it does not measure potential to change, of course) and the Registrar-General's

TABLE 9.2 Occupational class and housing tenure (%) (economically active married men) (N = 963[a])

Reg.-Gen. social class	Own outright	Own with mortgage	All owners	Rent privately	Rent from Council	All renters	Others	All
I and II	21·1	50·1	71·2	16·0	11·3	27·3	1·4	99·9
IIIa and IVa	20·7	34·0	54·7	18·0	27·3	45·3	0	100·0
IIIb	6·9	30·3	37·2	31·7	30·3	62·0	0·8	100·0
IVb	11·6	22·1	33·7	15·5	50·8	66·3	0	100·0
V	14·0	10·5	24·5	21·1	52·6	73·7	1·8	100·0
All	13·5	32·5	46·0	22·4	30·8	53·2	0·7	99·9

Source: Banbury and District, main sample.
[a] Married male respondents and husbands of female respondents.

social classes as a measure, albeit imperfect, of occupational status. Housing tenure has been listed in the order: own outright, own with a mortgage, rent privately (including the few dwellings which go with a business or a job), and rent from the Council. In a society which sets as high a value upon property as does British society this would appear to reflect some sort of ranking. Outright ownership gives control (although how much this control has been eroded by political action, particularly for older smaller properties is shown in Dennis's *People and Planning*).[17] Owning on a mortgage indicates an economic position which permits access to a building society or finance house and the promise of outright control in the future. Private tenants obviously include both those who rent cheaper and more expensive properties and implies dependence upon a landlord, but does not imply the dependence on a political administration that renting from the Council as landlord does. Three things must, therefore, be noted about this categorization by house tenure as an indicator of position in the housing market: (i) it is not free from influences derived from occupational status, income and wealth; (ii) wide differences may be found within the categories; (iii) the categories are discrete and do not form a continuum.

Given that the housing categories in Table 9.2 are in part at least determined by economic position, it is perhaps surprising that the association between the Registrar-General's social classes (which are really occupational classes) is not larger than it is. There is a tendency for ownership to decline through the occupational classes from I and II to V, and for renting to increase, but the correlation is not high. Over a quarter of classes I and II rent (including 11 per cent who rent from the Council), and nearly a quarter in class V own their own house. Outright ownership, as opposed to owning subject to mortgage, does not relate systematically to occupational status and neither does renting privately as opposed to renting from the Council.

Table 9.3 shows that while there are certain tendencies, e.g. for the more highly rated houses to be owned on a mortgage by those of occupational status I and II, there was no consistent or systematic relationship between tenure category, occupational status of the householder and the rateable value of the house in which he lived. The low-rated houses were found in all tenure categories, and representatives of all occupational statuses (the Reg.-Gen. social classes) were found in all tenures in these low-rated dwellings.

More important distinctions are found when place of origin is related to tenure and occupational class (Table 9.4): the migrant appears particularly dependent on the mortgage society or the Council for a dwelling; the native has greater access to private landlords and a greater likelihood of becoming an outright owner by inheritance or from the position of a sitting tenant.[18] This reduces the possibility of all those in one tenure category or potential housing class forming a 'class for itself', for each tenure category or potential housing class is not one but two quasi-groups, cross-cut by the factor of geographical mobility.[19] This is in addition to the cross-cutting of housing market and labour market positions in all categories.

TABLE 9.3 *Rateable value of houses by tenure*

| Reg.-Gen. social class | Rateable Value | | | |
	Less than £99	£100–149	£150+	All
I and II	4	16	12	32
IIIa and IVa	11	11	2	24
IIIb	8	13	1	22
IVb	11	7	0	18
V	6	1	0	7
All	40	48	15	103
Own with mortgage				
I and II	14	57	26	97
IIIa and IVa	13	27	1	41
IIIb	33	68	2	103
IVb	17	20	0	37
V	2	4	0	6
All	79	176	29	284
Rent privately				
I and II	6	17	1	24
IIIa and IVa	6	13	1	20
IIIb	34	16	0	50
IVb	18	1	0	19
V	10	1	0	11
All	74	48	2	124
Rent from Council				
I and II	14	7	2	23
IIIa and IVa	23	16	0	39
IIIb	82	80	0	162
IVb	49	39	0	88
V	18	12	0	30
All	186	154	2	342

Source: 6 per cent sample, Banbury and District.

TABLE 9.4 *Occupational class, house tenure and place of origin*
(% Banburian) (Economically active married men)

Reg.-Gen. social class	Own outright	Own with mortgage	Rent privately	Rent from Council	AU	N
I and II	34·1	20·7	38·2	20·8	27·0	211
IIIa and IVa	54·8	41·2	22·2	43·9	41·3	150
IIIb	40·0	46·8	55·7	41·0	45·3	362
IVb	72·7	43·9	68·0	37·0	47·2	180
V	(3/8)	(3/6)	(7/12)	60·0	56·1	57
All	46·9	36·7	57·0	40·5	41·7	960

Source: 6 per cent sample, Banbury and District.

Nor do other ranked statuses run together in such a way as to lead to distinct categories from which one might assume social class with appropriate class-consciousness might arise. The long-assumed close and increasing association between education received and occupational status achieved applies only to the geographically mobile. (See Table 9.5.) In this category, one may assume, are to be found Watson's 'spiralists' and Merton's 'cosmopolitans'.[20] It is not only in classes I and II that those with longer educations include those who are more geographically mobile, but in all other classes as well the proportion of immigrants with education to 17 or over is above average.

TABLE 9.5 *Place of origin, education and occupational status*
(% Banburians) (Economically active married men)

| Reg.-Gen. social class | Education completed at age | | | |
	15 or less	16	17 or older	All
I and II	41·25	44·7	14·0	29·9
IIIa and IVa	45·45	46·9	31·6	44·0
IIIb	50·6	38·1	20·0	48·6
IVb	48·5	(0/5)	20·0 (2/10)	45·0
V	57·4	(1/2)	(0/0)	58·1
All	49·0	41·8	17·5	43·6
N	702	98	137	937

Source: 6 per cent sample, Banbury and District.

But we have already seen that the more highly educated and higher occupation migrants are divided into spiralists and spiralist-locals.[21] The former play little part in the life of the town, but the latter are involved—some, for example, in the 'King's set'. These migrants are also divided by their style of life and political views: the 'Banbury intelligentsia' includes some who would not find themselves at ease in the 'King's' set. The category of long-education, high-occupational migrants is thus divided in at least two other ways. For women, education correlates more closely with occupation than it does for men (Appendix 5). But most women will have at least a spell as housewives, during which time their husband's occupational status will be more relevant than their own.

Apart from these two categories of people, the migrants and the women, the educational system in Banbury does not seem to be 'the means by which individuals are not merely trained for but allocated to their occupational roles'.[22] There are many other ways, some of them less formal, by which allocation and training take place.

Although large firms stress paper qualifications for some categories of employees, they, as well as the smaller firms, extensively practise promotion on the job. In addition, manual workers continue to set up small firms of their own in Banbury, as elsewhere. Of those in Registrar-General's classes I and II, 38 per cent left school at 15 years or earlier and 66 per cent of those in classes IIIa and IVa (see Table 9.6).

TABLE 9.6   *Age education terminated and occupational class (economically active married males)*

Reg.-Gen. social class	Education terminated[a]		
	At 15 years or earlier	At 16 years	At 17 years or over
I and II	38·1	18·1	43·8	100·0
IIIa and IVa	66·0	21·3	12·7	100·0
IIIb	90·0	5·8	4·2	100·0
IVb	91·7	2·8	5·5	100·0
V	96·6	3·4	0	100·0

Source: 6 per cent sample, Banbury and District.

[a] Where education was interrupted, it has for this purpose been counted as continuous. E.g., someone who left school at 15 and later took a year's full-time education course has been counted as if he left school at 16, and one who took two or more years' later education as if he had left school at 17 or over.

Nor is it only those who had parents in classes I and II who have achieved this occupational status. Eighty-seven per cent of sons now in classes I and II had no education beyond 15 years old *and* had fathers in class III or below (see Table 9.7).[23]

TABLE 9.7 *Occupational class of father, son's education and his occupational class (economically active married men)*

Father's occupational class	Son's occupational class[a]					
	Non-manual			Manual		All
	Higher	Lower	Skilled	Semi-skilled	Unskilled	
Non-manual	*Sons educated to 17 or over*					
Higher	27	2	2	1	0	32
Lower	16	4	4	2	0	26
Manual						
Skilled	8	5	4	1	0	18
Semi-skilled	5	2	5	2	0	14
Unskilled	0	0	2	0	0	2
Non-manual	*Sons educated to 16 or over*					
Higher	9	1	1	0	0	11
Lower	12	10	10	2	0	34
Manual						
Skilled	5	3	4	0	0	12
Semi-skilled	2	7	3	1	0	13
Unskilled	1	1	1	0	0	3
Non-manual	*Sons educated to 15 or less*					
Higher	8	5	6	1	0	20
Lower	22	20	51	18	6	117
Manual						
Skilled	20	21	78	40	5	164
Semi-skilled	9	11	62	30	10	122
Unskilled	3	3	22	7	11	46

Source: 6 per cent sample, Banbury and District.

[a] Derived from Reg.-Gen social class and socio-economic group.

While those in higher occupational classes do tend to have higher incomes, there is little difference between skilled manual and low non-manual categories. All sources of income are found in all income groups, salaries being the predominant source of income in classes I and II. The importance of wages increases as one moves to Class V, but even among the lowly paid profits and fees are earned.

Ownership of property, whether industrial, commercial, or domestic, does appear to be important in political behaviour. Chapter 4 demonstrated the higher proportion of Conservative voters among skilled manual workers who are outright house owners.[24]

A large and fluid middle social level is suggested by the evidence of interaction of beliefs and feelings and of statistical associations among socio-economic attributes. This middle social level, Parkin's buffer zone, comes between the social level which is largely outside Banbury (from which Parkin's dominant class is drawn) and a lower social level which is represented in town. The buffer zone is made up of those who, by reason of property ownership (domestic or other), education and training or occupational status, have some stake in the present distribution of resources and power. They may have some influence and authority, some limited power, in consequence of these resources. At a minimum they understand how to attempt to protect their interests. There are others whose chief stake is that in some areas they have some self-determination, as house owners or self-employed.

The lower class, in Parkin's terms, are without these stakes in the present institutionalized arrangements for the control and distribution of scarce resources. They have less skilled jobs, lower pay, and live in rented houses. They lack the social and political skills to perceive threats to their interests or to defend themselves against such threats.

But while it is possible in this sense to say that there are three social levels, it is as if those in the middle level may, for some parts of their lives and in some circumstances, be in the lower level. Similarly, while some in the middle level may exert power and influence over others at that and the lower level, they may also be quite powerless in the face of decisions taken by those in authority outside the town.

The relative powerlessness of the town leaders was well demonstrated in the expansion issue. Theirs was only the power of veto. They had little power or ability to influence the form the expansion might take, and were unable to discover what would be the real consequences for the town in terms of their notions of what was relevant. The expansion issue also showed clearly the quite different language and approach of those dominant in that issue and the extent to which their meanings were at variance with the meanings of local residents of all classes.

Nevertheless, the different life circumstances of those who might be called a dominant class within Banbury compared with an underclass is also well illustrated by the on-going expansion. Birds workers in Birmingham had a forced choice of losing their jobs or moving to Banbury. There was no chance for them to plan and attempt to control a working career. Similarly, most of those coming from London came because this was the only way they could get a decent house to live in, given their economic prospects.

The pattern of social class and social status which emerges is therefore one of marked and continuing inequality of wealth and life styles, influence and authority. But it is a pattern which is at the same time remarkably open and fluid. On Aron's criteria of (i) the psychosocial cohesiveness of the stratum, (ii) continuity from generation to generation, (iii) the individual's awareness of belonging to a certain stratum, (iv) the self-awareness of the stratum, one might agree with him that 'classes do exist more or less'.[25] But only more or less, there is no sense in which one can talk of a social class system or a stratification system in Banbury today. One can only speak of a broad division into social levels.

At the end of the first study it was concluded that it was not possible 'to construct for Banbury and district a simple *n*-fold class system'. It was possible to divide the total employed population of Banbury at that time into strata based on work situations. But among people in Banbury social relations of a kind which led one to suppose some equality among the participants were not confined to those within these strata. In addition there seemed to be marked divisions within the strata themselves, and then, as now, there was no consensus among residents about the nature of 'class' and 'status', some even denying the existence of 'class'.

But amid all the variety of attitudes and relationships found in the total population, there did, in 1950, appear to be groups of people articulated to each other in what could be called a 'social-class system' in the locality which linked to an assumed national system. Those involved in these groups validated their actions by reference to the excellence of things past, and so this 'system' or 'structure' was labelled 'traditional'. The majority of those who felt and acted in this way were locally born or brought up, but migrants who accepted the norms and values were also involved.

Among these people there appeared to be a fairly high degree of consensus about social class and social status and about the characteristics which qualified persons for a particular social class and which conferred high or low status. The system was not static, as some commentators appear to have supposed, nor were individuals immobile within it. Upward and downward mobility could and did occur. The inheritor of one business had let it go to pieces, he 'was not much good', the firm had collapsed, and his social standing declined as well. Of two men who had become rich, one who had done so by hard work associated with trade and who offered public service to the town was more highly esteemed than the other who had made his money through betting. Those in the middle class who maintained or improved an inherited position were those who felt most secure. For the majority in other classes the chances of upward mobility were limited. They shared with those they saw as above them a consensus about the characteristics, in terms of inherited position and personal behaviour, which gave clear social class and social status. Achievement of these characteristics was expected to be recognized in the end by acceptance, as was loss of them to lead to 'dropping' or to withdrawal to avoid being dropped. It now seems likely that the solidarity of the traditional social system was exaggerated for the time being in the late forties by the threats to it offered by the quick succession of new industry, war and Labour government. That there was a core of people who shared norms and values as well as multiplex role relations appears undoubted.

By 1966–8, as we have seen, there appears to be no such central core remaining. The finding for 1948–51 outside the central core, that there were no other stratification structures or systems which encompassed any great number of people or their values and attitudes, now seems to apply in a general sense to the whole town. But now, as then, relationships of equality and inequality, which one might expect to be related to some stratification system, appear fundamental to an understanding of social relations in Banbury.

Economic differences are marked at the extremes, but, throughout the society, differences of power and authority are perhaps more marked. The characteristic of these differences, however, would appear to be that there are a number of élites, of influential groups, of decision-makers. There is no evidence of one ruling class or power élite. The conception of an undifferentiated 'they' is one held by those who are furthest from the decision-makers.

Close inspection suggests that, within the town and without, 'they' are not one but many. Nor do 'they' act as one. One of the reasons that encouraged Banbury Borough Council to reject further expansion was the lack of co-ordination among the Ministries concerned with planning, which exaggerated problems of phasing expansion smoothly. In addition to planning and other administrative authorities, there are the leaders of industry (nationalized, public and private), of religion, of scholarship. There is a 'differentiation of ruling hierarchies', a 'dissociation of powers'.[26]

Just as there is no single hierarchy of social class or social status, so there appears to be no single hierarchy of power. At the same time there are marked inequalities in the society which appear remarkably persistent and those with more resources also tend to have more power and vice versa.[27]

The conclusion seems to be that the society is loosely stratified but that it is a pluralist rather than a unitary society. This concept is used not in the sense of two or more societies who meet only in the market-place,[28] or in the sense of the political scientists.[29] It is used to indicate a complex society within which are many different bases for groups to form, some, notably the industrial and commercial, including their own stratification systems. But individuals in this society are rarely encompassed within such groups; rather, they are associated with several. Thus a man's prestige may be high in one sector of his life and low in another. In some of his activities he may have considerable power or independence while in another he may be relatively powerless.

It might perhaps have been expected that we would have discussed the lack of clear divisions in the middle social levels in terms of the embourgeoisement hypotheses. We have not done this because our evidence suggests that these hypotheses, which the Luton studies have found not proven,[30] are predicated upon assumptions which are increasingly irrelevant in Banbury. They suggest that there are homogeneous and definable working and middle classes between which some assimilation is taking place. Our evidence suggests that, while there are social levels, these have so many divisions within them that they are not homogeneous and definable in the sense which the embourgeoisement hypotheses assume. As we read the evidence, those in lower social levels sometimes exhibit some attributes of those in higher levels and vice versa. There is quite wide variety in the normative, economic and relational aspects of all social levels.

Conclusion: the bases of group formation

The groups within which individuals interact are composed of people who tend to have the same sort of occupation and one or more other statuses in common, for example, age, marital state, family-cycle stage, education. Such people share at least two roles, and this forms the basis of groups. These groups tend to be associated with levels and with styles of life, but there are no hard lines between one level and another; indeed, quite the contrary, and the levels are themselves greatly sub-divided into groups, but not necessarily strata, which have remarkably different styles of life.

What we have perceived in Banbury is not a series of strata 'within a system of "classless inegalitarianism" offering no basis for or response to radical initiatives',[31] but complex and often cross-cutting categories. Some of these relate to positions in the system of production, some to positions in the consumption market, some to positions in the domestic housing market. Others have to do with familial statuses, or membership of age–sex categories. When we say that we do not think the dominant division in Banbury society is a social class one in the strict technical sense of that word, we do not imply either that the society is not divided or that it is not dynamic.

What we perceive is that people have many statuses, each one of which puts them into a particular social category. From time to time discontent with a status or blocked expectations about the way the role should be played leads to combination for action. This combination for action most generally occurs among people who share more than one status. Often the combination occurs within a social level— most often perhaps—but not invariably. We therefore find valuable notions such as Marx's of the 'class in itself' and 'the class for itself'[32] or Ginsberg's quasi-group[33] and Mayer's action set[34] where in certain circumstances a category can become a group.

It may be possible, objectively, to analyse inequality in Britain in terms of two major economic classes with related amounts of social and political power (and authority), a dominant class and an under-class which are in conflict, as Parkin does. Although in an analysis in these terms, one would have to pay more attention than Parkin does to the sizeable 'buffer zone'.[35] For Banbury, and we suspect for much of Britain, one must stress that a majority of the population do not see their society in these terms. The relatively small working-class movement has combined, at least in part, upon this basis and its social relations and political behaviour are associated with such perception.[36]

But we find that statuses in the productive system are only one of the many relevant types of status. Those who came together to act generally shared not only the status of, for example, manual worker, but that of manual worker in a particular industry or workshop.[37] The citizens who protested about the schools were not only parents of school children but also white-collar workers of particular kinds who had certain managerial skills, set a high value on educational achievement, lived in a particular locality, stood in a common relationship to government, i.e. were voters in a certain education authority's area. It was among people with this common cluster of statuses (but not including all such people) that the pressure group was formed. The roles the parents played led them to meet and to discover their shared interest: occupational, political, familial and residential roles crossed each other and led to the development of new roles altogether. Thus the society is complex, linked through many social relations with other parts of Britain and beyond, and pluralist in the sense of being composed of a kaleidoscope of interlocking and overlapping groups and networks. Associated with these were many sets of values, often inconsistent with each other, which people appeared to espouse depending on the situation they were in. This gave individuals at least some sense of a freedom of choice between various courses of action and some chance to manipulate affairs among groups. The kaleidoscope of groups is not without meaning or explanation: it depends upon the interests which are being pursued or are seen to be threatened at any one time.

Those in any social category have the potential to combine on the basis of shared interests at any time. We do not think that predictions of the Marxian kind that all members of a category will combine at a point of time can be made (but then neither did Marx; he said, rather, that they ought to and that it would be better for them if they did). In our view the potential is always there and, given knowledge of the complex of statuses and roles in any situation and their occupants' beliefs about the rights and duties attached to them, one could predict the probability of combination for action.

What has also emerged from our analysis of political action and political involvement is that many people do not in practice act in their individual or combined interests. The potential for combination and action is rarely fulfilled. The relative lack of interest and involvement in the expansion issue was a striking example of this. The complexities of the political and administrative system appear to be part of the explanation; the lack of consensus of interests and values between the governors and the governed, a structural and cultural gap, also forms part of the explanation, as does the powerlessness which derives not only from relative lack of economic means, but from lack of appropriate knowledge and skill.

So Banbury, we conclude, although it can be seen to be composed of two or three social levels, has no neat social class system but is dynamic, stratified, cross-cut by ties within and without. It is an ordered society without a formal social order.

Appendix 1   The samples

The survey

The survey was undertaken to achieve a number of ends. First, it was the only practicable means of collecting a good deal of information from large numbers of those living in the locality. Unlike 1950, there was an up-to-date 10 per cent Sample Census. This was useful, but it did not include data which we required, such as religious and political affiliation. These data we wished to cross-tabulate with factors which the census did include such as age, occupational status and sex. The only way to do this was to collect all the data afresh.

The 1967 sample differed in two important ways from that drawn for the 1950 study; first, the population sampled included people living in part of the surrounding rural area; second, in the 1967 survey we sampled individuals rather than addresses. We have already indicated (see pp. 12–13) the reasons for the first of these variations. Since the first study, and especially since 1960, not only has the population of the Borough increased but the population growth has flowed over into the rural area, so that many of the villages have now become effectively, if not administratively, dormitories of the borough. Accordingly, to take only the Borough as the population for the survey might have had attractions in terms of both replication and administrative ease, but it would not have been sociologically meaningful. Therefore the sample was drawn not only from the Borough but also from the surrounding rural areas. The decision as to how to delimit this area was inevitably to some degree arbitrary. Local knowledge and available data on such factors as shopping patterns and journeys to work indicated that roughly a five-mile radius from Banbury would include those villages which were most involved with the town. Accordingly, rural electoral areas which to any considerable extent came within this area were included in the population to be sampled: this included the villages of Bloxham, Bodicote, Bourton, Broughton, Cropredy, Drayton, East and West Adderbury, Hanwell, Horley, Milton, North Newington, Wardington, Wroxton, Shotteswell, Chacombe, King's Sutton, Middleton Cheney and Warkworth.

The second major difference between the two surveys was the sampling unit. The 1950 study sampled addresses. Interviews were conducted with any adult at a selected address concerning all those living there. Interviews at 930 addresses thereby gave data on 3,387 individuals, including all those under voting age. In the 1967 survey it was decided that, despite the loss of strict comparability, since our concern was primarily with individuals rather than addresses, it was more meaningful to sample individuals. It is this difference in the sampling unit which explains the apparently lower numbers to be found in the tables of this study as compared with those in *T. & C.*

The sample was drawn from the Electoral Registers covering the Borough along with the areas listed above, after eliminating Y voters, those in the armed forces, those with a business and those in institutions. This was the most suitable sampling frame available, but it should be noted that it had a number of weaknesses from our point of view. It only included those aged over 21 years, it excluded not only American servicemen but also those foreign immigrants who lived in the area and the most recent newcomers to the town. However, we were fortunate in that a new Electoral Register had been published a few months before our interviewing, and names and addresses for this had been collected only six months or so previously.

Six per cent of the names remaining on our amended Electoral Registers were selected for interview. The Registers were divided into blocks of 1,000 names, and 60 were drawn from each block by means of random numbers. At the same time reserves were also drawn, 15 from each block to be used as substitutes in the block from which they were drawn. Substitutes were used for non-contacts, i.e. moved, dead, house empty or gone, ill or in institution, and those not contacted after three attempts. Substitutes were not used for refusals. Table I shows the numbers drawn, the refusals, and the reasons for non-contact. Interviewing was carried out in April and May of 1967.

The questionnaire was primarily concerned with the following areas: household members and children, kin contact, migration, education, associational, political and religious affiliation, and occupation and employment details. Respondents in employment were asked which firm they worked for. Questionnaires were then sent to these firms, if we were ignorant of them, seeking information on numbers employed, ownership and whether or not it was a single plant company. Separate interview schedules were used for male and female respondents to ease the task of the interviewer, for the schedule was rather complex.[1] It was finally decided that a brief, large-scale survey of the kind we were undertaking should not include any attitudinal questions, although at one stage we had intended to ask a number of questions on class imagery.

TABLE I   *Response to the 6 per cent Sample Survey*

	No.	%
Names first drawn	1,564	100
Refusals	106	6·8
Non-contacts	220	14·1
Completed interviews first drawn	1,238	79·1
Substitutes drawn	220	100
Refusals of substitutes	9	4·1
Substitute interviews completed	211	95·9
Total interviews completed	1,449	
Over-all refusal rate		6·4
Reasons for non-contacts		
Moved	79	35·9
Dead	9	4·1
House gone or empty	3	1·4
Ill or in institution	9	4·1
Not contacted after three calls	120	54·5
Total non-contacts	220	100·0

Most of the interviewing was carried out by thirty or so interviewers who were selected after we had advertised in the local press (which resulted in over 100 applications), interviewed and selected applicants and they had undergone a training course. Many had had previous interviewing experience, but all underwent the several days of training which included the use of the pilot questionnaire in the field.[2] Interviewers were paid by the hour rather than by the interview since it was felt that the latter could encourage less care in interviewing and, more importantly, would be unfair to those interviewing in the less densely populated rural areas and areas where non-contacts might be especially high.

Coding of completed questionnaires was carried out by the research team with the aid of two of the most able interviewers. One in ten of the completed codings was checked for accuracy and where coding errors appeared particularly high (over 5 per cent) all questionnaires were checked and where necessary corrected on the relevant columns. For each respondent two computer cards were coded, the second card relating primarily to data on respondents' children. Punching of cards was carried out and checked by the School of Social Studies at Swansea University College, and further cleaning of the data was carried out by the Computer Centre at Swansea who also provided some tabulations. However, owing to changes in personnel and technical problems there, many of the tabulations were finally done on a counter-sorter by members of the research team.

TABLE II   *1966 Registrar-General's 10 per cent Sample Census and 1967 Banbury and District 6 per cent Sample Survey compared (%) (Banbury Municipal Borough only)*

	Registrar-General 1966				Banbury Social Survey 1967		
Age	*Persons*	*Males*	*Females*	*Age*	*Persons*	*Males*	*Females*
20–4[a]	9·8	10·1	9·4	21–4[a]	5·2	5·1	5·2
25–44	39·9	41·8	38·2	25–44	41·1	40·8	41·4
45–59	26·4	26·9	26·1	45–59	27·9	27·8	27·9
60–4	7·7	7·3	8·1	60–4	7·8	8·9	6·8
65+	16·1	13·9	18·2	65+	18·0	17·4	18·7
N	1,686	819	867		893	449	444

Number married as a per cent of the population over 20 or 21 years

	Persons	*Males*	*Females*
Registrar-General 1966 Over 20 years	76·9	79·4	74·6
Banbury Social Survey 1967 Over 21 years	79·7	82·3	77·0

[a] Note difference in this age category between the two samples.

Table II compares the age, sex and marital status distribution of our sample in the Municipal Borough only with that of the Registrar-General's 10 per cent sample of 1966. It is not possible to distinguish our survey area from his data for comparison. In addition our lowest age is 21 years, while his age-distribution break is at 20 years. In view of these difficulties, which have also made socio-economic group or social-class comparisons impossible, we display the figures for what they are worth and have not attempted sophisticated manipulations.

The sub-samples[3]

1. *On class imagery:* the 'model' sub-sample

Two samples of skilled and semi-skilled men were drawn from the employees of a large (48) add a small (27) firm. A comparison sample of 120 males was drawn from the main sample stratified to consist of 10 workers in small and 10 in large firms in Registrar General's classes I and II combined and IIIa and IVa combined; 20 each in small and large firms in class IIIb and IVb and V combined.

2. *On women and work:* the 'women' sub-sample

A sub-sample of the main sample was drawn from families in that stage of the cycle of the elementary family domestic group when all children are at home. This sub-sample was stratified into four categories: wives not working, wives working, both subdivided by whether husband's occupation is manual or non-manual.

3. *The family sub-sample*

This was also drawn from families in the stage of the cycle of the elementary family domestic group when all children are at home. This sub-sample was stratified into eight categories: it was divided into Banburians and immigrants; each of these was divided by occupational mobility defined by intergenerational movement from or to manual and non-manual occupations of father and husband. The aim was to have 20 respondents in each category.

Appendix 2   Immigrants

TABLE III   *The date of arrival of immigrants living in Banbury in 1967* (Banbury and District)

	N	%
Arrived before 1930	74	10
1930–9	110	16
1940–9	125	17
1950–9	116	16
1960–7	295	41
Total	720	100

Source: 6 per cent sample.

TABLE IV   Reasons for moving to Banbury in order of frequency of mention (%) (Banbury and District)

Men

Reason	%	
Work (not Birds)	53·1	} 59·7
Birds	6·6	}
London overspill	7·7	
With parents	7·4	
Kin reasons	5·8	
War reasons	5·5	
With spouse/on marriage	3·3	
Liked area	2·7	
House (not overspill)	1·4	
Other, inc. friends	6·5	

Women

Reason	%	
With spouse/on marriage	50·6	
Work (not Birds)	14·9	} 16·7[a]
Birds	1·8	}
With parents	9·1	
London overspill	5·6	
Kin reasons	5·1	
War reasons	4·1	
House (not overspill)	2·0	
Liked area	1·5	
Other, inc. friends	5·3	

Total

Reason	%	
Work (not Birds)	31·4	} 35·1
Birds	3·7	}
With spouse/on marriage	26·5	
With parents	10·9	
Kin reasons	5·9	
London overspill	5·6	
War reasons	5·0	
Liked area	2·1	
House (not overspill)	1·9	
Other, inc. friends	6·3	
D.K./Refuse	0·7	

Source: 6 per cent sample.

[a] Many of these responses are another way of saying 'with husband'.

Appendix 3 Voluntary associations

When voluntary associations in Banbury were studied in 1948–51 they were seen as a particular type of formal organization. They were characterized as having a constitution, voluntary membership, the qualifications for which had been defined by the members themselves, some continuity and a formal name. They were therefore distinguished from *ad hoc* bodies, sets, cliques and all other informal associations or groups. They were also distinguished from political organizations both governmental and party political. Governmental associations fail to qualify, either because membership is not voluntary, or because the members do not decide upon the membership qualifications. All statutory elected and appointed bodies were therefore dealt with separately. Political parties, although meeting the criteria, were kept separate because of their special relation to government bodies. Religious associations were also distinguished from voluntary associations because, while it is open to anyone to join a church, most people are initially attached to a religion by their parents and, furthermore, only in a few religious bodies are the criteria for membership determined by the members.

In 1966–8, as in 1948–50, voluntary associations were defined by five criteria; (i) they are formal associations having some kind of constitution by which the affairs of the group are ordered; (ii) membership is voluntary; (iii) the qualifications for membership are determined by the members themselves; (iv) the group has some continuity and is not convened merely for a special purpose or occasion; (v) the group has some formal name by which it is known.[1]

A further distinction proved important in the second study: that between voluntary associations which are open to anyone to join who has the appropriate membership qualifications and those associations which are composed of delegates from other associations.

These sometimes also have an individual membership. Many appointed statutory bodies effectively have the characteristics of delegate associations, but the members do not sit as representatives of other bodies. Nor are such organizations voluntary associations in our sense, although the members may serve in a voluntary capacity. The *delegate voluntary association* is one in which the committee members are appointed from other voluntary bodies. Sometimes government bodies also have the right of appointment. The Old Charitable Association in Banbury is an example.

Voluntary associations, which were studied in 1948–51 'as a guide to social structure and social behaviour',[2] were examined carefully in terms of their relations with each other and with the religious and political associations. The links that were made between associations by the actions of individuals who joined more than one association made connections between the groups. A similar analysis in 1966–8 was based on seventy-four associations in Banbury Municipal Borough. This is less than half the total known number but represents all for which adequate data became available.

A questionnaire was sent out during 1967 and followed through to 1968, to all those voluntary associations discovered by a search of the public library, the newspapers, advertisements and by word of mouth. This covered the name, aims, activities, size and recent history, and the names, occupations, sex and age range of committee members and the names of patrons or president. A similar schedule was used for interviewing officers of voluntary associations.[3]

In the 6 per cent sample survey (see Appendix 1) a question was asked about membership: 27 per cent of the population in the Borough reported that they belonged to one voluntary association and 30 per cent to two or more.

In both the first and second studies, voluntary associations were analysed descriptively in terms of their overt aims[4] and the nature of their memberships. The connections among the leaders of voluntary associations were also analysed. This was done by analysing links between committees having members in common. Thus, one link between two committees indicated that they shared one person in common, two links that they shared two persons and so on. To put the matter in the language of more recent discussions, it might be said that associations were treated as a 'social field'[5] and then within this field alone the 'sets' of the committee members were examined.[6]

Such an analysis is, of course, only a partial guide to the social structure and culture, for, despite the long history of associations in Britain among all social levels,[7] she has never been a nation of joiners.[8] Indeed, the very self-selection of the membership is part of the attraction of associations for sociological analysis. It is an analysis of the actions of defined individuals which accords full recognition to the element of choice in the urban situation.[9] Choice occurs at two levels: first the individual chooses to join more than one association and then he chooses to accept membership of the committees of more than one association. Included in his set, therefore, are other committee members, but these, of course, do not exhaust his set, which also includes rank-and-file members and persons who are not members of that or of any association. The analysis, therefore, is not one of personal networks of sets of individuals,[10] but is based upon specific aspects of parts of these.

There is obviously a difference in the nature of the links between voluntary bodies which have no formal connections and links which are themselves formally constituted. This distinction, along with that between the statutory and the voluntary committees, is of considerable importance, for in the second analysis we have found that the major concentrations of links are formal links of this kind.

Men and women in voluntary associations

TABLE V   *Number of associations joined, by sex: 1966–8*

No. of associations	Men	%	Women	%	Total	%
None	233	33	386	52	619	43
One or more	479	67	351	48	830	57
Total	712	100	737	100	1,449	100

Source: 6 per cent sample, Banbury and District.

TABLE VI   *Men and women on committees: 1950 and 1966–8 compared*

Committees	Committees 1950		Committees 1966–8	
	No.	%	No.	%
All male	39	55	32	43
Mixed	26	36	32	43
All female	6	9	10	14
Total	71	100	74	100

Source: Associations survey.

TABLE VII   *Committee members, by sex: 1950 and 1966–8 compared*

| | Committee members 1950 | | Committee members 1966–8 | |
	No.	%	No.	%
Men only	379		326	
Mixed: Male	265	78	262	67
Female	73	22	128	33
Women only	56		104	
Total	773		820	

Source: Associations survey.

Occupational status and voluntary associations

TABLE VIII   *Number of associations joined, by occupational status: 1966–8*

| No. of associations belonged to | Non-manual | | Manual | |
	No.	%	No.	%
None	185	36	409	46
One	121	24	253	29
Two or more	206	40	217	25
Total	512	100	879	100
6% sample survey		47·6		52·4

Source: 6 per cent sample, Banbury and District.

TABLE IX   *Occupational status of committee members compared with 6 per cent sample of Banbury Borough (%)*

Hall–Jones	All respondents Banbury M.B.	Voluntary association committee members
1	1·0	14·9
2	1·5	28·6
3	4·5	17·2
4	8·0	5·9
5a	30·0	8·4
All non-manual	45·0	75·0
5b	22·0	19·1
6	20·0	4·6
7	12·0	1·3
All manual	54·0	25·0
Total	99·0	100·0

Sources: 6 per cent sample, Banbury and District; associations survey.

Banburians, immigrants, and voluntary associations

TABLE X   *Committee members*

	% *Banburians*	*N*
Sports	40	65
Hobbies	47	126
Cultural	42	121
Social	49	82
Social service	46	61
Charity	80	36
Mutual aid	...	6
Occupational	39	53
All voluntary associations	47·5	550
All 6% sample	46·2	

Sources: Associations survey; 6 per cent sample, Banbury and District.

Appendix 4 Thrift clubs

There are about 150 Thrift Clubs in Banbury; they were found more often in older working-class areas and were more successful in such areas. Some are attached to work places and some to social clubs, but the more common form of neighbourhood thrift club is based on a pub which serves a particular locality. This itself is interesting. It is not only living together, but living together *and* going to the same pub which apparently provides the conditions for the development of a thrift club.[1] Thus three activities come together: residence, recreation and saving. At one time saving through a thrift club may have been predominantly for times of crisis: unemployment or death, for example. Now such clubs are used as a way of saving for times of heavy expenditure, particularly Christmas and, to a lesser extent, holidays. The Thrift Club acts as a further tie between those who are already neighbours and 'regulars' at the 'local' who are also already friends and perhaps kin as well. The treasurer of the club acts as an intermediary between the individual members and the bank where the money is paid in.

Thrift clubs based on pubs and streets in Banbury tend to concentrate in older areas where the average rateable value of the dwellings is £100 or less, i.e. predominantly the older working-class areas. Some are therefore found near the town centre, where there are still working-class residential areas, and many are found in the older working-class areas around the town. Some have grown up in newer areas. An analysis of the way in which money is collected in an older as compared with a newer neighbourhood shows how different these neighbourhoods are and is illustrated by the following two examples.

The first club is based on a pub in an old working-class area. One Christmas this club gave back to its 180 members more than £2,000. Money is usually taken to the pub by the men on Friday evening. But it is usually the wives who have collected the money. Wives collect from their neighbours and kin, give the money to their husbands, who take it to the thrift club 'bag-keeper' (treasurer)—so called because of his Gladstone bag into which the money disappears. The money was gathered by a number of women from their friends; they passed it to another, who amassed several collections; these again would be amassed by another woman whose husband or brother would then take the money to the pub. None of the women was ever known by the field-workers to take the money to the pub herself. The women have many multiplex role relations in the neighbourhood, so that if one should fail to collect by illness or other reason, another member of the neighbourhood would take her place and the money still come in.

The second club is also based on a pub, but in an area of new Council housing. It paid out over £3,000 to its members one Christmas. Husbands and wives often go to this pub together, and women as well as men may be payers-in. There is no clear sex division. In addition, the money is collected by one woman passing on her money to another, where each has only single-stranded role relations. The money passes along a chain whose links are single-stranded role relations, for each person in the chain in the new Council estate knows very few others. Thus if someone is ill or fails to collect, the link is broken; there is no one who can take over. Therefore members often fail to contribute to the club every week.

Appendix 5   Sex differences

TABLE XI   *Registrar-General's socio-economic groups, by sex*

Reg.-Gen. Socio-economic group	Men No.	Men %	Women No.	Women %	Total No.	Total %	Men %
1 and 2 Employers and Managers	63	9·0	7	1·0	70	5·1	90·0
3 and 4 Professional workers	27	3·9	6	0·9	33	2·4	81·8
5 Intermediate non-manual	42	6·0	93	13·8	135	9·8	31·1
6 Junior non-manual	65	9·3	214	31·8	279	20·4	23·3
7 Personal service workers	2	0·3	96	14·2	98	7·1	2·0
8 Foreman supervisors	30	4·3	5	0·7	35	2·6	85·7
9 Skilled manual	208	29·8	34	5·0	242	17·6	86·0
10 Semi-skilled manual	117	16·8	97	14·4	214	15·6	54·7
11 Unskilled manual	63	9·0	96	14·2	159	11·6	39·6
12 Own account	52	7·5	11	1·6	63	4·6	82·5
13 Farmers (employers)	7	1·0	0	0	7	0·5	100·0
14 Farmers own account	8	1·1	1	0·1	9	0·6	88·9
15 Agricultural workers	13	1·9	9	1·3	22	1·6	59·1
16 Armed forces	0	0	5	0·7	5	0·4	...

Source: 6 per cent sample, Banbury and District.

150

TABLE XII   *Net weekly earnings, by Registrar-General's social class and by sex (Full-time employment only)*

£	Males Non-manual No.	%	Manual No.	%	Females Non-manual No.	%	Manual No.	%
Under 10	2	1·3	11	3·5	36	45·6	30	83·3
10–14	25	16·8	105	33·8	24	30·4	5	13·9
15–19	36	24·2	120	38·6	9	11·4	1	2·8
20–9	53	35·6	69	22·2	10	12·6	0	0
30+	33	22·1	6	1·9	0	0	0	0
Totals	149	100·0	311	100·0	79	100·0	36	100·0

Source: 6 per cent sample, Banbury and District.

TABLE XIII   *Membership of occupational associations, by sex (%)*

	Males Non-manual	Manual	Females Non-manual	Manual
Members	47	48	11·5	15
N	139	277	176	106

Source: 6 per cent sample, Banbury and District.

TABLE XIV   Voting, by sex: 1950 and 1967 compared[a]

	1950[a] Male			1950[a] Female			1967[a] Male			1967[a] Female		
	No.	%	%	No.	%	%	No.	%	%	No.	%	%
Conservative	331	38·4	35·0	419	46	40·7	249	44·5	35·6	288	53·4	40·5
Labour	475	55·2	50·3	395	43·5	38·3	265	47·3	37·9	209	38·8	29·4
Liberal	55	6·4	5·8	95	10·5	9·2	46	8·2	6·6	42	7·8	5·9
Sub Total	861	100·0	91·1	909	100·0	88·2	560	100·0	80·1	539	100·0	75·8
Didn't (1967)/None (1950)	51		5·4	96		9·3	87		12·4	128		18·0
Rest (1967)/Floaters (1950)	33		3·5	24		2·3	52		7·4	44		6·2
Total	945		100·0	1,029		99·8	699		99·9	711		100·0

	1950[a] Cons.	%	Lab.	%	Lib.	%	1967[a] Cons.	%	Lab.	%	Lib.	%
Male	331	44·1	475	54·6	55	36·7	249	46·4	265	55·9	46	53·3
Female	419	55·9	395	45·4	95	63·3	288	53·6	209	44·1	42	47·7
Total	750	100·0	870	100·0	150	100·0	537	100·0	474	100·0	88	101·0

[a] Sample surveys of 1950 (Banbury M.B.) and 1967 (Banbury and District): in 1950 the question asked was 'What are your politics?'; in 1967 it was 'How did you vote at the last General Election?'.

TABLE XV *Voting, by sex and occupational class*

| | Male | | | | Female[a] | | | | All sample | | | |
| | Non-manual | | Manual | | Non-manual | | Manual | | Non-manual | | Manual | |
	%	No.	%	No.	%	No.	%	No.	%	No.	%	No.
Conservative	57·4	140	24·0	109	55·3	152	31·2	136	56·3	292	27·5	245
Labour	20·5	50	47·3	215	18·2	50	36·5	159	19·3	100	42·0	374
Liberal	7·4	18	6·2	28	6·5	18	5·5	24	6·9	36	5·8	52
Sub Total	85·3	208	77·5	352	80·0	220	73·2	319	82·5	428	75·3	671
Did not vote	7·8	19	15·0	68	13·5	37	20·9	91	10·8	56	17·8	159
Rest	7·0	17	7·7	35	6·5	18	6·0	26	6·7	35	6·8	61
Total	100·1	244	100·2	455	100·0	275	100·1	436	100·0	519	99·9	891

[a] All women are included here: single women by their own occupation; ever married by their husband's.

TABLE XV—*continued*

Those who did not vote, by sex and by manual/non manual:

		No.	%
Male	Non-manual	19	8·8
	Manual	68	31·6
Female	Non-manual	37	17·2
	Manual	91	42·3
Total		215	99·9

Source: 6 per cent sample, Banbury and District.

Appendix 6   Income

TABLE XVI   *Income and source of income (%) (economically active married men, married respondents and spouses of female respondents)*

Weekly income or equivalent (£)	Wage	Salary	Fees	%	N
10	85·2	3·7	11·1	100·0	27
10–14	95·0	3·8	1·2	100·0	160
15–19	83·5	13·8	2·7	100·0	260
20–4	61·9	31·3	6·8	100·0	147
25–9	45·3	51·6	3·1	100·0	64
30–4	8·0	76·0	16·0	100·0	25
35+	10·0	63·3	26·7	100·0	30
Total known	72·5	22·4	5·0	99·9	713
Refused	56·7	26·8	16·5	100·0	254
Total	68·3	23·6	8·1	100·0	967

Source: 6 per cent sample, Banbury and District.

TABLE XVII   *Source of income, by occupational class (%) (economically active married men, married respondents and spouses of female respondents)*

Reg.-Gen. social class	Wage	Salary	Fees	%	N
I and II	17·0	67·4	15·6	100·0	212
IIIa and IVa	56·1	35·1	8·8	100·0	148
IIIb	85·5	7·7	6·8	100·0	366
IVb	93·5	·2·7	3·8	100·0	184
V	100·0	0	0	100·0	57
All	68·3	23·6	8·1	100·0	967

Source: 6 per cent sample, Banbury and District.

Appendix 7   Party politics[1]

TABLE XVIII   *Voting at General Elections 1959–70*

	1959	1964	1966	1970
Conservative	26,413	27,281	28,932	36,712
Labour	19,699	22,159	24,529	25,166
Liberal	6,014	7,851	7,407	6,859
Conservative majority	6,714	5,122	4,403	11,546

Source: Official returns, North Oxfordshire constituency.

TABLE XIX   *Voting of Banburians and immigrants: 1950 and 1967 compared*

1950[a]	Banburian			Immigrant			Total		
	No.	%	%	No.	%	%	No.	%	%
Conservative	365	32·0	36·8	319	34·2	38·6	684	33·0	37·6
Labour	449	39·4	45·3	352	37·7	42·6	801	38·6	44·0
Liberal	74	6·5	7·5	63	6·7	7·6	137	6·6	7·5
Floaters and others[b]	27	2·3	2·7	26	2·8	3·1	53	2·6	2·9
None[a]	76	6·7	7·7	67	7·2	8·1	143	6·9	7·9
Total known	991	86·9	100·0	827	88·6	100·0	1,818	87·7	99·9
Rest	149	13·1		107	11·4		256	12·3	
Total	1,140	100·0		934	100·0		2,074	100·0	

[a] Source: 1950 sample, Banbury M.B. only. Question asked: 'What are your politics?'.
[b] The category 'floaters and others' used in 1950 is not relevant in 1967 because of the different question asked.

157

TABLE XIX—*continued*

1967[c]	Banburian No.	%	%	Immigrant No.	%	%	Total No.	%	%
Conservative	238	36·3	39·1	303	39·9	42·8	541	38·1	40·8
Labour	219	33·4	35·9	261	34·1	36·5	480	33·8	36·2
Liberal	42	6·4	6·9	47	6·1	6·6	89	6·3	6·7
Didn't[c]	110	16·8	18·1	105	13·8	14·8	215	15·1	16·2
Total known	609	92·9	100·0	716	93·9	100·0	1,325	93·3	99·9
Rest	46	7·0		49	6·4		95	6·7	
Total	655	99·9		765	100·3		1,420	100·0	

[c] Source: 1967 per cent sample, Banbury and District. Question asked: 'How did you vote at the last General Election?'.

TABLE XX   *Voting of non-manual and manual workers, by date of arrival in Banbury*

Non-Manual

Date of arrival	Since 1945 No.	%	1930–45 No.	%	Before 1930 No.	%	Banbury born or brought up No.	%	Total No.	%
Conservative	137	55·0	33	49·2	18	75·0	128	55·7	316	55·4
Labour	45	18·1	25	37·3	3	12·5	31	13·5	104	18·2
Liberal	21	8·4	3	4·5	2	8·3	15	6·5	41	7·2
Did not vote	30	12·0	1	1·5	1	4·2	38	16·5	70	12·3
Rest	16	6·4	5	7·5	0	0·0	18	7·8	39	6·8
Total	249	99·9	67	100·0	24	100·0	230	100·0	570	99·9

Manual

Date of arrival	Since 1945 No.	%	1930–45 No.	%	Before 1930 No.	%	Banbury born or brought up No.	%	Total No.	%
Conservative	69	25·7	25	25·8	17	34·7	134	28·1	245	27·5
Labour	118	44·0	45	46·4	19	38·8	192	40·3	374	42·0
Liberal	14	5·2	5	5·1	2	4·1	31	6·5	52	5·8
Did not vote	52	19·4	13	13·4	6	12·2	88	18·4	159	17·8
Rest	15	5·6	9	9·3	5	10·2	32	6·7	61	6·8
Total	268	99·9	97	100·0	49	100·0	477	100·0	891	99·9

Sources: 6 per cent sample; all sample.

TABLE XXI   Characteristics of Party committee members and Borough councillors: 1967 (the time of the expansion issue) and 1950ᵃ compared

% Party committee members

		Sex			Av. age	Occupational class H-J		Source of income		
		M	F	Total		Range	Average	Profits & fees	Salary	Wages
Conservative	1967	12	3	15	46·6	1–3	2·0	10	5	0
	1950	12	0	12	44	2–4	2·65	8	4	0
Labourᵇ	1967	14	1	15	44·5	2–5	4·13	2	3	10
	1950	9	2	11	44	3–6	4·30	0	4	7
Liberal	1967	7	4	11	39	1–4	2·36	2	7	–2
	1950	16	8	24	50	1–5	2·77	15	6	1

Borough councillors

		Sex			Av. age	Occupational class H-J					Source of income		
		M	F	Total		1 & 2	3 & 4	5	6	7	Profits & fees	Salary	Wages
Conservative	1967	9	3	12	44	9	2	1	0	0	5	6	1
	1950	12	4	16	44	10	5	1	0	0	9	6	1
Labour	1967ᶜ	12	0	12	49	1	4	6	0	0	2	2	7
	1950	7	1	8	50	0	3	3	2	0	21	1	5

Source: local documents.

ᵃ T. & C., p. 44.
ᵇ Labour party committee is taken as the President and two Vice-Presidents, Treasurer, and Secretary of the Borough party together with the Chairman and Secretary of the 5 Wards in which there is a Labour party (six are also Borough councillors and two appear twice—i.e. are on the central party committee and are Ward Secretary/Chairman).
ᶜ Including one Independent Labour.

159

Appendix 8   Family and kin

TABLE XXII   *Frequency of all forms of contact of those ever-married with parents alive (%)*

	Women		Men	
	Mothers	*Fathers*	*Mothers*	*Fathers*
Parents live in household	7	4	6	5
Some contact				
Within 24 hours	32	27	30	29
Within last week	47	48	46	50
A week to a month ago	11	13	10	11
Less frequently than monthly	3	8	8	5
N	293	240	274	235

Source: 6 per cent sample.

TABLE XXIII   *Views about rates of contact with relatives nowadays (men and women combined)*

	Non-manual		Manual		
	Occupational mobility				
	None	*Upward*	*None*	*Downward*	*All*
More	20	6	15	4	45
Same	11	23	16	14	64
More of some/					
Less of others	0	3	0	2	5
Less	0	2	0	0	2
All	31	34	31	20	116

Source: family sub-sample.

TABLE XXIV   *Views about what relatives do for each other nowadays (men and women combined)*

	Non-manual		Manual		
	Occupational mobility				
	None	*Upward*	*None*	*Downward*	*All*
More	10	1	2	2	15
Same	12	4	4	4	24
Varies	2	2	0	0	4
Less	7	17	25	12	61
Don't know	0	10	0	2	12
Totals	31	34	31	20	116

Source: family sub-sample.

Appendix 9　Age and sex of the population

TABLE XXV　*Age and sex of the population of Banbury Municipal Borough[a]*

Age in years	Male No.	%	Female No.	%
0–4	1,340	11·0	1,250	9·8
5–14	1,670	13·7	1,750	13·7
15–19	950	7·8	1,120	8·7
20–4	830	6·8	820	6·4
25–44	3,420	28·1	3,310	25·9
45–9	2,200	18·1	2,260	17·7
60–4	600	4·9	700	5·5
65+	1,140	9·4	1,580	12·3
Total	12,150	99·8	12,790	100·0

Sources: GRO 1966; 10 per cent Sample Census.

[a] It is not possible to extract the Banbury and District survey area from the 1966 sample census (GRO) because the data are not available for parishes.

TABLE XXVI   *Age and sex of the population of Banbury and District (%)*

Age in years	Male	Female
20–9	15·2	17·2
30–9	19·6	17·9
40–9	20·7	20·6
50–9	17·9	17·2
60–9	17·6	13·8
70+	8·9	13·2
N	709	721

Source: 6 per cent sample.

Glossary

AUTHORITY   Legitimated power, 'a recognised right to command',[1] but note Marshall's reservations.[2] *See also* POWER, POWERS, SELF-DETERMINATION.

CLASS   Economic class, i.e. a category of persons who occupy a similar position (status) in regard to the system of production. Generally in this book class is not used without a qualifying adjective. *See also* CLASS CONSCIOUSNESS, LEVEL CONSCIOUSNESS, LEGAL STATUS, OCCUPATIONAL CLASS, OCCUPATIONAL STATUS, SOCIAL CLASS, SOCIAL LEVELS, SOCIAL STANDING, SOCIAL STATUS, STATUS, STATUS-CONSCIOUS.

CLASS CONSCIOUSNESS   Used of individuals in a category who are all aware of the commonality of their position in the economic system,[3] who perceive stratification in terms of social class (*q.v.*) whether or not the society may objectively be said to be divided into such social classes. These social classes the actors perceive as pervasive of all social life and as being in conflict with each other. *See also* CLASS, LEVEL CONSCIOUSNESS, SOCIAL CLASS, STATUS-CONSCIOUS.

COMMUNITY   No longer operationally definable.[4] *See also* local social system.

DOMESTIC ELEMENTARY FAMILY GROUP   Members of the elementary family (*q.v.*) comprising a domestic group (*q.v.*) at any one time. *See also* EXTENDED FAMILY, HOUSEHOLD.[5]

DOMESTIC GROUP   a group of relatives who comprise a household (*q.v.*) at any one time. *See also* DOMESTIC ELEMENTARY FAMILY GROUP, ELEMENTARY FAMILY, EXTENDED FAMILY.

---

1 Chinoy, *Society*, p. 137.
2 Marshall, 'Reflections on Power', p. 146.
3 Aron, *Progress and Disillusion*, p. 42: 'In any case, such consciousness and purpose reside in a political party rather than in the class as a whole.'
4 Stacey, 'The Myth of Community Studies'.
5 Stacey (ed.), *Comparability in Social Research*, pp. 49–52.

164

ELEMENTARY FAMILY   Mates and their biological or legally adopted children.[1] *See also* DOMESTIC ELEMENTARY FAMILY GROUP, DOMESTIC GROUP, EXTENDED FAMILY, HOUSEHOLD.

EXTENDED FAMILY   Any persistent kinship grouping wider than the elementary family.[2] *See also* DOMESTIC ELEMENTARY FAMILY GROUP, DOMESTIC GROUP, ELEMENTARY FAMILY, HOUSEHOLD.

FAMILY   *See* ELEMENTARY FAMILY, EXTENDED FAMILY, DOMESTIC ELEMENTARY FAMILY GROUP, DOMESTIC GROUP.

HOUSEHOLD   Those who share a dwelling and have a common larder and accounts.[3] *See also* DOMESTIC ELEMENTARY FAMILY GROUP, DOMESTIC GROUP.

INCLUSIVE ROLES   Found in societies with little status differentiation, 'they include many aspects of behaviour rather than merely some limited segment of an individual's activities'.[4] Distinguish from multi-stranded roles and multiplex role relations (*q.v.*). *See also* MULTI-STRANDED ROLE RELATIONSHIP.

KIN   Relatives of the blood or marriage.

LEGAL STATUS   Denotes membership of a category 'carrying distinctive rights or duties, capacities or incapacities, determined and upheld by public law'.[5]

LEVEL CONSCIOUSNESS[6]   An awareness of social and economic differences associated with individual aspirations and attempts to modify life style, unlike class consciousness (*q.v.*) which promotes 'feelings of identification or collective involvement'.[7] Level consciousness and class consciousness may co-exist in a society and an individual. *See also* CLASS, SOCIAL LEVELS, STATUS CONSCIOUS.

LOCAL SOCIAL SYSTEM   Occurs when a set of interrelated social institutions (*q.v.*) is found in a geographically defined locality.[8] *See also* SOCIAL SYSTEM, COMMUNITY.

MULTIPLE ROLES   The many roles (*q.v.*) an actor has to play relating to his many statuses (*q.v.*).[9] *See also* MULTIPLEX ROLE RELATIONS, MULTI-STRANDED ROLE RELATIONSHIP, SINGLE-STRANDED ROLE RELATIONSHIP.

MULTIPLEX ROLE RELATIONS   Where the actor is an incumbent of two or more statuses (*q.v.*) and, in the roles (*q.v.*) he plays associated with these statuses, his role partners (*q.v.*) are one man who

1 Stacey, op. cit., p. 37.
2 Harris and Stacey, 'A Note on the Extended Family', p. 56.
3 Stacey, op. cit., p. 34.
4 Chinoy, op. cit., pp. 88, 89.
5 Marshall, op. cit., p. 134.
6 Marshall, *Sociology at the Crossroads*, p. 178; Nisbet, *The Social Bond*, p. 208.
7 Nisbet, op. cit.
8 Stacey, art. cit.
9 See Turner, 'Role: Sociological Aspects'.

occupies the appropriate complementary statuses.[1] *See also* MULTIPLE ROLES, MULTI-STRANDED ROLE RELATIONSHIP, SIMPLEX ROLE RELATIONS, SINGLE-STRANDED ROLE RELATIONSHIP, SEGMENTED ROLES, INCLUSIVE ROLES.

MULTI-STRANDED ROLE RELATIONSHIP   The relationship between two actors who have multiplex role relations.[2] *See also* INCLUSIVE ROLES, MULTIPLE ROLES, MULTIPLEX ROLE RELATIONS, ROLE, SEGMENTED ROLES, SIMPLEX ROLE RELATIONS, SINGLE-STRANDED ROLE RELATIONSHIP, STATUS.

OCCUPATIONAL CLASS   A category of persons who have similar occupational statuses (*q.v.*). *See also* CLASS, OCCUPATIONAL STATUS, SOCIAL CLASS, SOCIAL LEVELS.

OCCUPATIONAL STATUS   The status (*q.v.*) of an actor in relation to the labour market. *See also* OCCUPATIONAL CLASS, SOCIAL CLASS, SOCIAL LEVELS, SOCIAL STATUS, STATUS.

POWER   The capacity to control the actions of others,[3] part of the action frame of reference consisting in action, not the potential for action[4] and distinguished from powers (*q.v.*). *See also* AUTHORITY, SELF-DETERMINATION.

POWERS   The potential to influence the actions of others; it may relate to the man or his office and is distinguished from power (*q.v.*) and authority (*q.v.*). This concept relates to a structural–functional analysis of social systems.[5] *See also* SELF-DETERMINATION.

ROLE   The behaviour associated with a status (*q.v.*),[6] although any one status may involve a range of roles.[7,8] *See also* ROLE PARTNERS, MULTIPLE ROLES, MULTIPLEX/SIMPLEX ROLE RELATIONS, MULTI-STRANDED/SINGLE-STRANDED ROLE RELATIONSHIPS, INCLUSIVE/SEGMENTED ROLES.

ROLE PARTNERS   Those who play complementary roles, e.g. husband and wife, brother and sister, doctor and patient. *See also* ROLE, MULTIPLE ROLES, MULTIPLEX/SIMPLEX ROLE RELATIONS, MULTI-STRANDED/SINGLE-STRANDED ROLE RELATIONSHIPS, INCLUSIVE/SEGMENTED ROLES.

[1] Gluckman, *The Judicial Process among the Barotse of Northern Rhodesia;* Stacey, art. cit., although the use there of 'multiplex social roles' (p. 144) was an error for 'multiplex role relations'. Frankenberg, *Communities in Britain,* p. 287, uses 'multiple role relationships' following Southall, 'An Operational Theory of Role'.
[2] Cf. Banton, *Roles,* p. 203, 'interdependent' social relationships.
[3] Chinoy, op. cit, p. 137.
[4] Marshall, art. cit., pp. 146-7.   [5] Ibid., p. 146.
[6] Cf. Banton, op. cit., p. 29, '. . . a set of norms and expectations applied to the incumbent of a particular position'.
[7] Merton, *Social Theory and Social Structure,* p. 369.
[8] The twin concepts of status and role provide a link between a structural study of system and an action frame of reference. Cf. Chinoy, op. cit., p. 29.

SEGMENTED ROLES   Roles which 'are limited to specific contexts and confined to a narrow range of activity'.[1] *See also*   ROLE, ROLE PARTNERS, MULTIPLE ROLES, MULTIPLEX/SIMPLEX ROLE RELATIONS, MULTI-STRANDED/SINGLE-STRANDED ROLE RELATIONSHIPS.

SELF-DETERMINATION   An aspect of power, 'power over one's own life, i.e. independence'.[2]

SIMPLEX ROLE RELATIONS   Where there is only one pair of complementary statuses (*q.v.*) between two actors and one role partnership (*q.v.*).[3] *See also*   ROLE, ROLE PARTNERS, MULTIPLE ROLES, MULTIPLEX ROLE RELATIONS, MULTI-STRANDED/SINGLE-STRANDED ROLE RELATIONSHIPS, SEGMENTED ROLES.

SINGLE-STRANDED ROLE RELATIONSHIP   The relationship between two actors who have simplex role relations (*q.v.*).[4] *See also*   ROLE, ROLE PARTNERS, MULTIPLE ROLES, MULTIPLEX ROLE RELATIONS, MULTI-STRANDED/SINGLE-STRANDED ROLE RELATIONSHIPS, SEGMENTED ROLES.

SOCIAL CATEGORY   Persons who share a common social attribute.

SOCIAL CLASS   'Groups possessed both of real and vital common economic interests and of a group-consciousness of their general position in the social scale'.[5] *See also*   CLASS, CLASS CONSCIOUSNESS, LEVEL CONSCIOUSNESS, OCCUPATIONAL CLASS, SOCIAL STATUS, STATUS, STATUS-CONSCIOUS, SOCIAL LEVELS.

SOCIAL INSTITUTION   'Recognised and established usages governing the relations between individuals or groups'[6] or 'normative patterns which define what are felt to be . . . proper, legitimate, or expected modes of action or of social relationships'.[7]

SOCIAL LEVELS   Broad bands or strata of people with distinguishably different standards of living, styles of life, purchasing power, child-rearing habits, etc.,[8] but, unlike Nisbet, not necessarily implying normative consensus within the level.[9] *See also*   CLASS, CLASS CONSCIOUSNESS, LEVEL CONSCIOUSNESS, SOCIAL STATUS, STATUS, STATUS-CONSCIOUS.

SOCIAL STANDING   The honour or prestige which attaches to a face-to-face group or individual either holistically or in regard to a particular role (*q.v.*) or cluster of roles.[10] *See also*   SOCIAL STATUS, STATUS.

---

[1] Chinoy, op. cit., pp. 88, 89. [2] Marshall, op. cit., p. 203.
[3] Mitchell describes these relationships as 'uniplex': Mitchell (ed.), *Social Networks in Urban Situations*. Frankenberg, op. cit., p. 287 uses 'overlapping role relations', following Southall, op. cit.
[4] Cf. Banton, op. cit., 'isolated social relationships'.
[5] Marshall, op. cit., p. 149. [6] Ginsberg, *Sociology*, p. 42.
[7] Parsons, *Essays in Sociological Theory, Pure and Applied*, p. 203.
[8] Marshall, *Citizenship and Social Class;* Nisbet, op. cit., p. 207.
[9] Nisbet, op. cit., p. 207.
[10] Marshall, op. cit., p. 216.

SOCIAL STATUS   Stratification based upon consumption patterns or life styles and including the honour in which people are held. Cf. Weber's 'status groups'. Describes the position of an individual envisaged in his totality within the community as a whole.[1] *See also* CLASS, LEGAL STATUS, OCCUPATIONAL STATUS, SOCIAL CLASS, SOCIAL LEVELS, SOCIAL STANDING, STATUS.

SOCIAL SYSTEM   A set of interrelated social institutions (*q.v.*) covering all aspects of social life, familial, religious, juridical, etc., and the associated belief systems of each. Involves the notions of structure, process, and time.

STATUS   Position in society, not necessarily ranked. Every status has an associated role.[2] It provides a link between the structural study of social systems and the psychological study of personality and motivation.[3] *See also* ROLE and associated concepts, STATUS-CONSCIOUS.

STATUS-CONSCIOUS   Used by Goldthorpe *et al.* to indicate an awareness of ranked status.[4] Here level consciousness (*q.v.*) is used instead. *See also* CLASS CONSCIOUSNESS, SOCIAL CLASS, SOCIAL LEVELS, SOCIAL STATUS, SOCIAL STANDING, STATUS.

TRADITION   Used in *T. & C.* in a variety of ways. Used here as idea(s) valued and passed from one generation to the next and seen to be relevant in contemporary events,[5] a sense essentially similar to Firth's 'traditional tales' or 'traditional material' of societies, their quasi-history;[6] the means whereby Weber's traditional legitimation comes about. *See also* TRADITIONAL SOCIAL STRUCTURE/ SYSTEM, LOCAL SOCIAL SYSTEM, TRADITIONALISM, TRADITIONALISTS.

TRADITIONAL SOCIAL STRUCTURE OR SYSTEM   Used in *T. & C.* to describe a local social system (*q.v.*) in which the participants had multiplex role relations (*q.v.*) and overtly shared a consensus about the value of what-had-been as a means of legitimating present action. *See also* TRADITION, TRADITIONALISM, TRADITIONALISTS.

TRADITIONALISM   Used in *T. & C.* to describe the beliefs and values

[1] Ibid.
[2] The usual practice of social anthropologists and that set by Linton, *The Study of Man.* See also: Merton, op. cit, pp. 368 ff. and the dissenting note in Banton, op. cit., pp. 25–8 and 36–8. Our use departs from that of Weber, Runciman, and Goldthorpe *et al.*: Gerth and Mills, *From Max Weber: Essays in Sociology*, pp. 180 ff.; Weber, *The Theory of Social and Economic Organization*, pp. 424–9; Runciman, *Relative Deprivation and Social Justice;* Goldthorpe and Lockwood, 'Affluence and the British Class Structure', pp. 133–59; Goldthorpe, Lockwood, Bechhofer, Platt, *The Affluent Worker.*
[3] Marshall, op. cit., p. 208. The twin concepts of status and role provide a link between a structural study of system and an action frame of reference: Chinoy, op. cit., p. 29.
[4] Goldthorpe *et al.*, *The Affluent Worker*, vol. 3, p. 86.
[5] Radin, 'Tradition'.
[6] Firth, *History and Traditions of Tikopia.*

of 'traditionalists' (*q.v.*). Also the name of a sophisticated school of political philosophy. *See also*   TRADITIONAL, TRADITIONAL SOCIAL STRUCTURE OR SYSTEM.

TRADITIONALISTS   Used in *T. & C.* to describe those encompassed by the traditional social system (*q.v.*). *See also* TRADITIONAL, TRADITIONALISM.

Notes

Introduction

1 M. Stacey, *Tradition and Change: a study of Banbury* (O.U.P., 1960), hereinafter referred to as *T. & C.*

2 M. Gluckman, in A. L. Epstein, *The Craft of Social Anthropology* (Tavistock Publications, 1967), pp. xii ff.

3 For a recently published overview see Colin Bell and Howard Newby, *Community Studies* (Allen & Unwin, 1971).

4 C. M. Arensberg and S. T. Kimball, *Family and Community in Ireland* (Harvard Univ. Press, 1940).

5 R. S. and M. Lynd, *Middletown* (Harcourt, Brace, New York, 1929) and *Middletown in Transition* (Harcourt, Brace, New York, 1937).

6 e.g. W. Lloyd Warner and P. S. Lunt, *The Social Life of a Modern Community* (Yankee City series) (Yale Univ. Press, New Haven, 1941), W. Lloyd Warner, *Democracy in Jonesville*, (Harper, New York, 1949).

7 A. Davies, B. B. and M. R. Gardner, *Deep South* (Univ. of Chicago Press, Chicago, 1941).

8 *T. & C.*, p. v.

9 *T. & C.*, pp. 167–8.

10 *T. & C.*, p. 170.

11 *T. & C.*, p. 14.

12 R. Frankenberg, *Communities in Britain* (Penguin, Harmondsworth, 1966), p. 155.

13 R. K. Merton, *Social Theory and Social Structure* (Collier Macmillan, London, revised edn. 1965), p. 393.

14 *T. & C.*, p. 171.

15 *T. & C.*, p. 182.

16 *T. & C.*, p. 177.

17 *Brit. J. Sociol.*, vol. 20, no. 2, June 1969.

18 J. H. Goldthorpe, D. Lockwood, F. Bechhofer, J. Platt, *The Affluent Worker*, vols. 1–3 (C.U.P., 1968–9).

19 R. M. Titmuss, *Income Distribution and Social Change* (Allen & Unwin, 1962).

20 e.g. B. Abel-Smith and P. Townsend, *The Poor and the Poorest* (Bell, 1965); P. Townsend (ed.), *The Concept of Poverty* (Heinemann, 1970); T. Lynes, *National Assistance and National Prosperity* (Occ. Papers on Social Administration, no. 5, 1962).

21 R. S. and H. M. Lynd, *Middletown in Transition*.

22 Art Gallaher, Jr., *Plainville Fifteen Years Later* (Columbia Univ. Press, New York, 1961).

23 Oscar Lewis, *Life in a Mexican Village: Tepoztlan Restudied* (Univ. of Illinois Press, Urbana, 1951).

24 See pp. 76ff.

25 T. H. Marshall, 'Reflections on Power', *Sociology*, vol. 3, no. 2, 1969. See also Glossary p. 166.

26 See Appendix 1.

1 The changing face of Banbury: 1951–66

1 Cf. J. M. Mann, 'Sociological Aspects of Factory Relocation: a case study', D.Phil. thesis, University of Oxford, 1970.

2 Chapter 4.

3 Cf. *T. & C.*, p. 8.

4 *T. & C.*, p. 94.

5 Cf. *T. & C.*, pp. 92, et seq.

6 Chart XIV, *T. & C.*, p. 94.

7 *T. & C.*, pp. 91–101, 123–4.

8 See Appendix 1 for details of the sample survey made.

9 See Appendix 1 for details of this survey.

10 In 1950 Banburians and immigrants were roughly evenly divided, *T. & C.*, p. 12.

11 Cf. *T. & C.*, Table 2, p. 13.

12 R. K. Merton, *Social Theory and Social Structure*.

13 *T. & C.*, p. 13.

14 Cf. *T. & C.*, p. 10.

15 *T. & C.*, chap. 1.

16 Such permission from central government was, at the time of the study, essential before industrial development could take place.

17 See the detailed account in J. M. Mann, op. cit.

18 J. B. Cullingworth, *Town and Country Planning in England and Wales* (Allen & Unwin, 1964).

19 See Chapter 5.

20 Banbury and District Civic Society, *Bulletin* no. 8, April 1966.

2 Banburians, immigrants and work

1 *T. & C.*, pp. 21–4.

2 *T. & C.*, p. 24.

3 *T. & C.*, Table 8, p. 29.

4 *T. & C.*, Table 4, p. 25.

5 For a detailed account of this transfer see J. M. Mann, op. cit.

6 Cf. R. Aron, *Eighteen Lectures on Industrial Society* (Weidenfeld & Nicolson, 1967), p. 73, where he argues that an important feature of industrial society is 'large-scale industry' and P. Marris and A. Somerset, *African Businessmen* (Routledge & Kegan Paul, 1971), who argue the continuing importance of the small firm even in advanced industrial countries.

7 A special study of the attitudes of those working in small compared with those in large establishments was made, based on a sub-sample of the 6 per cent sample of residents. See Appendix 1 for further details. The study is fully reported in E. V. Batstone, 'Aspects of Stratification in a Community Context', Ph.D. thesis, University of Wales, 1970.

8 See also Batstone, op. cit.; D. Lockwood, 'Sources of Variation in Working Class Images of Society', *Soc. Rev.*, vol. 14, no. 3, 1966; J. H. Goldthorpe *et al.*, *The Affluent Worker*, vol. 1: *Industrial Attitudes and Behaviour* (C.U.P., 1968); and G. K. Ingham, 'Organizational Size, Orientation to Work and Industrial Behaviour', *Sociology*, vol. 1, no. 3, 1967.

9 Cf. the relationship between farmers and farm workers as described by J. Littlejohn, *Westrigg: The Sociology of a Cheviot Parish* (Routledge & Kegan Paul, 1963).

10 Cf. S. Cleland, *Influence of Plant Size on Industrial Relations* (Princeton Univ. Press, 1955). Also see B. P. Indik, 'Some effects of Organization size on members' attitude and behaviour', *Hum. Rel.*, vol. 16, no. 4, 1963, for a review of the literature; also M. Crozier, *The Bureaucratic Phenomenon* (Tavistock Publications, 1964); R. W. Revans, 'Big Firms', *New Soc.*, 5 Oct. 1967; E. O. Smigel, 'Public Attitudes toward stealing as related to the size of the victim organization', *A.S.R.*, vol. 21, no. 3, 1956.

11 A. Etzioni, *A Comparative Analysis of Complex Organizations* (Free Press, New York; Collier Macmillan, London, 1961).

12 A. W. Gouldner, *Wildcat Strike* (Routledge & Kegan Paul, 1955), p. 22.

13 E. V. Batstone, op. cit.

14 R. Frankenberg, *Communities in Britain*, p. 155.

15 *T. & C.*, p. 14.

16 W. Watson, 'Social Mobility and Social Class in Industrial Communities' in M. Gluckman (ed.), *Closed Systems and Open Minds* (Oliver & Boyd, Edinburgh, 1964).

17 Merton, op. cit., pp. 404–5, footnote.

18 *T. & C.*, especially p. 174, 'The non-traditional middle-class in the most mixed bag'.

19 Op. cit.

20 *T. & C.*, p. 48, also F. Bealey, J. Blondel, and W. P. McCann, *Constituency Politics: A study of Newcastle-under-Lyme* (Faber, 1965), especially pp. 306, 361, 400.

21 *T. & C.*, p. 16.

22 *T. & C.*, p. 174.

23 L. C. Goldberg *et al.*, 'Local-Cosmopolitan: Uni-dimensional or Multidimensional?' *A.J.S.*, vol. 70, no. 6, 1965, pp. 704–10, for example,

show that in some cases the dimensions of localism and cosmopolitanism are not distinct. See also P. M. Blau and W. R. Scott, *Formal Organizations* (Routledge & Kegan Paul, 1963) and B. G. Glaser, *Organizational Scientists* (Bobbs-Merrill, Indianapolis, Ind., 1964.)
24 *T. & C.*, pp. 21, 32–4.
25 Watson, op. cit.

3 Religion in Banbury

1 Cf. L. Paul, *The Deployment and Payment of the Clergy* (Church Information Office, 1964), p. 27.
2 Social Surveys Ltd., *Television and Religion* (Univ. of London Press, 1964), chap. 13.
3 A survey undertaken on a Sunday in March 1968 by the field-workers and members of an extra-mural class.
4 The 6 per cent sample survey: see Appendix 1.
5 The Chestnut Bowling Club. See *T. & C.*, p. 40, chart 5.
6 See Chapter 4.
7 B. Wilson, *Religion in Secular Society* (Watts, 1966), p. 139.
8 Church attendance in Banbury has fallen by two-thirds from 5,742 at the 1851 Ecclesiastical Census to 2,202 at a similar census made in the Borough in March 1968 by field-workers and extra-mural students. In this period the population of the Borough has trebled.
9 Cf. C. Rosser and C. C. Harris, *The Family and Social Change: a study of Family and Kinship in a South Wales Town* (Routledge & Kegan Paul, 1965), and C. C. Harris, 'Reform in a Normative Organization', *Soc. Rev.*, vol. 17, no. 2, July 1969, pp. 167–85.
10 R. Robertson (ed.), *The Sociological Interpretation of Religion* (Blackwell, Oxford, 1970).
11 Cf. J. Rex and R. Moore, *Race, Community and Conflict, A study of Sparkbrook* (O.U.P., 1967).
12 Cf. H. Richard Niebuhr, *The Social Sources of Denominationalism* (P. Smith, Gloucester, Mass., 1963), and R. Lee, *The Social Sources of Church Unity* (Abingdon Press, New York, 1960).

4 Political parties, voluntary associations and pressure groups

1 See p. 33.
2 *T. & C.*, pp. 88–9.
The definitions of voluntary and other associations and the method of analysis are described in Appendix 3.
3 *T. & C.*, pp. 41–2.
4 Cf. David Bartlett and John Walker, 'Inner Circle', *New Soc.*, 19 April 1973, p. 139.
5 David Berry, 'Party Membership and Social Participation', *Pol. Stud.*, vol. 17, no. 2, 1969, pp. 196–207, has argued following Kornhauser and Allardt that any voluntary association membership may be seen as political activity.

6 H. J. Laski, 'Freedom of Association', in *Encyclopaedia of the Social Sciences* (The Macmillan Co., New York, 1931), vol. 6, pp. 447–50.

7 *T. & C.*, p. 78. This accorded with many other findings both here and in America.

8 *T. & C.*, p. 79.

9 *T. & C.*, p. 80. It had been hoped to include a separate section on youth in Banbury, but in the event this proved impracticable.

10 64 per cent of non-manual workers and 54 per cent of manual workers are joiners compared with 48 per cent of non-manual workers and 52 per cent of manual workers in the sample as a whole.

11 *T. & C.*, p. 75. See Appendix 3 for the definition of a voluntary association and for the distribution of voluntary associations by overt aim.

12 That is, the links between advisory bodies and voluntary associations, excluding political parties and religious organizations.

13 T. Cauter and J. S. Downham, *The Communication of Ideas* (Chatto & Windus, 1954).

14 A. Rees in his paper 'Democracy in Local Government' in B. Lapping and G. Radice (eds.), *More Power to the People* (Longmans, Green, 1968), p. 137, comments on the growth of a new type of promotional pressure group.

15 J. Littlejohn, *Westrigg: The Sociology of a Cheviot Parish*. See also, Peter H. Rossi, *Why Families Move* (Free Press, Glencoe, Ill., 1955).

5 Running the town: power, authority and influence in Banbury

1 *T. & C.*, p. 55.

2 E. Goffman, *The Presentation of Self in Everyday Life*, Univ. of Edinburgh Social Science Research Centre, Monograph, no. 2, 1956 (Doubleday Anchor, New York 1959; Penguin, Harmondsworth, 1969).

3 The party system in local government in Banbury is what Bulpitt would call a 'secondary' system, i.e. neither party has a large or sure majority, as opposed to a 'one party' system. Furthermore, since the distribution of patronage is in dispute between the parties, Bulpitt would consider this an 'immature secondary' system. J. G. Bulpitt, *Party Politics in English Local Government* (Longmans, Green, 1967).

4 This Newton sees as the typically British kind of pressure group activity compared with the more public activity common among American pressure groups. K. Newton, 'City Politics in Britain and the United States', *Pol. Stud.*, vol. 17, no. 2, 1969, p. 214.

5 D. S. Morris and K. Newton note that in Birmingham actions through partisan channels are relatively infrequently undertaken by pressure groups (*Onymous Empire: Voluntary Organizations in Birmingham Politics*, Discussion Papers, Series F, No. 10, Birmingham Politics and Society, December 1970).

6 This does not appear in Chapter 4 because it serves an area wider than Banbury. Only Banbury town organizations were included in that analysis.

7 Morris and Newton, op. cit., found this a rare tactic in Birmingham.

8 See p. 62 n.

9 J. B. Cullingworth, 'The Swindon Social Survey: a Second Report on the Social Implications of Overspill', *Soc. Rev.*, vol. 9, no. 2, 1961, pp. 151–66.

10 N. Dennis, 'Changes in Function and Leadership Renewal', *Soc. Rev.*, vol. 9, no. 1, 1961, pp. 55–84.

11 For example, J. M. Mogey, *Family and Neighbourhood* (O.U.P., 1956); Liverpool University, Dep. of Social Science, *Neighbourhood and Community* (Liverpool Univ. Press, 1954). See also David L. Sills, 'The Succession of Goals' (1957) in A. Etzioni (ed.), *Complex Organizations: a Sociological Reader* (Holt, Rinehart and Winston, New York, 1965), pp. 146–59.

6 Making decisions: the example of expansion

1 All three field-workers say that throughout their two years living and studying in the town they were never present at so emotional and excited a gathering, political or other. Some townsmen claim that previous public inquiries had been even more excitable.

2 This illustrates the point made by Newton, K. in 'Community Decision-Making and Community Decision-Makers in England and the U.S.' (paper to International Sociological Association, Varna conference, 1970) of the overriding importance of party politics in English local government.

3 F. G. Bailey, *Stratagems and Spoils: A Social Anthropology of Politics* (Blackwell, Oxford, 1969), p. 59.

4 Hutson, J., has an interesting case history of a mayor in the Hautes-Alpes who backed a development plan for his village which proved unacceptable to influential sections of the village. He lost his position and left the village. In F. G. Bailey, (ed.), *Gifts and Poisons: the politics of reputation* (Blackwell, Oxford, 1971).

5 Readers may be tempted to compare the 'King' with the X family of *Middletown in Transition* (R. and H. M. Lynd), but this would be misleading. Neither he nor his family had the pervasive power reported for the Xs.

6 Newton, 'City Politics . . .', rightly says that English mayors have little power compared with U.S. mayors, but this event does illustrate one of the few occasions when an English mayor has political as well as ceremonial power. This derives entirely from the evenly balanced parties in the Council Chamber.

7 T. Cauter and J. S. Downham, *The Communication of Ideas*. See also pp. 87ff.

8 Hilda Jennings, *Societies in the Making, a study of development and redevelopment within a County Borough* (Routledge & Kegan Paul, 1962).

9 J. Rex and R. Moore, *Race, Community and Conflict, A Study of Sparkbrook;* H. B. Rodgers, A. B. de Vos, and D. T. Herbert, *Overspill in Winsford: a social and economic survey of the progress of the Winsford Town Expansion Scheme* (publ. for Winsford Council; printed by Guardian Press, Winsford, 1965). This study reports that Winsford

residents did not have much idea of what Winsford's expansion scheme entailed and a few did not seem to be aware that there was a scheme. This was after it had been in process for five years.

10 T. H. Marshall, 'Reflections on Power', *Sociology*, vol. 3, no. 2, 1969, p. 146.

11 Cf. N. Dennis, *People and Planning: the sociology of housing in Sunderland* (Faber & Faber, 1970), pp. 346 et seq.

12 Department of Environment and Welsh Office, *Local Housing Statistics England and Wales*, August 1973 (Londod, H.M.S.O.).

7 Neighbours and neighbouring

1 Cf. 'Little Rochdale' in 1940s, *T. & C.*, p. 109.

2 The interesting, and by no means simple, relationships between occupational classes and housing classes are discussed in Chapter 9.

3 See p. 38 and S. R. Lowe, *The Churches' Role in the Care of the Elderly* (1969). This is to take further the point made by Berger, who says, '. . . the degree of sociability is determined not primarily by ecological location but by the homogeneity of the population'. B. M. Berger, *Working Class Suburb* (Univ. of California Press, Berkeley, 1968), p. xvi. See also H. J. Gans, *The Levittowners* (Pantheon, New York, 1967), R. Pahl, *Urbs in Rure* (L.S.E. Geographical Paper, No. 2, 1965).

4 As, for example, in Sparkbrook, J. Rex and R. Moore, op. cit., or inner Liverpool, C. Vereker, J. B. Mays, E. Gittus and M. Broady, *Urban Redevelopment and Social Change* (Liverpool Univ. Press, 1961).

5 See p. 67.

6 The streets and the persons living therein have been disguised to avoid embarrassment to those who may still be living there. We do not believe that the alterations have changed the sociological point of the observations made in any material way.

7 Cf. Oldside St., *T. & C.*, p. 113.

8 In *T. & C.* the elderly of both sexes were noted as one of three categories particularly tied to and reliant upon the immediate vicinity of their homes. Upon consultation Cyril Smith, who undertook the neighbouring studies for *T. & C.*, reports that he observed mutual aid in neighbouring in which the old were involved, as is reported in *T. & C.*, but that there was no marked interaction of old men in the streets in his observations.

9 No one of Mr Mayor's socio-economic category would have done this around 1950. There is a sense in which the spread of car ownership has altered the conditions for neighbouring. See also the gossip group in the garages referred to in the discussion of Wychtree, below.

10 Cf., *T. & C.*, Mrs Morgan in Tracey Avenue who did not mind people borrowing from her but who herself would not borrow. Mrs Clayton in Sonniton Street behaved similarly. Both women had a number of neighbours who relied upon them, but they maintained their independence.

11 Many studies have reported the limited effects of propinquity on neighbour relations. Cf., for example, H. J. Gans, op. cit., pp. 155–6.

12 Cf. Gans, op. cit., p. 161.

13 Cf. the two separate children's play groups in Sky View, *T. & C.*, p. 107.

14 Cf. the few in that otherwise friendly and highly interacting neighbour-hood in Old Barton Hill who kept their front doors shut and did not interact with neighbours. Hilda Jennings, op. cit.

15 *T. & C.*, p. 112. Cf. also Gans, op. cit., pp. 45, 159.

16 R. Pahl, op. cit.

17 J. M. Mann says that this was not true of his sample: most wanted a house or bungalow on an estate near a field (op. cit., pp. 371, 380).

18 Cf. P. Rossi, *Why Families Move*, Table 9.7, p. 164.

19 Other studies have noted the partial nature of house-seekers' know-ledge of the housing market; e.g. M. Stacey, *Housing Study Report*, No. 1, Lower Swansea Valley Project, 1963, mimeo., University College of Swansea.

20 In the same study Stacey (ibid.) noted that 'middle class' residential areas appeared to be the result of the withdrawal to these areas of some 'middle class' people, which left the older areas of the town more mixed than working class.

21 See p. 91.

22 Gans remarks for Levittown that the place was far less homogeneous than notions of the American suburb would lead one to expect and despite the fact that Levittown was more homogeneous as to age, family-cycle stage and income than would be an old-established town or city (op. cit., pp. 165–6).

   Sylvia F. Fava, 'Contrasts in Neighbouring: New York City and a Suburban County', in Wm. M. Dobriner (ed.), *The Suburban Community* (Putnam, 1958), p. 127, suggests persistent differences in neighbouring patterns between city and suburbs when variables such as sex, age, marital state, education are held constant and associated with self-selection to suburbs on the basis of willingness to neighbour.

23 Cultural differences must also be taken into account. See H. E. Bracey, *Neighbours* (Routledge & Kegan Paul, 1964).

24 In Liverpool it was found that common work roles did not increase neighbouring: Liverpool University, Dept of Social Science, *Neighbour-hood and Community*. But see J. M. Mann, op. cit., who confirms the importance to Birds migrants of friendships among neighbours which followed contacts made on the shop floor (pp. 392, 395, 397), although when surveyed in Birmingham employees had on the whole been against having workmates for neighbours (p. 250).

25 R. Frankenberg, 'Participant Observers', *New Soc.* (no. 23), 7 Mar. 1963, p. 22. Also Gans, op. cit., p. 46.

26 Mogey, op. cit., Jennings, op. cit., T. Brennan, *Reshaping a City* (House of Grant, 1959); Gans, op. cit., B. M. Berger, op. cit. and others have described and analysed part of the process in private American estates, but studies of English middle-class estates are lacking.

27 Cf. P. Rossi (*Why Families Move*, p. 90), who found that having friends in a neighbourhood did not discourage from moving.

28 *T. & C.*, pp. 111, 115, 124.

29 B. S. Trinder, 'Banbury's Poor in 1850', *Cake and Cock Horse* (Ban-bury Historical Society, Winter 1966).

30 N. Elias and J. L. Scotson, *The Established and the Outsiders* (Cass, 1965).

31 P. Willmott, *The Evolution of a Community* (Routledge & Kegan Paul, 1963).

32 Op. cit.

33 *T. & C.*, p. 108.

34 *T. & C.*, p. 107.

35 *T. & C.*, p. 104.

36 *T. & C.*, pp. 104–6.

8 Women and the family

1 The proportion of women in the labour force had risen from 28 per cent in 1950 to a third in 1967. In England and Wales in 1966 women made up 35·5 per cent of the labour force: *Sample Census, Economic Activity Tables*, pt. 1 (H.M.S.O., 1966).

2 *T. & C.*, p. 135.

3 *Annual Abstract of Statistics*, no. 105 (H.M.S.O., 1968).

4 *T. & C.*, p. 25.

5 See p. 50.

6 *T. & C.*, p. 125.

7 *T. & C.*, p. 135.

8 *T. & C.*, p. 136.

9 This sub-sample drawn from the main 6 per cent sample consisted of 139 men and women, married, whose elementary families of marriage were in the child-rearing stage of the family cycles, and all children still lived with them. The sample was stratified according to whether or not the wife was in paid employment at the time of sub-sample interview, and by whether or not the husband's job was categorized as manual or non-manual. See Appendix 1.

10 H. Gavron, *The Captive Wife* (Routledge & Kegan Paul, 1966), p. 33.

11 *T. & C.*, p. 135.

12 In *Comparability in Social Research* (Heinemann, 1969), p. 45, Margaret Stacey analyses the terms used in discussions of the family and kin. She concludes that her own terminology in *T. & C.* was confusing. In this chapter, therefore, the terminology recommended in that paper is followed. This necessitates some translation from *T. & C.* Thus, what she then called 'the immediate family' is now called 'the elementary family domestic group'. In *T. & C.* she frequently used 'extended family' to mean any relatives outside an elementary family, i.e. where 'kin' would have been a more appropriate term. 'Extended family' will now be restricted to its definition as in the text above. See Glossary.

13 *T. & C.*, p. 134.

14 More than one reason was given per respondent; most frequently in addition to the ones already cited, was that of relieving the boredom experienced by the wife in the home all day; one or two respondents made the point that this, too, was valuable from the point of view of the family's welfare, in that she herself was thereby 'better adjusted' and so the family atmosphere was correspondingly improved.

15 With regard to Birmingham women working in Birds before it trans-ferred to Banbury, J. M. Mann says (op. cit., p. 308), 'they simply never considered following their jobs to another town'. Those who did come to Banbury were married to Birds employees.

16 Cf. *T. & C.*, p. 133. In 1950 there were more married people than household heads in the 20–35 age group, while the reverse was true in all higher groups.

17 Cf. W. M. Williams, *The Sociology of an English Village: Gosforth* (Routledge & Kegan Paul, 1956); J. Littlejohn, op. cit., pp. 9–10; M. Stacey, *Housing* (1963).

18 26 per cent were parent(s) of the household head or his wife; 12 per cent sibs of one of them; 14 per cent were spouses of their children; 22 per cent were other relatives.

19 Of the 152 cases where kin were household members, 89 were relatives of the wife (64) or daughter (24) compared with 63 who were relatives of the husband (47) or son (15). Two cases cannot be allocated. Cf., *T. & C.*, pp. 123–4.

20 *T. & C.*, p. 123.

21 C. Bell, *Middle Class Families* (Routledge & Kegan Paul, 1968).

22 C. C. Harris and M. Stacey, 'A Note on the Extended Family' in M. Stacey (ed.), *Comparability*. . . .

23 7 of 115 said 'yes' to the question 'Have you or your spouse ever worked in the same firm as a relative?': 2 not occupationally mobile non-manual Banburians, 2 not occupationally mobile manual Ban-burians; 1 non-mobile non-manual immigrant, 2 non-mobile manual immigrants. Only 4 of the 115 had ever worked for a relative: all were Banburians, 3 non-mobile non-manual and 1 downwardly occupation-ally mobile.

24 4 Banburian and 2 immigrant manual workers, all spoken for by mothers.

25 Jane Hubert has noted that the middle classes may pay for houses or give deposits to their children in order not to have them living at home. See 'Kinship and Geographical Mobility in a sample from a London middle-class area', *Int. J. of Comp. Soc.*, vol. 6, no. 1, 1965, p. 64. See also Stacey, *Housing* (1963).

9 Inequality and order: social class, social status and power

1 F. Parkin, *Class Inequality and Political Order* (MacGibbon & Kee, 1971).

2 See pp. 78–80.

3 T. H. Marshall, *Sociology at the Crossroads* (Heinemann, 1963), pp. 204, 216.

4 Ibid., p. 216.

5 See pp. 26–9.

6 See pp. 68–9.

7 M. Stacey, 'Myth of Community Studies'.

8 By *social level* we mean large categories of people with distinguishably different standards of living, styles of life, purchasing power: see

T. H. Marshall, *Sociology at the Crossroads*, p. 145, and R. A. Nisbet, *The Social Bond* (Knopf, New York, 1970), p. 207. We do not wish to include the notion of a larger sociological identity, normatively derived, associated with each level as Nisbet does. This in our view is a matter of empirical inquiry. We have avoided the use of *social class* in this context because we wish to restrict it to 'groups possessed both of real and vital common economic interests and of a group-consciousness of their general position in the social scale' (Marshall, op. cit., p. 149). Social levels may or may not be social classes in this sense. See also Glossary.

9 Cf. Marshall, *Sociology at the Crossroads*, p. 216.

10 W. M. Williams, op. cit.

11 See p. 41.

12 J. H. Goldthorpe and D. Lockwood, 'Affluence and the British Class Structure', *Sov. Rev.*, vol. 11, no. 2, July 1963, pp. 135–6.

13 A sub-sample of the main 6 per cent was interviewed. The sub-sample was stratified by skill and by the size of plant they worked in. It consisted of 79 manual workers, 38 in small plants and 41 in large plants, and 38 non-manual workers, 18 in small plants and 20 in large. Respondents were interviewed early in 1968. See Appendix 1.

14 Parkin, op. cit., p. 56.

15 We use *status* to mean position in society. See also Glossary.

16 J. Rex and R. Moore, op. cit.

17 N. Dennis, *People and Planning*.

18 It will also be remembered that migrants are more often in higher occupational status than Banburians. Chapter 2, p. 26.

19 Vere Hole, 'Housing in Social Research' in E. Gittus (ed.), *Key Variables in Social Research*, vol. 1: *Religion, Housing, Locality* (B.S.A./Heinemann, 1972), chap. 2. This refines the point made by Rex and Moore, op. cit.

20 Watson, op. cit.; Merton, op. cit., pp. 387 ff.

Academic sociologists also fall into this category; many of them have been upwardly mobile through educational achievement. In addition it is the academic's business to sell education. All these factors taken together may have led sociologists to over-estimate the importance of formal education.

21 See pp. 27–9.

22 O. Banks, *The Sociology of Education* (Batsford, 1968), p. 39.

23 These data are consistent with C. A. Anderson's 'Skeptical Note', derived from a re-analysis of Glass's social mobility data in A. H. Halsey *et al.* (eds.), *Education, Economy and Society* (Free Press, New York, 1961).

24 See p. 45.

25 Raymond Aron, *Progress and Disillusion* (Penguin, Harmondsworth, 1972), pp. 35–6.

26 R. Aron, *Progress and Disillusion*, p. 58.

27 Cf. Anthony Giddens, 'Élites in the British Class Structure', *Soc. Rev.* vol. 20, no. 3, Aug. 1972, pp. 345–72, especially p. 348: '. . . there can exist a "governing class" without it necessarily being a "ruling class":

... there can exist a "power élite" without there being either a "ruling" or a "governing class" ... there can be a system of "leadership groups" which constitutes neither "power élite" nor "governing class" nor "ruling class"; ... all ... compatible with ... an "upper class"; and ... *none* ... prejudices the relative primacy of the "political" and "economic" spheres within the class structure.'

28 For example, J. S. Furnivall, *Colonial Policy and Practice* (C.U.P., 1948), M. G. Smith, 'Social and Cultural Pluralism', *Annals of the New York Academy of Sciences*, 83, 20 Jan. 1960, pp. 763–77.
29 Cf. N. W. Polsby, *Community Power and Political Theory* (Yale Univ. Press, New Haven, Conn., 1963).
30 Goldthorpe *et al.*, *The Affluent Worker*, vols. 1–3.
31 Goldthorpe *et al.*, op. cit., vol. 3, p. 195.
32 K. Marx, *The Poverty of Philosophy*, trans H. Quelch (Chs. H. Kerr & Co., Chicago, 1910).
33 M. Ginsberg, *Sociology* (O.U.P., 1934), p. 40.
34 A. C. Mayer 'The Significance of Quasi-groups in the Study of Complex Societies' in M. Banton (ed.), *The Social Anthropology of Complex Societies* (Tavistock Publications, 1966), pp. 97–122.
35 Op. cit.
36 As Aron has pointed out, consciousness and purpose reside in a political party rather than in the class as a whole (*Progress and Disillusion*, p. 42).
37 Goldthorpe *et al.*, op. cit., vol. 3, p. 169.

Appendix 1   The samples

1 Copies of the schedule are available from the Department of Sociology and Anthropology, University College, Swansea.
2 The interviewer instructions are available with the schedules.
3 Copies of the schedules used are available from the Department of Sociology and Anthropology, University College, Swansea.

Appendix 3   Voluntary associations

1 *T. & C.*, p. 75.
2 *T. & C.*, p. 77. Cf. T. Brennan, E. W. Cooney, and H. Pollins, *Social Change in South West Wales* (Watts, 1954); T. Bottomore, 'Social Stratification in Voluntary Organizations', chap. 13 of D. V. Glass (ed.), *Social Mobility in Britain* (Routledge & Kegan Paul, 1954).
3 The schedules are available from University College, Swansea.
4 *T. & C.*, pp. 75–6.
5 M. Gluckman, 'Ethnographic data in British Social Anthropology', *Soc. Rev.*, vol. 9, no. 1, 1961, pp. 5–17.
6 Adrian C. Mayer, 'The Significance of Quasi-groups in the Study of Complex Societies' in M. Banton (ed.), *The Social Anthropology of Complex Societies* (Tavistock Publications, 1966), pp. 97–122.
7 H. J. Laski, 'Freedom of Association' in *Encyclopaedia of the Social Sciences* (The Macmillan Co., New York, 1931), vol. 6, pp. 447–50.

8 Cf. M. Hausknecht, *The Joiners: a sociological description of voluntary association membership in the United States* (Bedminster, Totowa, N. J., 1962).

9 J. Clyde Mitchell, 'Theoretical Orientations in African Urban Studies' in M. Banton (ed.), op. cit., pp. 37–68.

10 E. Bott, *Family and Social Network* (Tavistock Publications, 1957); J. A. Barnes, 'Class and Committees in a Norwegian Island Parish', *Hum. Rel.*, vol. 7, no. 1, 1954, pp. 39–58.

Appendix 4   Thrift clubs

1 It was an acknowledged omission of the first study that insufficient attention was paid to pubs in the context of neighbouring, although their importance was recognized throughout the study.

Appendix 7   Party politics

1 See also Appendix 5.

Bibliography

ANDERSON, C. A., 'A Skeptical Note on Education and Mobility' in A. H. Halsey, J. Floud, and C. A. Anderson (eds.), *Education, Economy and Society* (Free Press, New York, 1961).

Annual Abstract of Statistics, no. 105 (H.M.S.O., 1968).

ARENSBERG, C. M., *The Irish Countryman* (Harvard Univ. Press, Cambridge, Mass., 1950).

—— and KIMBALL, S. T., *Family and Community in Ireland* (Harvard Univ. Press, Cambridge, Mass., 1940).

—— —— *Culture and Community* (Harcourt, Brace and World, New York, 1965).

ARON, R., *German Sociology*, trans. T. B. and M. Bottomore (Heinemann, 1957).

—— *Eighteen Lectures on Industrial Society* (Weidenfeld & Nicolson, 1967).

—— *Progress and Disillusion, the dialectics of modern society* (Pelican, Harmondsworth, 1972).

AXELROD, M., 'Urban Structure and Social Participation', *A.S.R.*, vol. 21, no. 1, 1956, pp. 13–18.

BAILEY, F. G., *Stratagems and Spoils: a social anthropology of politics* (Blackwell, Oxford, 1969).

—— (ed.), *Gifts and Poisons: the politics of reputation* (Blackwell, Oxford, 1971).

BANBURY AND DISTRICT CIVIC SOCIETY, *Bulletin* no. 8, April 1966.

BANKS, O., *The Sociology of Education* (Batsford, 1968).

BANTON, M., *Roles* (Tavistock Publications, 1965).

—— (ed.), *The Social Anthropology of Complex Societies* (Tavistock Publications, 1966), pp. 97–122.

BARNES, J. A., 'Class and Committees in a Norwegian Island Parish', *Hum. Rel.*, vol. 7, no. 1, 1954, pp. 39–58.

BARR, J., 'What Place for the Family Firm?', *New Soc.*, 26 Oct. 1967.

BARTLETT D., and WALKER, J., 'Inner Circle', *New. Soc.*, 19 Apr. 1973, p. 139.

BATSTONE, E. V., 'Aspects of Stratification in a Community Context', Ph.D. thesis, University of Wales, 1970.

183

BEALEY, F., BLONDEL J., and MCCANN, W. P., *Constituency Politics: a study of Newcastle-under-Lyme* (Faber, 1965).

BECHHOFER, F., 'Occupations' in M. Stacey (ed.), *Comparability in Social Research* (Heinemann, 1969).

BELL, C., *Middle Class Families* (Routledge & Kegan Paul, 1968).

—— and NEWBY, H., *Community Studies* (Allen & Unwin, 1971).

BELL W., and FORCE, M. T., 'Urban Neighbourhood types and participation in Formal Associations', *A.S.R.*, vol. 21, no. 1, 1956, pp. 25–34.

BERGER, B. M., *Working Class Suburb* (Univ. of California Press, Berkeley, 1968).

BERGER, P., 'Religious Institutions' in N. J. Smelser (ed.), *Sociology: an introduction* (Wiley, New York, 1967).

—— and LUCKMANN, T., *The Social Construction of Reality* (Allen Lane, 1967).

—— —— 'Sociology of Religion and Sociology of Knowledge' in R. Robertson (ed.), *Sociology of Religion* (Penguin, Harmondsworth, 1969).

BERRY, D., 'Party Membership and Social Participation', *Pol. Stud.*, vol. 17, no. 2, 1969, pp. 196–207.

BEST, G. F. A., 'An Appraisal of Establishment' in W. S. F. Pickering (ed.), *Anglican–Methodist Relations* (Darton, Longman & Todd, 1961).

BIRCH, A. H., *Small Town Politics* (O.U.P., 1959).

BLAU, P. M., and SCOTT, W. R., *Formal Organizations* (Routledge & Kegan Paul, 1963).

BOTT, E., *Family and Social Network* (Tavistock Publications, 1957).

BOTTOMORE, T., 'Social Stratification in Voluntary Organizations' in D.V. Glass (ed.), *Social Mobility in Britain* (Routledge & Kegan Paul, 1954), chap. 13.

BRACEY, H. E., *Neighbours* (Routledge & Kegan Paul, 1964).

BRENNAN, T., *Reshaping a City* (House of Grant, 1959).

—— COONEY, E. W., and POLLINS, H., *Social Change in South West Wales* (Watts, 1954).

BROTHERS, J., *Religious Institutions* (Longman, 1971).

BROWN, L. C., 'Unionisation in Small Plants I', *Soc. Ord.*, vol. 6, no. 4, 1956.

BRUYN, S., *The Humanistic Perspective in Sociology* (Prentice-Hall, Englewood Cliffs, N.J., 1966).

BULPITT, J. G., *Party Politics in English Local Government* (Longmans, Green & Co., 1967).

CAUTER, T., and DOWNHAM, J. S., *The Communication of Ideas* (Chatto & Windus, 1954).

CENSUS, *Sample Census 1966, Oxfordshire County Report, Economic Activity Tables* (H.M.S.O., 1967).

CHAMBERS, R. C., 'A Study of Three Voluntary Organizations' in D. V. Glass (ed.), *Social Mobility in Britain* (Routledge & Kegan Paul, 1954), chap. 14.

CHINOY, E., *Society* (Random House, New York, 1961).

CLELAND, S., *Influence of Plant Size on Industrial Relations* (Princeton Univ. Press, 1955).

COULSON, M., and RIDDELL, D., *Approaching Sociology* (Routledge & Kegan Paul, 1970).

CROZIER, M., *The Bureaucratic Phenomenon* (Tavistock Publications, 1964).

CULLINGWORTH, J. B., 'The Swindon Social Survey: a Second Report on the Social Implications of Overspill', *Soc. Rev.*, vol. 9, no. 2, 1961, pp. 151–66.

—— *Town and Country Planning in England and Wales* (Allen & Unwin, 1964).

CURTIS, R. F., 'Occupational Mobility and Membership in Formal Voluntary Associations: a note on research', *A.S.R.*, vol. 24, no. 6, 1959, pp. 846–8.

DAVIS, A., and GARDNER, B. B. and M. R., *Deep South* (Univ. of Chicago Press, Chicago, 1941).

DENNIS, N., 'Changes in Function and Leadership Renewal', *Soc. Rev.*, vol. 9, no. 1, 1961, pp. 55–84.

—— *People in Planning: the sociology of housing in Sunderland* (Faber & Faber, 1970).

—— *Planning and Public Participation* (Faber & Faber, 1972).

DOBRINER, W. M. (ed.), *The Suburban Community* (Putnam, 1958).

DOTSON, F., 'Patterns of Voluntary Associations among Urban Working-Class Families', *A.S.R.*, vol 16, no. 5, 1951, pp. 687–93.

DUVIGNAUD, J., *Change at Shebika* (Pantheon, New York, 1970).

ELIAS, N., and SCOTSON, J. L., *The Established and the Outsiders* (Cass, 1965).

EPSTEIN, A. L., *The Craft of Social Anthropology* (Tavistock Publications, 1967).

ETZIONI, A., *A Comparative Analysis of Complex Organizations* (Free Press, New York; Collier Macmillan, London, 1961).

FAVA, S. F., 'Contrasts in Neighbouring: New York City and a Surburban County', in W. M. Dobriner (ed.), *The Surburban Community* (Putman, 1958).

FINER, S. E., *Anonymous Empire: a study of the lobby in Great Britain*, 2nd edn. (Pall Mall Press, 1966).

FIRTH, R., *History and Traditions of Tikopia* (Polynesian Soc., 1961).

FRANKENBERG, R., *Village on the Border* (Cohen & West, 1957).

—— 'Participant Observers', *New Soc.* (no. 23), 7 Mar. 1963.

—— *Communities in Britain* (Penguin, Harmondsworth, 1966).

FREEMAN, H., NOVAK, E., and REEDER, L. G., 'Correlates of Membership in Voluntary Associations', *A.S.R.*, vol. 22, no. 5, 1957, pp. 528–33.

FURNIVALL, J. S., *Colonial Policy and Practice* (C.U.P., 1948).

GALLAHER, JR., A., *Plainville Fifteen Years Later* (Columbia Univ. Press, New York, 1961).

—— 'Plainville: The Twice-Studied Town' in A. J. Vidich, J. Bensman and M. R. Stein, *Reflections on Community Studies* (Wiley, New York, 1964).

GANS, H. J., *The Levittowners* (Pantheon, New York, 1967).

GAVRON, H., *The Captive Wife* (Routledge & Kegan Paul, 1966).

GERTH, H., and MILLS, C. W., *From Max Weber: Essays in Sociology* (Routledge & Kegan Paul, 1947).

185

GIDDENS, A., 'Élites in the British Class Structure', *Soc. Rev.*, vol. 20, no. 3, Aug. 1972, pp. 345–72.

GINSBERG, M., *Sociology* (Butterworth, 1934).

GITTUS, E., 'Incomes' in M. Stacey (ed.), *Comparability in Social Research* (Heinemann, 1969).

—— (ed.), *Key Variables in Social Research*, vol. 1: *Religion, Housing, Locality* (B.S.A./Heinemann, 1972).

GLASER, B. G., *Organizational Scientists* (Bobbs-Merrill Co., Indianapolis, Ind., 1964).

GLASS, D.,(ed.), *Social Mobility in Britain* (Routledge & Kegan Paul, 1954).

GLUCKMAN, M., *The Judicial Process among the Barotse of Northern Rhodesia* (Manchester Univ. Press, 1955).

—— 'Ethnographic data in British Social Anthropology', *Soc. Rev.*, vol. 9, no. 1, 1961, pp. 5–17.

—— (ed.), *Closed Systems and Open Minds* (Oliver & Boyd, Edinburgh, 1964).

—— Introduction to A. L. Epstein, *The Craft of Social Anthropology* (Tavistock Publications, 1967).

GOFFMAN, E., *Presentation of Self in Everyday Life*, University of Edinburgh Social Science Research Centre, Monograph no. 2, 1956 (Doubleday Anchor, New York, 1959; Penguin, Harmondsworth, 1969).

GOLDBERG, L. C., *et al.*, 'Local Cosmopolitan: Uni-dimensional or Multidimensional?', *A.J.S.*, vol. 70, no. 6, 1965.

GOLDTHORPE, J. H., 'Orientation to Work and Industrial Behaviour' (unpublished, 1964).

—— and LOCKWOOD, D., 'Affluence and the British Class Structure', *Soc. Rev.*, vol. 11, no. 2, July 1963.

—— —— BECHHOFER, F., and PLATT, J., *The Affluent Worker* (C.U.P., 1968–9): vol. 1, *Industrial Attitudes and Behaviour* (1968); vol. 2, *Political Attitudes and Behaviour* (1968); vol. 3, *The Affluent Worker in the Class Structure* (1969).

GOODE, E., 'Social Class and Church Participation', *A.J.S.*, vol. 72, no. 1, July 1966.

GOULDNER, A. W., *Wildcat Strike* (Routledge & Kegan Paul, 1955).

HALL, R. H., and TITTLE, C., 'A note on bureaucracy and its "correlates" ', *A.J.S.*, vol. 72, no. 3, 1966.

HAMMOND, H., 'Continuity and Conscious Models in County Clare and Ashworthy: a reappraisal', *Sociology*, vol. 2, no. 1, 1968.

HARRIS, C. C., 'Reform in a Normative Organization', *Soc. Rev.*, vol. 17, no. 2, July 1969.

—— and STACEY, M. 'A Note on the Extended Family' in M. Stacey (ed.), *Comparability in Social Research* (Heinemann, 1969).

HARRIS, N., *Beliefs in Society* (Watts, 1968).

HAUSKNECHT, M., *The Joiners: a sociological description of voluntary association membership in the United States* (Bedminster, Totowa, N.J., 1962).

HENNINGSEN, G., 'Fatalism in Systematic Aspect and Fatalism in its Functional Context' in H. Ringgren (ed.), *Fatalistic Beliefs in Religion, Folklore and Literature* (Almquist, 1967).

HILL, C., *Puritanism and Revolution* (Secker & Warburg, 1958; Panther, 1968).

HINDESS, B., *Decline of Working Class Politics* (McGibbon & Kee, 1971).

HOBHOUSE, L. T., *Morals in Evolution* (Chapman & Hall, 1923).

—— WHEELER, G. C., and GINSBERG, M., *The Material Culture and Social Institutions of the Simpler Peoples* (Chapman & Hall, 1915).

HOLE, V., 'Housing in Social Research' in E. Gittus (ed.), *Key Variables in Social Research*, vol. 1: *Religion, Housing, Locality* (B.S.A./Heinemann, 1972).

HUBERT, J., 'Kinship and Geographic Mobility in a sample from a London middle-class area', *Int. J. Comp. Soc.*, vol. 6, no. 1, 1965.

HUTSON, J., 'A Politician in Valloire' in F. G. Bailey (ed.), *Gifts and Poisons* (Blackwell, Oxford, 1971).

INDIK, B. P., 'Some effects of Organization size on member attitudes and behaviour', *Hum. Rel.*, vol. 16, no. 4, 1963.

INGHAM, G. K., 'Organizational Size, Orientation to Work and Industrial Behaviour', *Sociology*, vol. 1, no. 3, 1967.

JACKSON, J. A., *Social Stratification* (C.U.P., 1968).

JENNINGS, H., *Societies in the Making, a study of development and re-development within a County Borough* (Routledge & Kegan Paul, 1962).

KLEIN, J., *Samples from English Cultures*, 2 vols. (Routledge & Kegan Paul, 1965).

KOMAROVSKY, M., 'The Voluntary Association of Urban Dwellers', *A.S.R.*, vol. 11, no. 6, 1946, pp. 686–98.

KRAUSZ, E., 'Religion as a key variable' in E. Gittus (ed.), *Key Variables in Social Research*, vol. 1 (Heinemann, 1972).

LAPPING, B., and RADICE, G., (eds.), *More Power to the People* (Longmans, Green & Co., 1968).

LASKI, H. J., 'Freedom of Association' in *Encyclopaedia of the Social Sciences* (The Macmillan Co., New York, 1931), vol. 6, pp. 447–50.

LEE, R., *The Social Sources of Church Unity* (Abingdon Press, New York, 1960).

LERNER, D., *The Passing of Traditional Society* (Free Press, Glencoe, Ill., 1958).

LEWIS, O., *Life in a Mexican Village: Tepoztlan Restudied* (Univ. of Illinois Press, Urbana, 1951).

LINTON, R., *The Study of Man* (Appleton-Century, New York, 1936).

LITTLEJOHN, J., *Westrigg: The Sociology of a Cheviot Parish* (Routledge & Kegan Paul, 1963).

LITWAK, E., 'Voluntary Associations and Neighbourhood Cohesion', *A.S.R.*, vol. 26, no. 2, 1961, pp. 258–71.

LIVERPOOL UNIVERSITY, Dept. of Social Science, *Neighbourhood and Community* (Liverpool Univ. Press, 1954).

LOCKWOOD, D., 'Sources of Variation in Working Class Images of Society', *Soc. Rev.*, vol. 14, no. 3, 1966.

LOWE, S. R., *The Churches' Role in the Care of the Elderly*, 1969 (from the Revd. S. R. Lowe, 28 Glaisdale Rd., Birmingham, 25).

LYND, R. S. and H. M., *Middletown* (New York, 1929).

—— —— *Middletown in Transition* (Harcourt Brace, New York, 1937).

187

MacKenzie, W. J. M., 'Pressure Groups in British Government' in R. Rose (ed.), *Studies in British Politics* (Macmillan, 1966). (Reprinted from *Brit. J. Sociol.*, vol. 6, no. 2, 1955.)

Malinowski, B., *Argonauts of the Western Pacific* (Routledge & Kegan Paul, 1964).

Mann, J. M., 'Sociological Aspects of Factory Relocation: a case study', D. Phil. thesis, Univ. of Oxford, 1970.

—— *Workers on the Move* (C.U.P., 1973).

Mann, P. H., *An Approach to Urban Sociology* (Routledge & Kegan Paul, 1965).

Marris, P., and Somerset, A., *African Businessmen: a study of entrepreneurship and development in Kenya* (Routledge & Kegan Paul, 1971).

Marshall, T. H., *Citizenship and Social Class* (C.U.P., 1950).

—— *Sociology at the Crossroads* (Heinemann, 1963).

—— 'Reflections on Power', *Sociology*, vol. 3, no. 2, 1969.

Martin, D., *A Sociology of English Religion* (S.C.M. Press, London, 1967).

—— *The Religious and the Secular* (Routledge & Kegan Paul, 1969).

Marx, K., *The Poverty of Philosophy*, trans. H. Quelch (Chs. H. Kerr & Co., Chicago, 1910).

Mayer, A. C., 'The Significance of Quasi-groups in the Study of Complex Societies' in M. Banton (ed.), *The Social Anthropology of Complex Societies* (Tavistock Publications, 1966), pp. 97–122.

Merton, R. K., *Social Theory and Social Structure* (Collier Macmillan, revised edn. 1965).

Mills, C. Wright, *The Sociological Imagination* (O.U.P., 1959).

Ministry of Labour, *Monthly Digest of Statistics* (H.M.S.O.).

Mitchell, J. Clyde, 'Theoretical Orientations in African Urban Studies' in M. Banton (ed.), *The Social Anthropology of Complex Societies* (Tavistock Publications, 1966), pp. 37–68.

—— (ed.), *Social Networks in Urban Situations* (Manchester Univ. Press, 1969).

Mogey, J. M., *Family and Neighbourhood* (O.U.P., 1956).

Moore, Jack, 'Town Development: a case study of Banbury,' unpub. thesis, Dept. of Land Use Studies, Schl. of Architecture and Bldng, Oxford, April 1966.

Morris, D. S. and Newton, K., *Onymous Empire: Voluntary Organizations in Birmingham Politics*, Discussion Papers, series F, no. 10, Birmingham Politics and Society, December 1970.

Newton, K., 'City Politics in Britain and the United States', *Pol. Stud.*, vol. 17, no. 2, 1969, pp. 208–18.

—— 'Community Decision-Making and Community Decision-Makers in England and the U.S.' (paper to Varna International Sociological Association Conference), 1970.

Niebuhr, H. R., *The Social Sources of Denominationalism* (P. Smith, Gloucester, Mass., 1963).

Nisbet, R. A., *The Social Bond* (Knopf, New York, 1970).

Pahl, R., *Urbs in Rure*, L.S.E. Geographical Paper, no. 2, 1965.

Parkin, F., *Class Inequality and Political Order* (MacGibbon & Kee, 1971).

PARSONS, T., *Essays in Sociological Theory, Pure and Applied* (revised edn., Free Press of Glencoe, Collier Macmillan, London, 1964).

PAUL, L., *The Development and Payment of the Clergy* (Church Information Office, 1964).

PICKERING, W. S. F., (ed.), *Anglican–Methodist Relations* (Darton, Longman & Todd, 1961).

PLOWMAN, D. E. G., MINCHINTON, W. E., and STACEY, M., 'Local Status in England and Wales', *Soc. Rev.*, vol. 10, no. 2 July 1962.

POLSBY, N. W., *Community Power and Political Theory* (Yale Univ. Press, New Haven, Conn., 1963).

PUGH, D. S., *et al.*, 'A Conceptual Scheme for Organizational Analysis', *A.S.Q.*, vol. 8, no. 3, 1963.

PUNNETT, R. M., *British Government and Politics* (Heinemann, 1968).

RADICE, Giles, 'Extending Democracy' in B. Lapping and G. Radice (eds.), *More Power to the People* (Longmans, Green & Co., 1968).

RADIN, M., 'Tradition' in *Encyclopaedia of the Social Sciences* (The Macmillan Co., New York, 1934), vol. 15.

REES, A., 'Democracy in Local Government' in B. Lapping and G. Radice (eds.), *More Power to the People* (Longmans, Green 1968).

REVANS, R. W., 'Big Firms', *New Soc.*, 5 Oct. 1967.

REX, J., and MOORE, R., *Race, Community and Conflict: a study of Sparkbrook* (O.U.P., 1967).

RICHARDS, P. G., *The New Local Government System* (Allen & Unwin, 1968).

ROBERTSON, R. (ed.), *Sociology of Religion* (Penguin, Harmondsworth, 1969).

—— (ed.), *The Sociological Interpretation of Religion* (Blackwell, Oxford, 1970).

RODGERS, H. B., VOS, A. B. de, and HERBERT, D. T., *Overspill in Winsford: a social and economic survey of the progress of the Winsford Town Expansion Scheme* (publ. for Winsford Council; printed by Guardian Press, Einsford, 1965).

ROHDEN, P., 'Traditionalism', *Encyclopaedia of the Social Sciences* (The Macmillan Co., New York, 1935), vol. 15.

ROSSER, C., and HARRIS, C. C., *The Family and Social Change: a study of family and kinship in a South Wales Town* (Routledge & Kegan Paul, 1965).

ROSSI, P. H., *Why Families Move* (Free Press, Glencoe, Ill., 1955).

—— 'The Organizational Structure of an American Community' (1961) in A. Etzioni (ed.), *Complex Organizations: a sociological reader* (Holt, Rinehart and Winston, New York, 1965).

RUNCIMAN, W. G., *Relative Deprivation and Social Justice* (Routledge & Kegan Paul, 1966).

SAYRE, W. S., and KAUFMAN, H., *Governing New York City* (Norton, New York, 1965).

SCOTT, Jnr., J. C., 'Membership and Participation in Voluntary Associations', *A.S.R.*, vol. 22, no. 3, 1957, pp. 315–26.

SHILS, E., 'Deference' in J. A. Jackson (ed.), *Social Stratification* (C.U.P., 1968).

SILLS, D. L., 'The Succession of Goals' (1957) in A. Etzioni (ed.), *Complex Organizations: a sociological reader* (Holt, Rinehart and Winston, New York, 1965).

SMIGEL, E. D., 'Public Attitudes toward stealing as related to the size of the victim organization', *A.S.R.*, vol. 21, no. 3, 1956.

SMITH, M. G., 'Social and Cultural Pluralism', *Annals of the New York Academy of Sciences*, 83, 20 Jan. 1960, pp. 763–77.

SOCIAL SURVEYS LTD., *Television and Religion* (Univ. of London Press, 1964).

SOROKIN, P., *Society, Culture and Personality* (quoted in T. H. Marshall, *Sociology at the Crossroads*, q.v.).

SOUTHALL, A., 'An Operational Theory of Role', *Hum. Rel.*, vol. 12, no. 1, 1959.

STACEY, F., *The Government of Modern Britain* (Clarendon Press, Oxford, 1968).

STACEY, M., *Tradition and Change: a study of Banbury* (O.U.P., 1960).

—— *Housing Study Report*, No. 1, Lower Swansea Valley Project University College of Swansea, 1963, mimeo.

—— (ed.), *Comparability in Social Research* (Heinemann, 1969).

—— *Methods of Social Research* (Pergamon, 1969).

—— 'The Myth of Community Studies', *Brit. J. Sociol.*, vol. 20, no. 2, June 1969.

Standard Industrial Classification (H.M.S.O., 1968).

STEIN, M., *The Eclipse of Community: an interpretation of American Studies* (Princeton Univ. Press, 1960; Harper and Row, New York (Harper Torchbooks), 1964).

TRADES UNION CONGRESS, *Selected Written Evidence submitted to the Royal Commission on Trade Unions and Employers Associations* (H.M.S.O., 1966).

TREVELYAN, G. M., *A Shortened History of England* (Penguin, Harmondsworth, 1959).

TRINDER, B. S., *The Methodist Church, Marlborough Road, Banbury* (in association with Banbury Historical Society, May 1965, printed by Banbury Advertiser Press Ltd.).

—— 'Banbury's Poor in 1850', *Cake and Cock Horse*, Banbury Historical Society, Winter 1966.

TURNER, R. H., 'Role: Sociological Aspects' in D. Sills (ed.), *International Encyclopaedia of the Social Sciences* (Macmillan and Free Press, New York, 1968), vol. 13, p. 555.

VEREKER, C., MAYS, J. B., GITTUS, E., and BROADY, M., *Urban Redevelopment and Social Change* (Liverpool Univ. Press, 1961).

VIDICH, A. J., and BENSMAN, J., *Small Town in Mass Society* (Doubleday Anchor, New York, 1960).

WARNER, W. Lloyd, *Democracy in Jonesville* (Harper, New York, 1949).

—— and LUNT, P. S., *The Social Life of a Modern Community* (Yankee City series) (Yale Univ. Press, New Haven, Conn., 1941).

WATSON, W., 'Social Mobility and Social Class in Industrial Communities' in M. Gluckman (ed.), *Closed Systems and Open Minds* (Oliver & Boyd, Edinburgh, 1964).

WEBER, M., *The Theory of Social and Economic Organization* (Free Press, Glencoe, Ill., 1964).

WELLS, A., *Social Institutions* (Heinemann, 1970).

WHEELDON, P. D., 'The Operation of Voluntary Associations' in J. Clyde Mitchell (ed.) *Social Networks in Urban Situations* (Manchester Univ. Press, 1969).

WICKHAM, E. R., *Church and People in an Industrial City* (Lutterworth Press, 1957).

WILLIAMS, R., 'Literature and Rural Society', *The Listener*, vol. 78, 16 November, 1967, pp. 630–2.

WILLIAMS, W. M., *The Sociology of an English Village: Gosforth* (Routledge & Kegan Paul, 1956).

WILLMOTT, P., *The Evolution of a Community* (Routledge & Kegan Paul, 1963).

—— and YOUNG, M., *Family and Class in a London Suburb* (Routledge & Kegan Paul, 1960).

WILSON, B., *Religion in Secular Society* (Watts, 1966).

WRIGHT, C. R., and HYMAN, H. H., 'Voluntary Association Memberships of American Adults: evidence from National Sample Surveys', *A.S.R.*, vol. 23, no. 3, 1958, pp. 284–94.

YOUNG, M., and SHILS, E., 'The Meaning of the Coronation', *Brit. J. Sociol.*, vol. 1, 1953.

—— and WILLMOTT, P., *Family and Kinship in East London* (Routledge & Kegan Paul, 1957).

Index

Routledge Social Science Series

Routledge & Kegan Paul   London and Boston

68–74 Carter Lane   London EC4V 5EL
9 Park Street   Boston   Mass 02108

Contents

*Authors wishing to submit manuscripts for any series in
this catalogue should send them to the Social Science Editor,
Routledge & Kegan Paul Ltd, 68–74 Carter Lane,
London EC4V 5EL*

● *Books so marked are available in paperback*
All books are in Metric Demy 8vo format (216 × 138mm approx.)

International Library of Sociology

General Editor John Rex

GENERAL SOCIOLOGY

Barnsley, J. H. The Social Reality of Ethics. *464 pp.*
Belshaw, Cyril. The Conditions of Social Performance. *An Exploratory Theory. 144 pp.*
Brown, Robert. Explanation in Social Science. *208 pp.*
● Rules and Laws in Sociology. *192 pp.*
Bruford, W. H. Chekhov and His Russia. *A Sociological Study. 244 pp.*
Cain, Maureen E. Society and the Policeman's Role. *326 pp.*
Gibson, Quentin. The Logic of Social Enquiry. *240 pp.*
Glucksmann, M. Structuralist Analysis in Contemporary Social Thought. *212 pp.*
Gurvitch, Georges. Sociology of Law. *Preface by Roscoe Pound. 264 pp.*
Hodge, H. A. Wilhelm Dilthey. *An Introduction. 184 pp.*
Homans, George C. Sentiments and Activities. *336 pp.*
Johnson, Harry M. Sociology: *a Systematic Introduction. Foreword by Robert K. Merton. 710 pp.*
Mannheim, Karl. Essays on Sociology and Social Psychology. *Edited by Paul Kecskemeti. With Editorial Note by Adolph Lowe. 344 pp.*
Systematic Sociology: *An Introduction to the Study of Society. Edited by J. S. Erös and Professor W. A. C. Stewart. 220 pp.*
Martindale, Don. The Nature and Types of Sociological Theory. *292 pp.*
●**Maus, Heinz.** A Short History of Sociology. *234 pp.*
Mey, Harald. Field-Theory. *A Study of its Application in the Social Sciences. 352 pp.*
Myrdal, Gunnar. Value in Social Theory: *A Collection of Essays on Methodology. Edited by Paul Streeten. 332 pp.*
Ogburn, William F., and **Nimkoff, Meyer F.** A Handbook of Sociology. *Preface by Karl Mannheim. 656 pp. 46 figures. 35 tables.*
Parsons, Talcott, and **Smelser, Neil J.** Economy and Society: *A Study in the Integration of Economic and Social Theory. 362 pp.*
●**Rex, John.** Key Problems of Sociological Theory. *220 pp.*
Discovering Sociology. *278 pp.*
Sociology and the Demystification of the Modern World. *282 pp.*
●**Rex, John** (Ed.) Approaches to Sociology. *Contributions by Peter Abell, Frank Bechhofer, Basil Bernstein, Ronald Fletcher, David Frisby, Miriam Glucksmann, Peter Lassman, Herminio Martins, John Rex, Roland Robertson, John Westergaard and Jock Young. 302 pp.*
Rigby, A. Alternative Realities. *352 pp.*
Roche, M. Phenomenology, Language and the Social Sciences. *374 pp.*
Sahay, A. Sociological Analysis. *220 pp.*
Urry, John. Reference Groups and the Theory of Revolution. *244 pp.*
Weinberg, E. Development of Sociology in the Soviet Union. *173 pp.*

FOREIGN CLASSICS OF SOCIOLOGY

●**Durkheim, Emile.** Suicide. *A Study in Sociology. Edited and with an Introduction by George Simpson. 404 pp.*
Professional Ethics and Civic Morals. *Translated by Cornelia Brookfield. 288 pp.*

●**Gerth, H. H.,** and **Mills, C. Wright.** From Max Weber: *Essays in Sociology. 502 pp.*

●**Tönnies, Ferdinand.** Community and Association. (*Gemeinschaft und Gesellschaft.) Translated and Supplemented by Charles P. Loomis. Foreword by Pitirim A. Sorokin. 334 pp.*

SOCIAL STRUCTURE

Andreski, Stanislav. Military Organization and Society. *Foreword by Professor A. R. Radcliffe-Brown. 226 pp. 1 folder.*

Coontz, Sydney H. Population Theories and the Economic Interpretation. *202 pp.*

Coser, Lewis. The Functions of Social Conflict. *204 pp.*

Dickie-Clark, H. F. Marginal Situation: *A Sociological Study of a Coloured Group. 240 pp. 11 tables.*

Glaser, Barney, and **Strauss, Anselm L.** Status Passage. *A Formal Theory. 208 pp.*

Glass, D. V. (Ed.) Social Mobility in Britain. *Contributions by J. Berent, T. Bottomore, R. C. Chambers, J. Floud, D. V. Glass, J. R. Hall, H. T. Himmelweit, R. K. Kelsall, F. M. Martin, C. A. Moser, R. Mukherjee, and W. Ziegel. 420 pp.*

Jones, Garth N. Planned Organizational Change: *An Exploratory Study Using an Empirical Approach. 268 pp.*

Kelsall, R. K. Higher Civil Servants in Britain: *From 1870 to the Present Day. 268 pp. 31 tables.*

König, René. The Community. *232 pp. Illustrated.·*

●**Lawton, Denis.** Social Class, Language and Education. *192 pp.*

McLeish, John. The Theory of Social Change: *Four Views Considered. 128 pp.*

Marsh, David C. The Changing Social Structure of England and Wales, 1871-1961. *288 pp.*

Mouzelis, Nicos. Organization and Bureaucracy. *An Analysis of Modern Theories. 240 pp.*

Mulkay, M. J. Functionalism, Exchange and Theoretical Strategy. *272 pp.*

Ossowski, Stanislaw. Class Structure in the Social Consciousness. *210 pp.*

Podgórecki, Adam. Law and Society. *About 300 pp.*

SOCIOLOGY AND POLITICS

Acton, T. A. Gypsy Politics and Social Change. *316 pp.*

Hechter, Michael. Internal Colonialism. *The Celtic Fringe in British National Development, 1536–1966. About 350 pp.*

Hertz, Frederick. Nationality in History and Politics: *A Psychology and Sociology of National Sentiment and Nationalism. 432 pp.*

Kornhauser, William. The Politics of Mass Society. *272 pp. 20 tables.*

Laidler, Harry W. History of Socialism. *Social-Economic Movements: An Historical and Comparative Survey of Socialism, Communism, Co-operation, Utopianism; and other Systems of Reform and Reconstruction. 992 pp.*

Lasswell, H. D. Analysis of Political Behaviour. *324 pp.*

Mannheim, Karl. Freedom, Power and Democratic Planning. *Edited by Hans Gerth and Ernest K. Bramstedt. 424 pp.*

Mansur, Fatma. Process of Independence. *Foreword by A. H. Hanson. 208 pp.*

Martin, David A. Pacifism: *an Historical and Sociological Study. 262 pp.*

Myrdal, Gunnar. The Political Element in the Development of Economic Theory. *Translated from the German by Paul Streeten. 282 pp.*

Wootton, Graham. Workers, Unions and the State. *188 pp.*

FOREIGN AFFAIRS: THEIR SOCIAL, POLITICAL AND ECONOMIC FOUNDATIONS

Mayer, J. P. Political Thought in France from the Revolution to the Fifth Republic. *164 pp.*

CRIMINOLOGY

Ancel, Marc. Social Defence: *A Modern Approach to Criminal Problems. Foreword by Leon Radzinowicz. 240 pp.*

Cain, Maureen E. Society and the Policeman's Role. *326 pp.*

Cloward, Richard A., and **Ohlin, Lloyd E.** Delinquency and Opportunity: *A Theory of Delinquent Gangs. 248 pp.*

Downes, David M. The Delinquent Solution. *A Study in Subcultural Theory. 296 pp.*

Dunlop, A. B., and **McCabe, S.** Young Men in Detention Centres. *192 pp.*

Friedlander, Kate. The Psycho-Analytical Approach to Juvenile Delinquency: *Theory, Case Studies, Treatment. 320 pp.*

Glueck, Sheldon, and **Eleanor.** Family Environment and Delinquency. *With the statistical assistance of Rose W. Kneznek. 340 pp.*

Lopez-Rey, Manuel. Crime. *An Analytical Appraisal. 288 pp.*

Mannheim, Hermann. Comparative Criminology: *a Text Book. Two volumes. 442 pp. and 380 pp.*

Morris, Terence. The Criminal Area: *A Study in Social Ecology. Foreword by Hermann Mannheim. 232 pp. 25 tables. 4 maps.*

Rock, Paul. Making People Pay. *338 pp.*

● **Taylor, Ian, Walton, Paul,** and **Young, Jock.** The New Criminology. *For a Social Theory of Deviance. 325 pp.*

SOCIAL PSYCHOLOGY

Bagley, Christopher. The Social Psychology of the Epileptic Child. *320 pp.*

Barbu, Zevedei. Problems of Historical Psychology. *248 pp.*

Blackburn, Julian. Psychology and the Social Pattern. *184 pp.*

●**Brittan, Arthur.** Meanings and Situations. *224 pp.*

Carroll, J. Break-Out from the Crystal Palace. *200 pp.*

●**Fleming, C. M.** Adolescence: Its Social Psychology. *With an Introduction to recent findings from the fields of Anthropology, Physiology, Medicine, Psychometrics and Sociometry. 288 pp.*

● The Social Psychology of Education: *An Introduction and Guide to Its Study. 136 pp.*

Homans, George C. The Human Group. *Foreword by Bernard DeVoto. Introduction by Robert K. Merton. 526 pp.*

● Social Behaviour: *its Elementary Forms. 416 pp.*

●**Klein, Josephine.** The Study of Groups. *226 pp. 31 figures. 5 tables.*

Linton, Ralph. The Cultural Background of Personality. *132 pp.*

●**Mayo, Elton.** The Social Problems of an Industrial Civilization. *With an appendix on the Political Problem. 180 pp.*

Ottaway, A. K. C. Learning Through Group Experience. *176 pp.*

Ridder, J. C. de. The Personality of the Urban African in South Africa. *A Thematic Apperception Test Study. 196 pp. 12 plates.*

●**Rose, Arnold M.** (Ed.) Human Behaviour and Social Processes: *an Interactionist Approach. Contributions by Arnold M. Rose, Ralph H. Turner, Anselm Strauss, Everett C. Hughes, E. Franklin Frazier, Howard S. Becker, et al. 696 pp.*

Smelser, Neil J. Theory of Collective Behaviour. *448 pp.*

Stephenson, Geoffrey M. The Development of Conscience. *128 pp.*

Young, Kimball. Handbook of Social Psychology. *658 pp. 16 figures. 10 tables.*

SOCIOLOGY OF THE FAMILY

Banks, J. A. Prosperity and Parenthood: *A Study of Family Planning among The Victorian Middle Classes. 262 pp.*

Bell, Colin R. Middle Class Families: *Social and Geographical Mobility. 224 pp.*

Burton, Lindy. Vulnerable Children. *272 pp.*

Gavron, Hannah. The Captive Wife: *Conflicts of Household Mothers. 190 pp.*

George, Victor, and **Wilding, Paul.** Motherless Families. *220 pp.*

Klein, Josephine. Samples from English Cultures.

1. Three Preliminary Studies and Aspects of Adult Life in England. *447 pp.*

2. Child-Rearing Practices and Index. *247 pp.*

Klein, Viola. Britain's Married Women Workers. *180 pp.*

The Feminine Character. *History of an Ideology. 244 pp.*

McWhinnie, Alexina M. Adopted Children. *How They Grow Up. 304 pp.*

● **Myrdal, Alva,** and **Klein, Viola.** Women's Two Roles: *Home and Work. 238 pp. 27 tables.*

Parsons, Talcott, and **Bales, Robert F.** Family: Socialization and Interaction Process. *In collaboration with James Olds, Morris Zelditch and Philip E. Slater. 456 pp. 50 figures and tables.*

SOCIAL SERVICES

Bastide, Roger. The Sociology of Mental Disorder. *Translated from the French by Jean McNeil. 260 pp.*

Carlebach, Julius. Caring For Children in Trouble. *266 pp.*

Forder, R. A. (Ed.) Penelope Hall's Social Services of England and Wales. *352 pp.*

George, Victor. Foster Care. *Theory and Practice. 234 pp.*
  Social Security: *Beveridge and After. 258 pp.*

George, V., and **Wilding, P.** Motherless Families. *248 pp.*

●**Goetschius, George W.** Working with Community Groups. *256 pp.*

Goetschius, George W., and **Tash, Joan.** Working with Unattached Youth. *416 pp.*

Hall, M. P., and **Howes, I. V.** The Church in Social Work. *A Study of Moral Welfare Work undertaken by the Church of England. 320 pp.*

Heywood, Jean S. Children in Care: *the Development of the Service for the Deprived Child. 264 pp.*

Hoenig, J., and **Hamilton, Marian W.** The De-Segregation of the Mentally Ill. *284 pp.*

Jones, Kathleen. Mental Health and Social Policy, 1845-1959. *264 pp.*

King, Roy D., Raynes, Norma V., and **Tizard, Jack.** Patterns of Residential Care. *356 pp.*

Leigh, John. Young People and Leisure. *256 pp.*

Morris, Mary. Voluntary Work and the Welfare State. *300 pp.*

Morris, Pauline. Put Away: *A Sociological Study of Institutions for the Mentally Retarded. 364 pp.*

Nokes, P. L. The Professional Task in Welfare Practice. *152 pp.*

Timms, Noel. Psychiatric Social Work in Great Britain (1939-1962). *280 pp.*

● Social Casework: *Principles and Practice. 256 pp.*

Young, A. F. Social Services in British Industry. *272 pp.*

Young, A. F., and **Ashton, E. T.** British Social Work in the Nineteenth Century. *288 pp.*

SOCIOLOGY OF EDUCATION

Banks, Olive. Parity and Prestige in English Secondary Education: a Study in Educational Sociology. *272 pp.*

Bentwich, Joseph. Education in Israel. *224 pp. 8 pp. plates.*

●**Blyth, W. A. L.** English Primary Education. *A Sociological Description.*
  1. Schools. *232 pp.*
  2. Background. *168 pp.*

Collier, K. G. The Social Purposes of Education: *Personal and Social Values in Education. 268 pp.*

Dale, R. R., and **Griffith, S.** Down Stream: *Failure in the Grammar School. 108 pp.*

Dore, R. P. Education in Tokugawa Japan. *356 pp. 9 pp. plates.*

Evans, K. M. Sociometry and Education. *158 pp.*

●**Ford, Julienne.** Social Class and the Comprehensive School. *192 pp.*

Foster, P. J. Education and Social Change in Ghana. *336 pp. 3 maps.*

Fraser, W. R. Education and Society in Modern France. *150 pp.*

Grace, Gerald R. Role Conflict and the Teacher. *About 200 pp.*

Hans, Nicholas. New Trends in Education in the Eighteenth Century. *278 pp. 19 tables.*

● Comparative Education: *A Study of Educational Factors and Traditions. 360 pp.*

Hargreaves, David. Interpersonal Relations and Education. *432 pp.*

● Social Relations in a Secondary School. *240 pp.*

Holmes, Brian. Problems in Education. *A Comparative Approach. 336 pp.*

King, Ronald. Values and Involvement in a Grammar School. *164 pp.*

School Organization and Pupil Involvement. *A Study of Secondary Schools.*

●**Mannheim, Karl,** and **Stewart, W. A. C.** An Introduction to the Sociology of Education. *206 pp.*

Morris, Raymond N. The Sixth Form and College Entrance. *231 pp.*

●**Musgrove, F.** Youth and the Social Order. *176 pp.*

●**Ottaway, A. K. C.** Education and Society: An Introduction to the Sociology of Education. *With an Introduction by W. O. Lester Smith. 212 pp.*

Peers, Robert. Adult Education: *A Comparative Study. 398 pp.*

Pritchard, D. G. Education and the Handicapped: *1760 to 1960. 258 pp.*

Richardson, Helen. Adolescent Girls in Approved Schools. *308 pp.*

Stratta, Erica. The Education of Borstal Boys. *A Study of their Educational Experiences prior to, and during, Borstal Training. 256 pp.*

Taylor, P. H., Reid, W. A., and **Holley, B. J.** The English Sixth Form. *A Case Study in Curriculum Research. 200 pp.*

SOCIOLOGY OF CULTURE

Eppel, E. M., and **M.** Adolescents and Morality: *A Study of some Moral Values and Dilemmas of Working Adolescents in the Context of a changing Climate of Opinion. Foreword by W. J. H. Sprott. 268 pp. 39 tables.*

●**Fromm, Erich.** The Fear of Freedom. *286 pp.*

● The Sane Society. *400 pp.*

Mannheim, Karl. Essays on the Sociology of Culture. *Edited by Ernst Mannheim in co-operation with Paul Kecskemeti. Editorial Note by Adolph Lowe. 280 pp.*

Weber, Alfred. Farewell to European History: *or The Conquest of Nihilism. Translated from the German by R. F. C. Hull. 224 pp.*

SOCIOLOGY OF RELIGION

Argyle, Michael and **Beit-Hallahmi, Benjamin.** The Social Psychology of Religion. *About 256 pp.*
Nelson, G. K. Spiritualism and Society. *313 pp.*
Stark, Werner. The Sociology of Religion. *A Study of Christendom.*
Volume I. *Established Religion. 248 pp.*
Volume II. *Sectarian Religion. 368 pp.*
Volume III. *The Universal Church. 464 pp.*
Volume IV. *Types of Religious Man. 352 pp.*
Volume V. *Types of Religious Culture. 464 pp.*
Turner, B. S. Weber and Islam. *216 pp.*
Watt, W. Montgomery. Islam and the Integration of Society. *320 pp.*

SOCIOLOGY OF ART AND LITERATURE

Jarvie, Ian C. Towards a Sociology of the Cinema. *A Comparative Essay on the Structure and Functioning of a Major Entertainment Industry. 405 pp.*
Rust, Frances S. Dance in Society. *An Analysis of the Relationships between the Social Dance and Society in England from the Middle Ages to the Present Day. 256 pp. 8 pp. of plates.*
Schücking, L. L. The Sociology of Literary Taste. *112 pp.*
Wolff, Janet. Hermeneutic Philosophy and the Sociology of Art. *About 200 pp.*

SOCIOLOGY OF KNOWLEDGE

Diesing, P. Patterns of Discovery in the Social Sciences. *262 pp.*
●**Douglas, J. D.** (Ed.) Understanding Everyday Life. *370 pp.*
●**Hamilton, P.** Knowledge and Social Structure. *174 pp.*
Jarvie, I. C. Concepts and Society. *232 pp.*
Mannheim, Karl. Essays on the Sociology of Knowledge. *Edited by Paul Kecskemeti. Editorial Note by Adolph Lowe. 353 pp.*
Remmling, Gunter W. (Ed.) Towards the Sociology of Knowledge. *Origin and Development of a Sociological Thought Style. 463 pp.*
Stark, Werner. The Sociology of Knowledge: *An Essay in Aid of a Deeper Understanding of the History of Ideas. 384 pp.*

URBAN SOCIOLOGY

Ashworth, William. The Genesis of Modern British Town Planning: *A Study in Economic and Social History of the Nineteenth and Twentieth Centuries. 288 pp.*
Cullingworth, J. B. Housing Needs and Planning Policy: *A Restatement of the Problems of Housing Need and 'Overspill' in England and Wales. 232 pp. 44 tables. 8 maps.*

Dickinson, Robert E. City and Region: *A Geographical Interpretation* *608 pp. 125 figures.*
The West European City: *A Geographical Interpretation. 600 pp. 129 maps. 29 plates.*
● The City Region in Western Europe. *320 pp. Maps.*
Humphreys, Alexander J. New Dubliners: *Urbanization and the Irish Family. Foreword by George C. Homans. 304 pp.*
Jackson, Brian. Working Class Community: *Some General Notions raised by a Series of Studies in Northern England. 192 pp.*
Jennings, Hilda. Societies in the Making: *a Study of Development and Re-development within a County Borough. Foreword by D. A. Clark. 286 pp.*
●**Mann, P. H.** An Approach to Urban Sociology. *240 pp.*
Morris, R. N., and **Mogey, J.** The Sociology of Housing. *Studies at Berinsfield. 232 pp. 4 pp. plates.*
Rosser, C., and **Harris, C.** The Family and Social Change. *A Study of Family and Kinship in a South Wales Town. 352 pp. 8 maps.*

RURAL SOCIOLOGY

Chambers, R. J. H. Settlement Schemes in Tropical Africa: *A Selective Study. 268 pp.*
Haswell, M. R. The Economics of Development in Village India. *120 pp.*
Littlejohn, James. Westrigg: *the Sociology of a Cheviot Parish. 172 pp. 5 figures.*
Mayer, Adrian C. Peasants in the Pacific. *A Study of Fiji Indian Rural Society. 248 pp. 20 plates.*
Williams, W. M. The Sociology of an English Village: *Gosforth. 272 pp. 12 figures. 13 tables.*

SOCIOLOGY OF INDUSTRY AND DISTRIBUTION

Anderson, Nels. Work and Leisure. *280 pp.*
●**Blau, Peter M.,** and **Scott, W. Richard.** Formal Organizations: *a Comparative approach. Introduction and Additional Bibliography by J. H. Smith. 326 pp.*
Eldridge, J. E. T. Industrial Disputes. *Essays in the Sociology of Industrial Relations. 288 pp.*
Hetzler, Stanley. Applied Measures for Promoting Technological Growth. *352 pp.*
Technological Growth and Social Change. *Achieving Modernization. 269 pp.*
Hollowell, Peter G. The Lorry Driver. *272 pp.*
Jefferys, Margot, *with the assistance of Winifred Moss.* Mobility in the Labour Market: *Employment Changes in Battersea and Dagenham. Preface by Barbara Wootton. 186 pp. 51 tables.*

Millerson, Geoffrey. The Qualifying Associations: *a Study in Professionalization. 320 pp.*

Smelser, Neil J. Social Change in the Industrial Revolution: *An Application of Theory to the Lancashire Cotton Industry, 1770-1840. 468 pp. 12 figures. 14 tables.*

Williams, Gertrude. Recruitment to Skilled Trades. *240 pp.*

Young, A. F. Industrial Injuries Insurance: *an Examination of British Policy. 192 pp.*

DOCUMENTARY

Schlesinger, Rudolf (Ed.) Changing Attitudes in Soviet Russia.
   2. The Nationalities Problem and Soviet Administration. *Selected Readings on the Development of Soviet Nationalities Policies. Introduced by the editor. Translated by W. W. Gottlieb. 324 pp.*

ANTHROPOLOGY

Ammar, Hamed. Growing up in an Egyptian Village: *Silwa, Province of Aswan. 336 pp.*

Brandel-Syrier, Mia. Reeftown Elite. *A Study of Social Mobility in a Modern African Community on the Reef. 376 pp.*

Crook, David, and **Isabel.** Revolution in a Chinese Village: *Ten Mile Inn. 230 pp. 8 plates. 1 map.*

Dickie-Clark, H. F. The Marginal Situation. *A Sociological Study of a Coloured Group. 236 pp.*

Dube, S. C. Indian Village. *Foreword by Morris Edward Opler. 276 pp. 4 plates.*

   India's Changing Villages: *Human Factors in Community Development. 260 pp. 8 plates. 1 map.*

Firth, Raymond. Malay Fishermen. *Their Peasant Economy. 420 pp. 17 pp. plates.*

Firth, R., Hubert, J., and **Forge, A.** Families and their Relatives. *Kinship in a Middle-Class Sector of London: An Anthropological Study. 456 pp.*

Gulliver, P. H. Social Control in an African Society: a Study of the Arusha, Agricultural Masai of Northern Tanganyika. *320 pp. 8 plates. 10 figures.*

   Family Herds. *288 pp.*

Ishwaran, K. Shivapur. *A South Indian Village. 216 pp.*

   Tradition and Economy in Village India: *An Interactionist Approach. Foreword by Conrad Arensburg. 176 pp.*

Jarvie, Ian C. The Revolution in Anthropology. *268 pp.*

Jarvie, Ian C., and **Agassi, Joseph.** Hong Kong. *A Society in Transition. 396 pp. Illustrated with plates and maps.*

Little, Kenneth L. Mende of Sierra Leone. *308 pp. and folder.*

   Negroes in Britain. *With a New Introduction and Contemporary Study by Leonard Bloom. 320 pp.*

Lowie, Robert H. Social Organization. *494 pp.*

Mayer, Adrian,C. Caste and Kinship in Central India: *A Village and its Region. 328 pp. 16 plates. 15 figures. 16 tables.*
Peasants in the Pacific. *A Study of Fiji Indian Rural Society. 248 pp.*

Smith, Raymond T. The Negro Family in British Guiana: *Family Structure and Social Status in the Villages. With a Foreword by Meyer Fortes. 314 pp. 8 plates. 1 figure. 4 maps.*

SOCIOLOGY AND PHILOSOPHY

Barnsley, John H. The Social Reality of Ethics. *A Comparative Analysis of Moral Codes. 448 pp.*

Diesing, Paul. Patterns of Discovery in the Social Sciences. *362 pp.*

●**Douglas, Jack D.** (Ed.) Understanding Everyday Life. *Toward the Reconstruction of Sociological Knowledge. Contributions by Alan F. Blum. Aaron W. Cicourel, Norman K. Denzin, Jack D. Douglas, John Heeren, Peter McHugh, Peter K. Manning, Melvin Power, Matthew Speier, Roy Turner, D. Lawrence Wieder, Thomas P. Wilson and Don H. Zimmerman. 370 pp.*

Jarvie, Ian C. Concepts and Society. *216 pp.*

Pelz, Werner. The Scope of Understanding in Sociology. *Towards a more radical reorientation in the social humanistic sciences. 283 pp.*

Roche, Maurice. Phenomenology, Language and the Social Sciences. *371 pp.*

Sahay, Arun. Sociological Analysis. *212 pp.*

Sklair, Leslie. The Sociology of Progress. *320 pp.*

International Library of Anthropology

General Editor Adam Kuper

Brown, Paula. The Chimbu. *A Study of Change in the New Guinea Highlands. 151 pp.*

Lloyd, P. C. Power and Independence. *Urban Africans' Perception of Social Inequality. 264 pp.*

Pettigrew, Joyce. Robber Noblemen. *A Study of the Political System of the Sikh Jats. 284 pp.*

Van Den Berghe, Pierre L. Power and Privilege at an African University. *278 pp.*

International Library of Social Policy

General Editor Kathleen Jones

Bayley, M. Mental Handicap and Community Care. *426 pp.*

Butler, J. R. Family Doctors and Public Policy. *208 pp.*

Holman, Robert. Trading in Children. *A Study of Private Fostering. 355 pp.*

Jones, Kathleen. History of the Mental Health Service. *428 pp.*
Thomas, J. E. The English Prison Officer since 1850: *A Study in Conflict.*
258 pp.
Woodward, J. To Do the Sick No Harm. *A Study of the British Voluntary Hospital System to 1875. About 220 pp.*

International Library of Welfare and Philosophy
General Editors Noel Timms and David Watson

● **Plant, Raymond.** Community and Ideology. *104 pp.*

Primary Socialization, Language and Education
General Editor Basil Bernstein

Bernstein, Basil. Class, Codes and Control. *2 volumes.*
1. *Theoretical Studies Towards a Sociology of Language. 254 pp.*
2. *Applied Studies Towards a Sociology of Language. About 400 pp.*
Brandis, W., and **Bernstein, B.** Selection and Control. *176 pp.*
Brandis, Walter, and **Henderson, Dorothy.** Social Class, Language and Communication. *288 pp.*
Cook-Gumperz, Jenny. Social Control and Socialization. *A Study of Class Differences in the Language of Maternal Control. 290 pp.*
● **Gahagan, D. M.,** and **G. A.** Talk Reform. *Exploration in Language for Infant School Children. 160 pp.*
Robinson, W. P., and **Rackstraw, Susan D. A.** A Question of Answers. *2 volumes. 192 pp. and 180 pp.*
Turner, Geoffrey J., and **Mohan, Bernard A.** A Linguistic Description and Computer Programme for Children's Speech. *208 pp.*

Reports of the Institute of Community Studies

Cartwright, Ann. Human Relations and Hospital Care. *272 pp.*
● Parents and Family Planning Services. *306 pp.*
Patients and their Doctors. *A Study of General Practice. 304 pp.*
● **Jackson, Brian.** Streaming: *an Education System in Miniature. 168 pp.*
Jackson, Brian, and **Marsden, Dennis.** Education and the Working Class: *Some General Themes raised by a Study of 88 Working-class Children in a Northern Industrial City. 268 pp. 2 folders.*
Marris, Peter. The Experience of Higher Education. *232 pp. 27 tables.*
Loss and Change. *192 pp.*

Marris, Peter, and Rein, Martin. Dilemmas of Social Reform. *Poverty and Community Action in the United States. 256 pp.*

Marris, Peter, and Somerset, Anthony. African Businessmen. *A Study of Entrepreneurship and Development in Kenya. 256 pp.*

Mills, Richard. Young Outsiders: *a Study in Alternative Communities. 216 pp.*

Runciman, W. G. Relative Deprivation and Social Justice. *A Study of Attitudes to Social Inequality in Twentieth-Century England. 352 pp.*

Willmott, Peter. Adolescent Boys in East London. *230 pp.*

Willmott, Peter, and Young, Michael. Family and Class in a London Suburb. *202 pp. 47 tables.*

Young, Michael. Innovation and Research in Education. *192 pp.*

●Young, Michael, and McGeeney, Patrick. Learning Begins at Home. *A Study of a Junior School and its Parents. 128 pp.*

Young, Michael, and Willmott, Peter. Family and Kinship in East London. *Foreword by Richard M. Titmuss. 252 pp. 39 tables.*
The Symmetrical Family. *410 pp.*

Reports of the Institute for Social Studies in Medical Care

Cartwright, Ann, Hockey, Lisbeth, and Anderson, John L. Life Before Death. *310 pp.*

Dunnell, Karen, and Cartwright, Ann. Medicine Takers, Prescribers and Hoarders. *190 pp.*

Medicine, Illness and Society

General Editor W. M. Williams

Robinson, David. The Process of Becoming Ill. *142 pp.*

Stacey, Margaret, *et al.* Hospitals, Children and Their Families. *The Report of a Pilot Study. 202 pp.*

Monographs in Social Theory

General Editor Arthur Brittan

●Barnes, B. Scientific Knowledge and Sociological Theory. *About 200 pp.*

Bauman, Zygmunt. Culture as Praxis. *204 pp.*

● Dixon, Keith. Sociological Theory. *Pretence and Possibility. 142 pp.*

●Smith, Anthony D. The Concept of Social Change. *A Critique of the Functionalist Theory of Social Change. 208 pp.*

Routledge Social Science Journals

The British Journal of Sociology. *Edited by Terence P. Morris. Vol. 1, No. 1, March 1950 and Quarterly. Roy. 8vo. Back numbers available. An international journal with articles on all aspects of sociology.*

Economy and Society. *Vol. 1, No. 1. February 1972 and Quarterly. Metric Roy. 8vo. A journal for all social scientists covering sociology, philosophy, anthropology, economics and history. Back numbers available.*

Year Book of Social Policy in Britain, The. *Edited by Kathleen Jones. 1971. Published annually.*

Printed in Great Britain by Unwin Brothers Limited
The Gresham Press Old Woking Surrey
A member of the Staples Printing Group